A GAME THAT WOULD PAY

A GAME THAT WOULD PAY

A Business History of
Professional Football in Bradford

A.J. Arnold

Duckworth

First published in 1988 by
Gerald Duckworth & Co. Ltd.
The Old Piano Factory
43 Gloucester Crescent, London NW1

ISBN 0 7156 2506 3

British Library Cataloguing in Publication Data

Arnold, A.J.
    A game that would pay : a business history
of professional football in Bradford.
    1. Soccer — Economic aspects — England
— Bradford (West Yorkshire)
    I. Title
    338.4′7796334′0942817   GV93.3

    ISBN 0-7156-2506-3

Photoset in North Wales by
Derek Doyle & Associates, Mold, Clwyd
and printed in Great Britain by
Redwood Burn Limited, Trowbridge

Contents

Contents

1958 – 1985: The Old Order Changes

Plates

(between pages 84 and 85)

Preface

Bradford is the ninth largest city in England, yet neither of its Football League clubs have been in the First Division since 1922, and between them they have won only one major honour, the FA Cup in 1911.

Bradford Park Avenue were voted out of the Football League in 1970 and their liquidation soon followed. Park Avenue's ground has changed in ten years from a distinctive, well maintained stadium to a desolate shell with sawn-off floodlight pylons, grassed-over terraces and scrub-filled turnstiles. Valley Parade's old main stand burst into flames in May 1985, as Bradford City were celebrating their return to the Second Division. Fifty-six people died and many more were severely injured in the worst disaster in English football.

The obvious question is why did it happen in Bradford? How did the city allow the ground where Greenwood, Shackleton and Scoular regularly entertained the crowds to become a sad wasteland, and why were Bradford City still using a wooden main stand dating back to 1908?

Answers to these questions can be obtained by examining the nature and development of professional football, the relationships between playing success and financial success, the reasons for the delayed entry of Bradford into the Football League, and by considering the reasons why the men who ran football in Bradford were never able to work together to provide the facilities that could have brought sporting success to their city.

In some senses the development of professional football has followed, in Bradford, a unique path. In other ways it illustrates processes common to many other clubs and has much wider implications.

The towns and cities in West Yorkshire, formerly part of the West Riding, have dominated the United Kingdom's woollen textile industry since industrialisation. Each town specialised in particular aspects of the trade, Bradford in wool dealing (in which it became a world centre) and the worsted trade. This gave the city its own pattern of industrial growth and decline, both of which have been quite dramatic because of the extent to which the industry has relied on overseas trade and has thus been vulnerable to foreign competition, tariff changes and even demand changes dependent on the level of military hostility in Europe. Industrial growth and decline does not have a direct impact on

ix

professional sport, but it does shape the social context in which that sport operates and affects the supply of business capital and the level of potential support.

The West Riding textile district had, and still has, a traditional social ethic; the respect for 'masculine' values, the rivalry if not hostility between some local communities, and the absence of any public school ethos combined to implant cup rugby in Yorkshire. The violence and popularity of the game contributed to the early development of commercial rugby, to the split between rugby league and rugby union and to difficulties in establishing a more national professional sport, association football, in the district.

In every other major industrial area professional soccer was established in Victorian times, in the adjacent Lancashire cotton textile towns as early as 1880, but in the West Riding it needed the changed commercial prospects for rugby early in the twentieth century and the patronage of the football authorities to establish soccer in the area.

Bradford is the only city to have had two senior clubs leave rugby for soccer, and the only city to have had two First Division sides that fell to the Fourth Division; the reasons for this in part relate to factors specific to the city but also in large measure exemplify the difficulties and rewards of operating in the Football League.

Football has obvious importance as a recreational and social outlet, as a national game that commits loyalties and enthusiasm far beyond its economic significance, but it is also a business with most unusual features. The controls on players' contracts, the dividend restraints, the prohibitions on remunerating directors and the openness of the cartel-type arrangements have no parallel in any other business and yet have been only thinly researched.

In this book the consequences of these constraints for football clubs in general, particularly on the supply of equity capital and on its investment in ground developments, are examined with reference to the temptations, rewards and disappointments facing small clubs in the Football League which, like Bradford, have been in pursuit of prestige and of 'a game that would pay'.

Neither club had any archive material; Park Avenue had been liquidated and City had not kept more than immediately necessary documents. The process of reconstructing the dealings of the two clubs involved the retrieval of material from a wide variety of sources including financial statements stored in accountants' basements, documents filed at Companies House and the Public Record Office, pamphlets and papers in local library collections and material contained in family scrapbooks.

I am therefore particularly grateful to Phillip Woodrow of Baker Rooke, Bradford for the help he offered at the start of my researches, to Stafford Heginbotham, Chairman, and Terry Newman, Secretary, of Bradford City, to David Oxley, Secretary-General of the Rugby Football League, to Kathryn Grace and Kim Hutchinson of the Bradford Telegraph and Argus library, to several members of the Leeds, Bradford, Huddersfield and Halifax reference libraries, the Leeds Business Archives and the staff at Companies House, London for a willingness to help which went far beyond the call of duty. I am also very grateful to Pamela Keech and Elizabeth Blundell for the efficiency with which, at various times in the preparation of the book, they have converted my writings into readable form. Above all thanks are due to my wife, Jo, for her encouragement and help. Any mistakes that remain are, of course, mine.

University of Essex   A.J.A.
January 1988

Acknowledgements

The photographs of Tyrrel Street, Bradford, the Manningham district of Bradford and the aerial view of Park Avenue's grounds appear by permission of C.H. Wood and Co, Bradford.

The remaining photographs appear by permission of the *Telegraph and Argus*, Bradford.

The extended quotation in Chapter 3 is included with the permission of T.W.J. Auty and Headingley RUFC.

BEFORE 1903

THE SEARCH FOR
'A GAME THAT WOULD PAY'

1. Bradford and the Textile Trade

The West Riding is almost synonymous, industrially, with woollen textiles. The region has dominated the British woollen textile market since industrialisation in the eighteenth century; until the post-war contraction in the industry, and the severe rationalisation that followed, the various branches of the trade employed a substantial proportion of the region's work force.

Industrialisation came early to the West Riding, where domestic industry had been established for some two hundred years. The close proximity of land suitable for sheep rearing, plentiful water power and local supplies of coal and soft water enabled the West Riding to dominate the trade, and the spread of new machinery was accelerated by the closeness of Lancashire.

Woollen textiles need a sequence of specialised treatments which vary according to the cloth produced. Particular towns developed distinctive skills in their own sector of the trade, and the hilly countryside prevented many neighbouring towns from merging. In consequence civic pride and 'a self-assertive attitude of independence' dominated its nineteenth-century history,[1] an outlook which helped to shape the development of the region's professional sport.

Bradford was noted for wool dealing, worsted weaving and merchanting. The worsted trade was transformed by innovations in machinery and fabrics, and increasingly concentrated in the West Riding. By 1850, out of 79,000 employees in the English worsted industry, 71,000 were in Yorkshire, including 35,000 in the parish of Bradford.[2]

The population of Bradford increased fivefold between 1801 and 1841 and its transformation from a small market town on the eastern slopes of the Pennines to a major industrial centre was 'one of the most striking phenomena in the history of the British Empire'.[3] This explosive growth led in 1832 to parliamentary borough status for Bradford, bringing together the townships of Bradford, Bowling, Horton and Manningham, but expansion was not without its social and environmental problems; a

[1] Asa Briggs, *Victorian Cities*, (London 1968), p. 150.
[2] See Gary Firth, 'The Bradford Trade in the Nineteenth Century' in D. G. Wright and J. A. Jowitt, *Victorian Bradford*, (Bradford 1981).
[3] Asa Briggs, op cit, p. 140.

Health of Towns Commissioner described it as 'the dirtiest, filthiest and worst regulated town in the Kingdom'.

In 1873 Bradford's ornate Town Hall was opened, but the woollen trade, which had been highly successful for forty years, started to decline. French competition, which had been almost eliminated by the Franco-Prussian war of 1870, increased rapidly and their superior dyes proved more popular than the colours in Bradford's woven pieces, which were affected by the oiling of combed wool. Tariff wars started with a 10% levy by France on Bradford worsted goods in 1874, an example quickly followed by other European countries. The worsted trade fared particularly badly and the McKinley tariff in 1891 halved Bradford's trade with America.

Manufacturers were now more pessimistic, and reports of low profits universal.[4] The early 1890s were a period of economic depression, with strikes and disputes over wage rates and cuts,[5] and a recurrent problem, particularly in Bradford, was the replacement of male workers by female by managements eager to lower wages during the trade depression. The most serious dispute was the strike at Manningham Mills; on 14th April 1891 the town was 'in uproar' and the Durham Light Infantry made fixed bayonet charges until late at night in order to clear the streets.[6]

This depression intensified in 1894, a year described in the Bradford Chamber of Commerce Annual Report as 'one full of disappointments for the wool trade in general and the Bradford trade in particular'. A short-lived recovery caused by the reduction in American tariffs was curtailed by the 1898 Dingley tariff which reduced trade, especially in Bradford, to its lowest level since early in the century.

During the last quarter of the nineteenth century, a period in which association football emerged in England as a recreational outlet in the industrial areas, the dominant trade in the West Riding had suffered a prolonged decline, and this was most marked in the worsted trade centred on Bradford. None the less the nineteenth century had transformed the region. The West Riding had become the pre-eminent woollen textile district, providing jobs for 70% of England's wool textile work force. Four of the country's largest urban districts were now here, Leeds (5th), Bradford with a population of 265,000 (8th), Halifax (26th) and Huddersfield (27th), and in 1897 Bradford successfully petitioned Queen Victoria for designation as a city.

[4] D. Jenkins and K. Ponting, *British Wool Textile Industry 1770-1914*, (London 1982), p. 234.

[5] J. Reynolds and K. Laybourn, 'The Emergence of the ILP in Bradford', *International Review of Social History* 20 (1975), p. 345.

[6] C. Pearce, 'The Manningham Mills Strike', *University of Hull Occasional Paper* (1975), p. 10, and J. Reynolds and K. Laybourn, op cit, p. 327.

2. The Growth of Leisure

As Britain industrialised, the population grew and, partly due to the effects of the enclosure of open fields, moved from rural areas to the towns and cities. This trend continued through the nineteenth century; the population doubled in the sixty years from 1821, but the proportion in rural areas fell from 50% in 1851 to 22% in 1911.

The growth of new industries had cultural as well as demographic effects. In the eighteenth century the traditional working day had been long but relatively flexible. The work rhythm was 'self-imposed, and often leisurely, weekends had been elastic and holidays numerous'.[1] Industrialisation subjected employees to a strictly controlled working day, with long hours and few holidays. In the industrial towns work and recreation became sharply distinguished and leisure itself confined into 'time marked off from work'.

Faced with an increasingly rationalised working day, and 'the extensive and indiscriminate inclosure of commons which were playgrounds',[2] many turned for respite and sociability to the public houses, which provided newspapers and books as well as their more obvious attractions.

This was important in the development of leisure opportunities, as a coalition of temperance reformers and rational recreationalists attempted to offer 'attractions of a higher kind', such as railway excursions and cheap concerts, and to encourage more ordered and improving leisure through the public provision of parks, monuments, museums, libraries and concert halls. Clergymen also tried to combat such 'pernicious pastimes' as drink and dance by introducing organised sport to urban working people.[3] The policy was only partly succesful as the consumption of alcohol rose to a peak in the mid-1870s and was still seen by the respectable classes as a serious problem as late as 1905, when Professor Sims Woodhead addressed a largely medical audience in Leeds Town Hall on 'Alcohol and Physical Degeneration', and identified a marked and adverse effect on the birthrate, on the quality of nutrition

[1] P. Bailey, *Leisure and Class in Victorian England*, (London 1978), pp. 11-12.
[2] Hugh Cunningham, *Leisure in the Industrial Revolution*, (London 1980), p. 81.
[3] R. F. Wheeler, 'Organised Sport and Organised Labour: The Workers' Sports Movement', *Journal of Contemporary History*, XIII, No 2 (1978), p. 192.

provided to the newly born and on the 'efficiency rate among army recruits'.[4] In Bradford, however, the number of licensed premises declined from a peak of 1219 in 1882 to 926 in 1894, and arrests for drunkenness also fell.[5]

Employees in the textile districts of Lancashire and Yorkshire achieved a reduced working week sooner than workers in many other areas. The Ten Hours Bill of 1847, which also limited Saturday work to eight hours, was followed by a Factory Act of 1850 which stopped work in the textile mills at 2 pm on Saturdays, primarily because women and children were such an important part of the workforce. The legislation had been mainly concerned with the employment conditions of women and children, and once they were not permitted to work on Saturday afternoons it was uneconomic to keep the mills open merely for male employees.[6] In the early 1870s the 'unexampled prosperity' of the Bradford trade led other local employers, notably in the engineering and foundry trades, to give employees a Saturday half-holiday in order to avoid the labour disputes that had arisen elsewhere.

Employees were not alone in their desire for Saturday half-holidays. Sabbatarians felt it would help to keep Sunday holy, and many employers assumed that it would reduce absenteeism on 'Saint Monday'. By the 1870s, when Bank Holidays were becoming national holidays, many large groups of workers had Saturday afternoons off, and Saturday night began to replace Saint Monday as the climax of the working week.

During the latter part of the nineteenth century there was a marked increase in leisure facilities, provided by a combination of entrepreneurial, municipal and evangelical initiative.

The music hall was developed by entrepreneurs as an extension of singing saloons. The Alhambra was run by a limited company which was known to pay high dividends, and four theatres were opened in Bradford by 1876. In 1877 the Bradford Skating Rink Company was founded near Manningham Lane and a similar company was formed in Halifax.[7]

St George's Hall was built and opened in 1853 to offer music without alcohol to working people. The first public baths in Bradford were opened in 1864 and Peel Park (1863), Samuel Lister's deer park in Manningham (1873) and Horton Park (1876) were bought by the corporation for public use. The parks were also used to host the Great West Riding Galas which dated from 1844. These Galas were usually

[4] *Huddersfield Daily Examiner*, 15 February 1905, p. 3.
[5] D. Russell 'The Pursuit of Leisure' in D. G. Wright and J. A. Jowitt, op cit, p. 210.
[6] J. Ryder and H. Silver, *Modern English Society*, (London 1970), p. 78.
[7] Bradford Skating Rink Company founded 1877, Companies House No 11,117 and Halifax Skating Rink Company founded 1876, Companies House No 10,257.

held at Whitsuntide for a period of up to three days, and persisted until 1936. They were 'one of the few great corporate and communal occasions of the Bradford year' and in 1866 an audience over the two days of almost 100,000 people enjoyed morris and maypole dancing, acrobatics, military manoeuvres and a firework display.[8]

The Leeds and Bradford Railway was opened in 1846, partly to lower the cost of carrying wool from, and building stone to, the southern counties. In 1867 a station was opened at Manningham to service a suburb which was working-class but also contained some of the most impressive surburban villas in Bradford. The new station had a considerable effect on attendances at the Peel Park Gala, and subsequently increased the attractiveness of nearby Valley Parade as a site for commercial rugby. The Bradford and Thornton Railway also opened a station in 1878 at Horton Park which was immediately opposite the cricket and rugby grounds.

Sport by now was far more respectable than it had been previously. The most popular local sports during the eighteenth century had been prize fighting, cock fighting, 'pedestrianism' and horse racing, each of which was the focus for serious betting. In 1775 in Leeds, in a pit at the back of the Shambles, a three-day fight had taken place between stags belonging to the 'gentlemen of Yorkshire and Lincolnshire',[9] and as late as 1843 authorities in Manchester had found it necessary to ban dog and cock fighting, and bull and badger baiting. The Crimean War and the rise of Prussia had, however, increased military preparedness, and respect for physical education. Huddersfield's rugby club began with a meeting of gentlemen in 1864 to form an athletic club with a basement gymnasium in the town;[10] the Chairman in his address of 1870 said that 'anyone who wished this country to be as powerful as it had been hitherto would not hesitate to support these clubs', and connected the victories won by the Germans with the existence of a gymnasium in every large German town.[11]

Most of the senior rugby sides began as part of a multi-sports club. The Huddersfield Cricket and Athletic Club initially saw rugby as a branch of athletics, but the growth of membership and crowds that it caused led to a change of emphasis. Halifax was formed as a cricket and (rugby) football club in 1877. Leeds Athletic Club amalgamated two years after its formation in 1868 with a rugby football club, but in 1871 its main

[8] J. Reynolds, *The Great Paternalist: Titus Salt and the Growth of Nineteenth-Century Bradford*, (Bradford 1983), p. 176.

[9] E. M. Sigsworth, 'Leeds and its Industrial Growth: 22 Sport (1)', *Leeds Journal*, March 1957, p. 78.

[10] Huddersfield Cricket and Athletic Club, October, 1895 Grand Bazaar Programme, Huddersfield Reference Library, p. 81.

[11] Huddersfield Athletic Club, 1869-70, Annual Report, pp. 4-5.

focus was the gymnasium with its instructor, Professor Lacon. They had distinct athletics, cricket, cycling, rugby, tennis, harrier and bowling sections and, like Huddersfield, experimented with an association football side between 1895 and 1898 before losses caused the section's closure.

As elsewhere in the country, churchmen were also influential in the establishment of sporting clubs. The choice of sport was essentially a pragmatic consideration according to the popular game in the locality; in the West Riding the church established mainly rugby clubs.

3. The Northern Union Game

Rugby union was the first winter team game to prove popular in the West Riding, and in Lancashire. Rugby union in the South and Midlands was initially monopolised by members of the upper middle classes, and even in Lancashire the impact of former public school boys was important; Manchester, the oldest club in the county, was formed by old boys of Rugby School in 1860.

In Yorkshire, the public school influence was slight, and from the outset Yorkshire clubs were 'less socially exclusive than elsewhere in the country'.[1] Leeds Athletic, one of the oldest clubs, originated with an advertisement placed in a local newspaper[2] by a railway clerk, and Halifax RFC was formed after an advertisement by a brass founder, who was soon supported by a number of local traders including a boot manufacturer, a wool and waste dealer and a victualler.

Few of those who ran rugby clubs in Yorkshire had been to public school, and they did not share the amateur ethos which characterised southern rugby. This ethic expected that norms of fair play and friendly rivalry would be willingly observed, that enthusiasm in victory and disappointment in defeat would be subdued and that the game would be seen as an end in itself.

In 1877 the five senior Yorkshire clubs, Bradford, Leeds, Huddersfield, York and Hull, met to consider a suggestion by Messrs Schutt, a wool merchant, Garnett, a borough magistrate of the Bradford club, and Hudson, a mill owner from Leeds, that a Challenge Cup competition be inaugurated. The clubs were in favour and duly presented the County Committee with a cup worth fifty guineas for annual competition.

The competition was an immediate success, at least in Yorkshire, partly because of the strong community ties within, and hostility and rivalry between the different mill towns and mining villages. The identification of town with team and the presence of highly partisan crowds meant that attendances were large, and that players performed for the benefit of their community as much as for themselves.

[1] E. Dunning and K. Sheard, *Barbarians, Gentlemen and Players: A Sociological Study of the Development of Rugby Football*, (1979), p. 135.
[2] *Leeds Mercury*, 7 March 1864.

The southern rugby establishment was highly critical, however, feeling that such a valuable prize would change the game from a mock fight to a real one. The evidence certainly supported their fears, and a contemporary writer[3] commented that, 'whatever the class of players', cup ties provoked unnecessary roughness. The Midlands was the only other area to adopt a similar competition and in a different social context it caused far less ferment.

By the 1890s Yorkshire rugby was based on a remarkably successful Challenge Cup allied to a league competition which provided regular gates. The enthusiasm of the public remained unabated and for real excitement there was 'still nothing like a Cup-tie', excepting poorly matched encounters such as the 70-2 victory of Leeds over Wakefield St. Austins in 1892.

Crowds were growing; a match at Fartown, Huddersfield in November 1891 between Yorkshire and Lancashire attracted 23,250 and a gate of £845 and in March 1893 22,000 paid £410 to see Bradford play Halifax in the Yorkshire Cup. Bradford attracted crowds of over 10,000 on several occasions during the 1880s and early 1890s, and 18,000 paid to see a Yorkshire Challenge Cup match against Manningham in 1886. Yorkshire established clear dominance in the County Championship that began in 1888 (the year that the Football League was started), winning seven of the first eight annual contests and often providing a majority of the England team.

The popularity of rugby was due to a number of factors. The high degree of local rivalry boosted the Challenge Cup competition into a lucrative activity welcomed by club officials who were usually local traders rather than gentlemen. Rugby players also displayed traditional masculine values which were well received by their local communities. Rugby was less restrained than association football, placed more emphasis on team work than individuality, and on sheer strength, and allowed more physical violence.

It was certainly a rough sport, and contemporary newspaper reports regularly spoke of the game's toughness. A table in a Wakefield newspaper[3] claimed that there had been 71 deaths and 208 broken limbs in Yorkshire rugby matches between 1890 and 1893, although these claims may well have been exaggerated. Local fixtures could be particularly hazardous, as a member of Headingley's side for a match in Pudsey related:

> It was my second visit to the ground; on my first I had received two black eyes, and they were a rough and tough crowd in those days, though Headingley could give as well as take. Pudsey, for some reason which I

[3] Montague Shearman, *Athletics and Football*, (London 1887), pp. 327-30.
[4] *Wakefield Express*, 8 April 1893.

never found out, was always a joke in the West Riding. It used to be said that if a stranger arrived in the town, one Pudsey lad would say, 'Who's yon across t'street, Bill?' Bill would say, 'A stranger,' and the reply would be, "Eave a brick at 'im.' To revert to the game, from the beginning it was a rough one, and I received my usual black eye. Afterwards we went to the pub near the station to hoist a few 'Woolsorters' before our train came in. I and my pals, Toddy Mellish, a very likeable and mischievous chap, and Harold Mawson, a very heavy and powerful lad, were sitting at a table when four of the Pudsey lads came in looking for 'the beggar wit't'light coat', which was yours truly. Well, they would not have a drink with us, but wanted a rough house, so Toddy Mellish told them I could lick them at 'rat trap and ball', whatever that may be. They were up at once wanting to have a go at me, but this brought the landlord in, who asked me to come out with him, as he did not want the police in. He took me out and guided me to a side door telling me to get into the station waiting room and wait there until the train came in, as they were a very tough lot. When the train arrived we all three made a mad rush and just got on in time, or I suspect I should have had at least another black eye.[5]

There existed a gulf between the increasingly commercial rugby clubs of Yorkshire and Lancashire, who wanted to put their clubs' affairs, including the relationship with the players, on a more open, businesslike footing, and the attitudes of the London amateur clubs, with their distaste for the ethics of trade.

The senior clubs in Yorkshire had also made sizeable investments in their grounds, and formalised their organisational structures. Manningham had recently constructed a ground for 18,000 people, and were a company limited by member guarantees. Bradford Park Avenue had spent heavily on new grandstands and been incorporated in 1892. The Huddersfield Cricket and Athletic Club were incorporated as early as 1879 and they spent £8,600 on ground development in 1890-1. When the work was finished an athletics festival was held, complete with American athletes, before a crowd of 15,000. Halifax Cricket and Football Club were incorporated in 1888, while the Leeds Cricket, Football and Athletic Company Limited spent £9,000 (£C 275,000)[6] in 1890-1 on two pavilions, three grandstands, entrances and other ground improvements. The result was a 30,000 capacity stadium, with facilities for other sports, at an accumulated cost of £30,300 (£C 940,000).

In September 1893 two representatives of the Yorkshire Union decided to head off the anti-professionalism campaign of the Rugby Union by proposing at the General Meeting that 'players be allowed compensation for bona fide loss of time'. Their attempt to legitimise broken-time payments, whereby players were compensated for wages lost due to playing rugby, was defeated, and a counter motion which

[5] *Headingley Football Club*, 1878-1978,(Leeds 1978), p. 23.
[6] In 1987 £'s.

described the Yorkshire approach as contrary to the interests and spirit of the game was carried by 282 votes to 136.[7]

The Rugby Union was also suspicious of gate-taking leagues and ruled that competitions would only be acceptable if they included promotion and relegation. This was unattractive to the senior Yorkshire clubs, who gained more revenue by playing each other in a closed league, and when they learnt that rules were to be proposed at the General Meeting of the Rugby Union in September 1895 that would outlaw even the receipt of medals as *de facto* professionalism they decided to act.

On August 29th 1895 a private meeting was held at the George Hotel, Huddersfield, between the representatives of the twenty-one senior rugby clubs of Yorkshire and Lancashire. There were officials present from eleven West Riding clubs: Bradford, Manningham, Leeds, Hunslet, Halifax, Huddersfield, Dewsbury, Batley, Brighouse, Liversedge and Wakefield. After a three-hour meeting the clubs decided to form a Northern Rugby Football Union, to be based on the principle of payment for broken time only. Twenty clubs, including Bradford and Manningham, resigned from the Rugby Union (only Dewsbury did not) and two other clubs subsequently joined them.

The first Northern Rugby Football Union season started on 7th September 1895, the *Pall Mall Gazette* commenting sardonically that 'professional football set in on Saturday, but no deaths are recorded'.

The Northern Union was hardly a month old before there were demands for a more open and spectacular game, to be achieved by reducing the number of forwards by two, abolishing lineouts and using a round ball! It was not until June 1906, however, that the number of players in a team was reduced to thirteen, after which the game was faster and more open.

The first competition, a league for twenty-two clubs, was won by Manningham in 1896, with Halifax second.

Eight more sides joined the Northern Union and the organisers decided to reform into separate Lancashire and Yorkshire Senior Competitions, supplemented by a Challenge Cup for all the clubs.

In 1898 the players were able to capitalise on their crowd appeal when the Northern Union adopted professionalism but, unlike the Football League, players had to have legitimate employment in another part-time job.

The new competition was not proving as successful as anticipated and by 1900 there were ominous reports[8] of the financial strains even on

---

[7] See E. Dunning and K. Sheard, 'The Bifurcation of Rugby Union and Rugby League: A Case Study of Organisational Conflict and Change', *International Review of Sports Sociology* II, (1976), pp. 31-72.

[8] See, for example, *Yorkshire Post*, 12 February 1900, p. 10.

senior clubs. At the same time association code matches in Sheffield were generating record receipts.

A particular problem was that the Union was keen to extend its influence by accepting new clubs, but only encounters between the top sides were particularly lucrative so the senior clubs were not keen to play in a large league which included sides with limited crowd appeal. There were a number of changes made to the competition structures in an attempt to find an acceptable compromise.

In 1901 the top seven clubs in each county's league resigned to form a new league, but the following season an attempt was made to expand the senior competition and meet the complaints of clubs left to play in the depleted county competitions.

Two divisions, of eighteen clubs each, were formed, but the Second Division contained a number of sides who were unable to compete properly at this level and also contained sides who were widely dispersed geographically, including South Shields (Durham) and Millom (Cumberland).

The consequent increase in travel costs and fall in attendances exacerbated the serious financial problems of many clubs, particularly those in Division Two. The refusal of the Northern Union to reduce the number of players enabled inferior sides to deny space to opponents and led to a stagnant pattern of play in which strength in the maul counted rather than speed. One match at Halifax in 1902 had included 110 scrummages, which could be protracted mauls, and excitement and spectator interest dwindled. The points system, of five points for a goal kicked from a try, four points for a dropped goal or goal from a rolling ball, three points for a penalty goal and only two points for a try, also did nothing to encourage width in the play and contributed to a congestion of players in the middle of the pitch.

By 1903 the Northern Union was in a state of crisis, and the *Yorkshire Post* in May of that year[9] doubted whether any of the Division Two sides from Yorkshire had made rugby football pay that season.

[9] ibid, 26 May 1903, p. 12.

4. The Association Code

Football has a long history, probably dating back to 200 A.D. when 'faction fights over the ball between the ecclesiastical districts of Derby were in vogue'.[1]

Early mob-football was uncontrolled and violent. It was commonly played on holidays, particularly Shrovetide, and was disapproved of and regularly banned by authority, either because it threatened public order or because it interfered with more important national priorities, such as archery. Edward II outlawed it in 1314, and Edward III forbade it and such 'other useless games' as tennis, skittles, hand-ball, club-ball and cock fighting in 1349, as did Richard II, Henry IV and Henry VIII. In 1572 an edict threatened imprisonment for those who played 'foteball within the City of London', for the game 'gave no pleasure, but beastlie furie and violence'.[2] By 1667 it had been banned at least thirty times, either by reigning monarchs or local authorities, particularly in London and Manchester.[3]

Football continued to be unpopular with authority, both because of its intrinsic nuisance and because the game was sometimes played as a protest on open fields due for enclosure until the players were removed by force.[4]

Boys at the old public schools played football in their free time, although not all were enthusiastic; one Etonian in 1831 considered football 'not at all gentlemanly. It is a game which the common people of Yorkshire are particularly partial to.'[5]

Football, undifferentiated between association and rugby codes, was gradually adopted by the public schools, each of whom invented rules according to the nature and size of their own cloisters or fields. The dribbling game developed mainly at schools where the confined areas made running with the ball and tackling the runners particularly

---

[1] A. Gibson and W. Pickford, *Association Football and the Men Who Made It*, (London 1906), Vol. 1, p. 5.

[2] ibid, p. 6.

[3] E. Dunning and K. Sheard, *Barbarians, Gentlemen and Players*, p. 22.

[4] S. Tischler, *Footballers and Businessmen: The Origins of Professional Soccer in England*, (New York 1981), p. 18.

[5] H. J. C. Blake, *Reminiscences of Eton by an Etonian*, (Chichester 1831), p. 47.

dangerous to both clothes and limbs.

In 1847 rules were drawn up at Eton that outlawed the use of hands, except for stopping the ball. The early rules at Rugby school forbade hacking on or above the knee and, unless a player in a maul refused to put the ball down, required that no player be hacked and held at the same time.

The public schools were vital in the process of adapting the 'open scrambles of the country' to the confined spaces that would be available in urban areas, but the variation in their rules was a potential problem.

In 1863 the Football Association was formed and attempted to agree on common rules for inter-club matches. Blackheath, who were soon to be instrumental in the formation of the Rugby Union, could not accept the prohibitions on running with the ball and hacking, without which 'all the courage and pluck of the game would be at an end'. The Blackheath secretary, however, F. W. Campbell, continued as Treasurer to the FA for some time; clearly differences between the two camps could be accommodated within the norms of public school etiquette.

The members of the FA contributed to a modest Challenge Cup costing £20 which was first played for in the 1871-2 season. By 1873 there were twenty-eight entries, but the process of harmonising the rules was still far from complete; the Engineers' match against Sheffield Association was played half under London rules, and half under Sheffield rules.

In 1878-9 came the first signs that the role of the public schools would merely be to provide a transition between mob-football and the permanent domination of the representatives of the industrial towns; Darwen reached the fourth round before losing to Old Etonians after two draws, all three matches being played in London, and Nottingham Forest reached the semi-final.

The early success of Darwen, Blackburn Rovers and Blackburn Olympic was partly due to their ability to attract Scottish players, who were particularly adept at combination play rather than the individual dribbling initiatives preferred by the southern sides. The Scots were paid higher wages for their work in the mills than they could earn at home, but as their numbers increased so did the suspicion that they were being paid to play and that gate returns were being falsified.

The Lancashire sides were also less encumbered by traditional patterns of play, and were prepared to innovate tactically in pursuit of victories. In 1883 Blackburn Olympic's combination of close passing and wing-to-wing moves enabled them to beat Old Etonians in the FA Cup Final. The Cup was never to be won by an amateur side again.

The excitement of this victory and its implications for the commercial future of the association code weakened the hold of rugby in many other areas, although not in the West Riding. Gibson and Pickford concluded that the rugby code did attract an earlier and stronger following than association in the province as a whole, but that association began to oust rugby from the early 1880s,[6] a process undoubtedly stimulated by the ending of southern amateur supremacy.

Certainly Lancashire had been a 'hotbed' of rugby with few association clubs until the first success of Darwen prompted the formation of the Lancashire Football Association in 1878. Preston had played rugby since 1877, but four years later the achievements of their neighbouring towns encouraged them to change to association. By now it was 'the common talk of the mill and foundry hands' that the players were paid, and Mr Sudell, a cotton mill owner from the Preston club, responded to a complaint by readily admitting to the FA the payment of players, which he said was a common practice.

A series of meetings followed, including one by rebel clubs willing to form a British Football Association rather than accept a continued ban on professionalism.

Finally at a meeting in London on 20th July 1885 professionalism was legalised within 'stringent restrictions' somewhat similar to those that applied in cricket; professionals were allowed to compete in cup matches provided they were qualified by birth or residence for two years within six miles of the ground or headquarters of their club. Most senior clubs were optimistic that they would be able to make better arrangements with paid players, and that business would now be cheaper.[7]

Attendances increased considerably and crowds of over 20,000 at important matches were not uncommon, so the senior clubs were eager to take steps to realise their full commercial potential.

Until now professional football had existed in a disorganised form of competition. Cup ties, although lucrative, were unpredictable and 'interfered' with the arrangement of other 'friendly' matches, leading to hastily rearranged games against teams that did not attract the public.[8] Also, the desire of clubs to win honours and prestige led them actively to poach each other's players. Clubs had at first merely paid match fees but increasingly had come to provide a weekly wage well in excess of average earnings, and paid even though the clubs could not rely on regular fixtures. Paying players was, however, a necessity for real success. A committee man at Burnley said 'the public will not go to see inferior players. During the first year we did not pay a single player and

[6] Gibson and Pickford, op cit, Vol. I, p. 75.
[7] *Athletic News*, 28 July 1885, p. 4.
[8] C. E. Sutcliffe, J. A. Brierley, F. Howarth, *The Story of the Football League 1888-1938*, (Preston 1938), pp. 2-3.

nobody came to see us.'[9] A national league would bring regular fixtures that would improve gate receipts, and a degree of organisation that could restrict the freedom of financial arrangements with players and reduce wage payments.

The Football League was formed in 1888, although its founder, W. McGregor, a director of Aston Villa, attempted to find another name at first because the activities of the Irish Land League had given pejorative overtones to the word 'League'.[10] Its original objects included the regulation of players' terms of employment by agreement on a maximum wage, and a requirement that all players should be registered with one club who had a veto over any transfer. The latter was adopted by the Football League as a rule in 1890. In May 1889 the residency conditions for professionalism were abolished; they had lasted less than four years. The competing Football Alliance was also absorbed by the formation of a Second Division in 1892.

The maximum wage was brought into effect for the 1901-02 season at £4 a week with the signing-on bonus at £10; benefits could be paid after five years subject to the FA's approval. The wealthy clubs preferred an open market but the arguments of clubs like Wolverhampton Wanderers that they could not compete with neighbours like Aston Villa without such a rule proved decisive. The rules were often broken, however, and several clubs fined.

The adequacy of the pay level varied. Certainly the maximum wage was well above the rate paid to a skilled workman or even foreman, but clubs had large playing staffs, not all of whom were on the maximum wage. (At the end of the 1901-02 season clubs in the two divisions of the Football League retained 1,315 players and released 1,065 for transfer.)[11] W. J. Baker concluded that on average most players were paid under £2 per week, about the same as a skilled artisan, although better-class players were paid the maximum wage[12] and presumably also enjoyed their status as local folk heroes who 'went to the wars in saloon carriages, and were attended by supporters on their departure and met on their return'.[13]

The amassing of large playing staffs was partly a speculation leading, it was hoped, to transfer-fee revenues, and was also caused by a managerial perception that players were highly specialised and unable to switch positions effectively.

[9] *Athletic News*, 10 February 1885, p. 3.

[10] Gibson and Pickford, op cit, Vol. II, p. 4.

[11] *Yorkshire Post*, 26 May 1902.

[12] W. J. Baker, 'The Making of a Working Class Football Culture in Victorian England', *Journal of Social History*, XIII, No 2, 1979, p. 246.

[13] C. Edwardes, 'The New Football Mania', *Nineteenth Century*, XXXII, (1892), p. 5.

Large playing staffs were possible as a result of the increase in match attendances. First Division aggregate attendances more than trebled from 602,000 in 1888-9 (12 clubs) to 1,900,000 in 1895-6 (16 clubs),[14] although admission prices were fairly low. Between 1890 and the First World War the minimum admission fee was 6d (£C1) for men and 3d for ladies and boys, with clubs charging at least an extra 6d for entrance to the stands.

Crowds at Cup Finals rose from 45,000 in 1893 to the 114,000 who saw the final at Crystal Palace in 1901, and some contemporary writers saw football as a 'popular fever'; even in 1892 football was thought to be ruining the country by absorbing all the mental energies of young men and distracting them from proper performance of their jobs.

Members of Parliament and Mayors 'quite frequently set the ball moving at a match to show their sympathy with the popular ferment',[15] while people in the League districts were seen as smitten by the football fever. Many women and old people were so caught up by it that they would not, on any account, miss a local match, and could be seen 'wedged in the crowds of youths and young men who patronise the excursion trains to fields of combat fifty or a hundred miles from home.'[16]

Crowds in the first twenty years were not always as peaceable as this account suggests. When Blackburn fielded only three first-team players for a local derby against Darwen in December 1890 and Darwen retaliated by taking their players off and putting their reserves on, the rival supporters overran the ground, breaking goal posts and dressing-room windows.[17] In 1901 a match between Newcastle and Sunderland was abandoned when the pitch became a battleground between rival supporters. The affray was so enjoyable to the participants that it took the police until five o'clock to clear the pitch.[18]

Such outbreaks of violence were naturally occasional rather than routine events, but Dunning, Murphy et al. concluded that 'spectator disorderliness was a recurrent and relatively frequent accompaniment of association football before the First World War',[19] although by contemporary standards the problems were probably not all that serious: 'as a rule half-a-dozen flat-footed Robertos serve to keep both the

[14] Tony Mason, *Association Football and English Society 1863-1915*, (Brighton 1980), p. 140.

[15] C. Edwardes, op cit, p. 5.

[16] ibid, p. 6.

[17] W. Vamplew, 'Ungentlemanly Conduct: the Control of Soccer Crowd Behaviour in England, 1888-1914' in T.C. Smout, *Search for Wealth and Stability*, (London 1979), p. 141.

[18] Simon Inglis, *The Football Grounds of England and Wales*, (London 1983), p. 86.

[19] E. Dunning, P. Murphy, J. Williams and J. Maguire, 'Football Hooligan Violence before the First World War' in A. Tomlinson, Explorations in Football Culture, Brighton Polytechnic Working Papers, 1983 (unpublished), p. 42.

members and ticket holders and the casual sixpenny gentlemen as well in order.'[20]

Disorderly or not, it was this increase in spectator interest that transformed many clubs from multi-sports clubs into Limited Liability Companies specialising in professional soccer. Bradford Park Avenue was a multi-sports club, but this was not a particularly distinctive feature; Bolton's Burnden Park was opened by the town's annual athletic festival and had a cycling track installed, Goodison Park had a cinder running track until 1907 and Preston had been a cricket, rugby and athletics club (a familiar combination in the West Riding) before taking up the association code in 1881.

If football was to pay it was clearly necessary to employ professional players, and in order to cover these regular costs (which were far higher than in the 'broken-time' Northern Union) large crowds had to be attracted and housed.

The construction of purpose-built stands transformed football from a game into a leisure business, for it necessitated both raising finance and bearing the ever-present risks of financial loss and liquidation. Similar considerations, of course, applied to horse racing, music hall and theatre developments and the promotion of seaside resorts (including piers), the other emergent leisure industries of the late Victorian era.

In horse racing the gentry and their womenfolk had obtained seclusion in purpose-built stands since the 1770s, but it was the railway that made horse racing a national spectator sport and prompted the new enclosed courses of the 1870s directly linked to railway stations and, in some cases, railway company sponsorship. £1,500,000 (£C46,000,000) was invested in courses and grandstands between 1875 and 1895.[21]

In association football major ground development came after the formation of the Football League in 1888. The first large grandstands were at Goodison Park in 1892, Anfield 1895, and Villa Park in 1897. Major building work took place at about twenty grounds before the First World War, encouraged by an era of relatively low building costs.[22] The period before 1910 was decisive in the location of clubs. Sixty-six of the current league clubs had moved to their present grounds by then,[23] and the strength of local loyalties and traditions did not encourage clubs to move. Grounds were generally primitive; in the 1880s vehicles were often brought onto them to be used as makeshift stands, grandstands were invariably built of wood, few spectators were under cover, while terracing consisted of banks of earth or cinders edged with wood.

[20] Simon Inglis, op cit, p. 70.
[21] Hugh Cunningham, op cit, pp. 159, 177.
[22] Simon Inglis, op cit, p. 20.
[23] ibid, p. 13.

The economics of football, and the risks and finance associated with ground construction, had profound organisational implications. At Woolwich Arsenal, the only club to move any considerable distance, the club went professional in 1891 but rejected Limited Liability to avoid 'degenerating into a proprietory or capitalist club'.[24] Under the financial pressures of buying their own ground they reversed their position in 1893, a fairly typical reaction, for the level of gate money income was very unpredictable.

At least one contemporary writer in the 1890s thought that as financial property, football was not very valuable;[25] already professional football was offering more by way of community involvement and recognition than direct monetary return. The Football League had, from its inception, sought to control player costs and mobilities, but in turn the Football Association rules made it impossible for football to be commercially exploited, by prohibiting directors' remuneration, and limiting dividends to a maximum of 5%. Although this was a far more respectable return than it would appear from the perspective of the 1980s (interest rates averaged about 3% from 1880-1914), it was still not commensurate with the risks involved, and the price of protecting the sport against financial greed was to deny the incentives that might have widened the supply of managerial talents and investment funds. In consequence the newly incorporated clubs which had lost democratic, grass-roots involvement gained only the time and money of those who could afford to offer them on a non-commercial basis. As football was essentially a working-class activity, and offered little social cachet to the monied gentry, the development of association football was to suffer from a rationing of organisational talents and funds.

In Bradford these effects were to be reinforced by local factors and distinctions integral to the pattern of historical development of commercial sport in the city.

---

[24] *Woolwich Gazette and Plumstead Times*, 15 May 1891.
[25] C. Edwardes, op cit, p. 4.

5. The Origins of Bradford City AFC

Manningham Football Club was established in 1880 and played its early (rugby union) matches on a ground in Carlisle Road, west of Manningham Lane, until the land was required for a Board School in 1886.

The club was fairly successful, and when a suitable site east of Manningham Lane, between Valley Parade and Midland Road, was obtained on a favourable lease from the Midland Railway Company, the members decided to place the club on a firmer foundation. At the Sixth Annual General Meeting on 21st May 1886 the members resolved that the club be incorporated under the Companies Acts, with the liability of each member limited by guarantee to £1.

The club's primary objective was to play (rugby) football, particularly in the Yorkshire Challenge Cup, but they also anticipated that cricket matches, athletic festivals and 'assaults at arms' would be organised, with prize money and admission charges for entry to the grounds and stands of the club. An area was left at the present 'Spion Kop' end as a proposed site for lawn tennis courts.

The structure was democratic; although there were seven-year members who subscribed £2 (£C60), and ordinary members who paid at least 6/- (£C9) a year, every member had only one vote, to be exercised in person. The club was managed by a committee of fifteen, elected annually, three of whom were to be players.[1]

The new ground at Valley Parade was opened in late September 1886, for the visit of Wakefield Trinity.

Four acres of steep hillside had been leased from the Midland Railway Company. The ground was close on the top side to the tram service that ran along Manningham Lane, a main thoroughfare, and on the lower side to Manningham Station on the railway line immediately below Midland Road.

In three months the hillside was turned into a ground suitable for serious rugby. The field was laid with layers of ballast, ashes and soil and covered with turf, and the ground was so stony that drainage work was almost entirely dispensed with.

[1] Manningham FC Memorandum and Articles PRO BT 31-3700/23007.

The playing area was 120 yards by 80 and the actual field of play 100 yards by 70. A three-yard wide cinder track was included for athletics, being nearly 400 yards long.

The stand from the previous ground at Carlisle Road was transported to Valley Parade and fixed at the top of the ground, parallel to South Parade, and a new enclosure constructed in front, stepped and holding 2,000 people, thus making a main stand. Dressing-rooms were built under the stand, with entrance to the field along the side of the stand, but this arrangement did not prove satisfactory for very long. Walls were built with stone quarried on site.

Apart from the stand, which ran less than half the length of the playing area, the spectator slopes provided 'a good view' for 4,000 people on the top side, 6,000 on the low or Midland Road side, and 6,000 behind the goals, for a capacity of 18,000.[2]

Although the Manningham club was incorporated, it was not a 'capitalist club'; there was no transferable share capital, and no distribution of profits was allowed, even on winding up.

The structure was a sensible compromise. The club had been founded and subsequently run by working men[3] but now needed to provide them with protection against the risks associated with ground development, even though this was on a fairly modest scale appropriate to the needs and finances of gate-taking rugby.

The occupational composition of its committee in 1886, the year it was incorporated, shows the strong, although not exclusive, influence of working men on the management of the club (see Appendix 3a).

Manningham were only recently founded, but they soon developed into a strong side, although their membership and attendances were lower than at neighbouring Bradford. They were one of the senior Yorkshire clubs that withdrew in 1895 from the Rugby Union over broken-time payments.

The formation of the Northern Union came when Manningham's side was at its strongest and they became the first champions of the Northern Union in 1896, winning 33 out of 42 matches.

The Northern Union then decided to operate separate Yorkshire and Lancashire Leagues so as to accommodate the other clubs who had left the Rugby Union. Manningham finished second, but the following season, 1897-8, they finished fifth, well behind Bradford (Park Avenue) who only just failed to win the Yorkshire Senior Competition, losing the decisive playoff.

Manningham's gate receipts fell 15% to £1,075 (£C33,000), and total income to £1,800 (£C56,000) giving rise to a loss of £125 (£C4,000).

[2] *Illustrated Weekly Telegraph*, 25 September 1886, p. 1.
[3] *Bradford Daily Telegraph*, 30 April 1903, p. 5.

However, broken-time payments (£305) and travel costs (£120) were still quite a small proportion of gate receipts, and accumulated profits from previous years amounted to £460 (£C14,000).[4]

The management structure was gradually tightened. By 1899 the committee was down to seven, with only two retiring and reapplying for election each year, and it was stipulated that none of the committee could be a playing member. Additionally the category of life-member was instituted, requiring a payment of over £5 (£C150).

When the Northern Union was restructured again in 1901 Manningham were near the foot of the Yorkshire Senior Competition. The top seven clubs in both Yorkshire and Lancashire formed a new Northern Union League, but Manningham were forced to play in the depleted Yorkshire competition.

This was soon to prove decisive to their entry into professional soccer, for they lost money heavily on the season; the annual accounts for 1901-02 showing a loss of £200 (£C6,000) which wiped out 40% of the accumulated surpluses. Although assets of £2,200 (including £1,550 spend on the ground) still exceeded liabilities (£1,900 including a mortgage of £1,100), gate receipts had halved (£1,275 to £685), members' subscriptions were down 30% (to £160), and a loss had been made in spite of 'a series of economies' which covered all items of expenditure, other than payments to players, which increased slightly (to £455).

The management assured the public that they were still a 'sound and solvent body', but the direction of events was clearly a worrying one.[5]

There was widespread dissatisfaction amongst the stronger clubs in the two county competitions, and the Northern Union responded by forming a Second Division. Manningham had no alternative to entering this division, for to have remained in the further depleted Yorkshire competition would have been commercial suicide. On the other hand rapid promotion to lucrative fixtures in the First Division was essential as the Second Division included a number of highly marginal clubs, dispersed over a wide area offering a prospect of poor gate receipts and increased travelling expenses.

Manningham spent more money in 1902-03 than in previous seasons on players' wages in an attempt to escape from Division Two, but they were unsuccessful, finishing in the middle of the league table. (The risk was worthwhile; Leeds lost £800 in a successful pursuit of promotion the same year and recouped the loss the following year, increasing rugby membership from 650 to 2,275).[6] Gate receipts were even lower than the

[4] *Yorkshire Post*, 21 May 1898, p. 14.
[5] *Bradford Daily Telegraph*, 23 May 1902, p. 3.
[6] Leeds Cricket, Football and Athletic Co Ltd, 15th Annual Report, 26 June 1903.

previous year and members' subscriptions fell again. The outcome was a loss of £660 (£C19,000), three times the previous year and enough to turn accumulated surpluses into losses. Payments to players of £605 were 90% of gate receipts and total income of £870 compared poorly with expenses of £1,470 (which included travel costs of £140).

Liabilities now exceeded assets, and although an athletics carnival made a notable profit which safeguarded their financial position and took the club out of debt, the longer-term prospects for Northern Union rugby had never looked worse.

An article appeared in the *Bradford Daily Telegraph* in January, 1903, which was highly convenient for those who sought to establish 'socker' in Bradford, and may well have been sponsored.

A gradual but sure decline of public interest in rugby was noted, and gates at the two Bradford clubs were said to have declined from 13,000 to 4,000 in a few years. Unnamed but 'sound' judges were also said to contend that soccer was more subtle than its rival and, by implication, more likely to prove popular. On the basis of a comparison of attendances at rugby and soccer matches in Manchester over Christmas, and the comparative populations of Manchester and Bradford, a highly tenuous prospect of soccer gates of 27,000 in Bradford was constructed.

The article went on to say that £1,000 (£C31,000) was needed to found a team of professional players and that nothing would please the football authorities more than to extend their influence to the densely populated West Riding. 'We have authority for saying that the FA will do all in its power to assist the club who will take the first step. Shall it be Bradford or Leeds?'[7]

The message was reinforced two days later when the paper spoke of the 'parlous state' of Northern Union rugby in Leeds, and the probability that Headingley would next year be in the hands of a professional association team.[8]

In the same month the Bradford and District FA issued a circular for a meeting to discuss how best to set up a 'first-class association club in Bradford'.

At this time there were about a hundred school teams and junior clubs in the district; school teams were numerous because the schools' authorities had abandoned rugby in favour of association, apparently after a boy's leg was badly broken playing rugby.

A private meeting took place at Market Tavern, Bradford, on 14th February, 1903, and the 'thirty gentlemen' present confirmed their interest, appointing a committee of seven, comprising J. T. Whyte, a newspaper sub-editor who had played association in Scotland, and J.

[7] *Bradford Daily Telegraph*, 14 January 1903.
[8] ibid, 16 January 1903, p. 6.

Brunt, who had both issued the original circular, together with A. J. Foxcroft, W. Harland, A. Ayrton, Colonel Armitage and J. E. Fattorini.[9]

The main work took place in private. By the end of February an announcement was made that support had been promised by Football League clubs and 'should a club be formed little doubt now exists as to the question of securing admission to the Second Division of the League'. Moreover the Manningham club had been approached with a view to making the Valley Parade ground the new club's headquarters.[10]

It was against this background that seventeen members requisitioned an Extraordinary General Meeting of Manningham FC on 26th March 1903.

The committee had already been approached by the promoters of a professional soccer club in Bradford and seemed already in sympathy with them; revealingly the meeting was limited to life members and excluded the 6/- members. The committee did have a general power to manage and superintend the affairs of the club, but this procedure seemed in complete breach of their Articles of Association, item 14 of which stated that 'every member shall have one vote and no more'.

The Chairman and Secretary made the committee's position clear; the club had lost money for several years and although they were now out of debt (due to the athletics carnival) they would not stay that way under rugby rules.

'Rugby was a dismal failure, and as businessmen they must look to something better', said H. Jowett, the Treasurer.

The association promoters had undertaken to provide £2,000 (£C62,000) if Manningham provided the ground, and £500 (£C15,000) capital, for the two bodies to go into partnership and run the two codes on alternate weeks. Furthermore eighteen clubs had promised to assist Bradford get into the Second Division.

The Committee, amidst applause, was then empowered to play both codes, the soccer section under the name Bradford City.[11]

Momentum was maintained when a leading side, Sheffield United, came to the city in April 1903 and played a West Yorkshire XI as a sort of 'missionary game'.

The decisive step came at the Annual General Meeting of the Football League on 24th May when Burnley, Doncaster Rovers and Stockport County sought re-election against would be entrants. Bradford City topped the list of eight clubs with thirty votes, above Stockport and Football League founders Burnley, and above Doncaster who were forced to leave the League. The size of Bradford's vote indicates their

[9] ibid, 16 February 1903, p. 3.
[10] ibid, 26 February 1903, p. 5.
[11] ibid, 27 March 1903, p. 3.

powers of persuasion, and the desire of the soccer movement to establish itself in the one densely populated area it had failed to enter, the West Riding textile district.

Bradford City thus became the only side to join the Football League without having played a soccer match of any kind. Although they had signed on several players, and although the committee and life members of Manningham had agreed to share facilities, the general members had not yet sanctioned the use of their ground for soccer.

The day after Bradford City were accepted into the Football League, on 25th May 1903, there was a special meeting of Manningham FC, attended by 160 members and by the successful London delegation, Foxcroft, Whyte and Fattorini.

Fattorini was a member of the Bradford family who built the chain of jewellers' shops, Messrs Fattorini and Son, that made the second FA Cup in 1911 and subsequently created Empire Stores, a large mail-order business.

Sensing the euphoria that admission into the Football League had brought, the committee's official position had already shifted; they were prepared to play both codes at Valley Parade *if necessary*, but they were also prepared to leave the rugby code to Bradford (PA) with whom they could not compete while their rivals were in the First Division of the Northern Union, and Manningham were in the Second Division. (In fact no one was able to compete with Bradford (PA) that season as they won the First Division of the Northern Union.) 'They had tried it, and lost money, and therefore they were prepared to drop it,' said H. Jowett the Treasurer.

The committee were willing to put all their energies into the Bradford City club, and Whyte anticipated home gates of at least 7,000, 2,000 more than necessary for financial success; 7/6 tickets would give admission to all matches, 10/6 to a special stand and 21/- to the covered stand.[12]

Final ratification of the changes proposed at Manningham came at the 23rd Annual General Meeting on 29th May 1903, at a noisy, crowded meeting, attended by the President A. Ayrton, and the committee, W. Knowles, H. Jowett, J. Nunn, I. Newton, A. Lancaster, W. Wyrill and E. W. Wilkinson.

Financial considerations dominated the discussion. The Treasurer felt that the decay of the rugby game was absolute and recognised on all sides, and they would be wise to abandon it and go in for a game they were convinced would pay.

A further, and final, shift in the Committee's position was then made

---

[12] ibid, 26 May 1903, p. 5.

clear; they had decided it was impossible to play both codes next year, and wanted to abandon rugby completely 'for twelve months' and run two soccer teams, the second in the West Yorkshire League.

The financial commitments were not to be excessive; the ground would not need to be extended, as it held 15,000, and if they got 10,000 they would be satisfied.

Although a proposal that the club stick to rugby was 'greeted with great cheers' the counter-proposal that they adopt soccer in place of rugby was carried by 75 votes to 34.

The only faint consolation to the rugby enthusiasts was that, although the soccer team played under the name Bradford City from its inception, the company did not change its name from Manningham FC until a new company was formed in 1908. None the less few could have been deceived; Manningham had taken an irreversible decision in pursuit of 'a game that would pay'.

6. Park Avenue as an Elite Rugby Club

Of the eleven senior rugby clubs in the West Riding that attended the decisive meeting at Huddersfield in 1895, Manningham (1880) were one of the most recently established, and Bradford (1863) were the oldest. Bradford's origins as a club, focussed initially on cricket, in fact went back to 1836.

After a meeting at the White Lion Hotel on the 18th July 1836 the Bradford Cricket Club was formed, to play on 'Mr Booths field' in Great Horton Road, close to the town centre. The first match was played on 1st August 1836. Although cricket was often sponsored by religious organisations as a form of distraction from less worthy activities, it was not entirely remote from gambling and drink; each member of Bradford Cricket Club put up a 5/- stake for the first match, against Bradford West End, and tents were customarily pitched at matches to act as public houses. Meetings were usually held in local hostelries and tickets for important matches were allocated to the various inns for distribution.[1]

Cricket had been played in the West Riding since at least 1757, when the Church Burgesses paid players to entertain the populace on Shrove Tuesday and prevent the infamous practice of throwing at cocks.[2] In 1824 there were 17,000 spectators at a match in Sheffield. From the 1840s cricket went through a period of intense competition between travelling professional sides, embryonic county clubs, and the MCC, which had been formed in 1788, and this led eventually to the arrangement of a County Championship competition in 1873.[3]

Bradford were sufficiently well established for the All-England XI to visit them for a fixture in September 1852 and they were hosts for a county match as early as 1863 when Yorkshire played Kent at the Trinity Fields. By 1866 Bradford and York provided the main challenge to Sheffield's ambitions to provide the focus of Yorkshire County Cricket aided in the case of Bradford by a 'liberal' subscription list. The Horton Lane ground was 'good and well sited', but too small to be ideal, as 'only

[1] *Bradford Cricket Club* (Bradford 1973), p. 8.
[2] R. S. Holmes, *The History of Yorkshire County Cricket*, 1833-1903, (London 1904), p. 11.
[3] J. A. Schofield, 'The Development of First Class Cricket in England', *Journal of Industrial Economics*, XXX, No 4 (1982), p. 338.

square hits can be run out', so an enlargement was considered.[4]

Also in 1863, a Mr. Ingham of Lingfield Dyeworks, Bradford, and some fellow students from Bramham College formed a rugby football club. They played on Horton Cricket Club's field for two winters, but this damaged the field and they moved to a succession of other grounds in the Bradford area, before giving up for some time.

This was a fruitful time for launching sports clubs; the Huddersfield Rugby Club started the following year with a meeting where those present decided to form an athletics club and obtain a gymnasium. The first of a series of annual athletics festivals was held in 1865, and rugby began in 1869, promoting a large growth in membership.

By the mid 1870s the Bradford rugby club was playing again at Applerley Bridge, on the eastern edge of Bradford, under the name Bradford FC. They were by now one of the senior clubs in Yorkshire and were instrumental in the presentation of the Challenge Cup to the county rugby authorities. Bradford Cricket Ground, which was where Pemberton Drive now is, across Great Horton Road from the present University of Bradford, was required for building, so alternative grounds were found further out on Great Horton Road, just south of Dirk Hill, and near the intersection of two railway lines. The location was the more attractive commercially as the Bradford and Thornton Railway had opened in 1878 with a station immediately outside the grounds.

These grounds at Park Avenue were acquired by trustees on behalf of the club in 1879, and construction took place during 1879 and 1880. Talks were taking place between the cricket club and Bradford FC and an amalgamation was agreed, with the rugby club moving from Apperley Bridge to Park Avenue and the combined organisation playing under the name Bradford Cricket Athletic and Football Club.

On 21st July 1880 the ground was opened by the Mayor, Alderman A. Holden. The area covered was eight acres, and of the two pavilions the one at the top of the grounds had a 130-foot frontage onto the cricket ground. This pavilion had a grandstand in front, a two-storey structure 'in a modified Italian style of architecture', while at the back of the building was a 60-foot long refreshment bar. The south gable of the upper storey contained a 130-seat dining-room. The lower pavilion had frontages onto both the cricket and football grounds, and was particularly suited to the latter. These structures were to remain virtually unchanged for more than seventy years.[5]

A rugby match was played on 28th September 1880 and the first season's receipts of £520 (£C18,000) yielded a profit of £300 (£C10,000). The cricket side was also doing well and Yorkshire played Derbyshire at

[4] R. S. Holmes, op cit, p. 43.
[5] *Bradford Daily Telegraph*, 19 July 1950.

Park Avenue the following season.

Although Park Avenue was further from the centre of Bradford than the previous ground, the city was expanding even more rapidly; in 1886 the local historian Cudworth had to remind his readers that Horton was once a 'distinct place divided from the town by a long stretch of green fields';[6] fifty years previously the walk from Horton to Bradford 'took the pedestrian through two miles of meandering country lanes'.[7]

The combined organisation had made an encouraging start and they soon became a successful club. In 1884 when they reached the final of the Yorkshire Challenge Cup, 6,000 people travelled to Leeds and a large crowd gathered for news at the telegraph office, making traffic movements very difficult.

The victorious Bradford side were met at the Midland Station by the Great Horton Brass Band and a crowd of several thousand who carried them shoulder-high to a celebration meal at a local hotel.[8]

Their financial position was just as assured, and by 1885-86 receipts were £3,120, including the half-guinea subscriptions of 2,050 members. As there were no players' wages to meet, expenses were moderate and the profit reported was £2,000 (£C62,000).[9]

The growing importance and financial strength of the rugby and cricket sections encouraged the committee to attempt to secure their position at Horton Park Avenue for the foreseeable future.

With this in mind the members voted on 17th December 1891 to form the Incorporated Bradford Cricket, Athletic and Football Club, with a licence from the Board of Trade to hold lands, to take over the unincorporated club. This took advantage of a section of the 1862 Act which allowed incorporation of organisations formed for the purpose of promoting commerce, art, science, religion, charity or any useful object and where the profits were to be used to promote the objectives and could not be paid out as dividends to the members. Manningham had been similarly incorporated five years before.

This met the wishes of Mr. F. S. Powell who was prepared to transfer the field in Park Avenue to the club on a 999-year lease at nominal ground rent, for a reasonable sum as long as he could be assured that the field would be used for cricket, football and athletics.[10]

Incorporation took place in March 1892. The president was the Mayor of Bradford, T. Priestley, a worsted manufacturer, and the club was organised into a general committee and a football committee, an

---

6 Asa Briggs, op cit, p. 28.
7 J. Reynolds, op cit, p. 26.
8 D. J. Wright and J. A. Jowett, op cit, p. 214.
9 Bradford Rugby Union FC Centenary Brochure.
10 *Bradford Observer*, 18 December 1891, p. 6.

arrangement which recognised the importance of the rugby side of the club and gave exclusive control of rugby to a committee of twelve, five of whom were on the ten-member general committee. These five, A. Barrett, an iron manufacturer from Harrogate, T. Corry, S. Haigh, J. Hickson and R. N. Rhodes were committed to rugby, but among the other early committee members were E. Briggs and H. Geldard who were to play a major role in the subsequent switch to the association code.

In 1895 Bradford was among the clubs who broke away from the English Rugby Union and formed the Northern Union. Their disaffected rugby union players remained together but had serious problems finding a suitable ground which were not resolved satisfactorily until 1919.

The club's commitment to rugby was not as wholehearted as it might have seemed. At the same time that the club were joining the Northern Union they also formed a new association team, and they defeated Moss Side Manchester on 14th September 1895 in the first 'regular association fixture' at Park Avenue. (Many years before, the ground had been used for an exhibition match between Blackburn Rovers and Blackburn Olympic.)

On this occasion the crowd was 3,000, and the newspaper report noted with some incredulity that 'many persons amongst the crowd evidently understood the association rules'.[11] Ten days later their amateur soccer team were visited by First Division Bolton Wanderers, who played a 'sort of missionary match' before a crowd of 5,000.[11]

The financial position of the club was under severe strain in 1895 due to the substantial demands of a programme of ground purchase and development which included a large rugby stand that backed onto the cricket ground. The overdraft had now risen to a level which concerned the bank, so a special meeting was held in October 1895, at which E. Briggs presided, to consider some solutions to the financial problems.

The meeting was told there were 2,000 football and 560 cricket members, that membership had declined by 800 in the last year and that if the club was to continue there was a need for more guinea members. A proposal was made to levy subscriptions at 10/6 except for playing members, but to offer those who paid a guinea a year membership of both the cricket and football sections, and to allow only the guinea members to vote.

This was probably more of a procedural device to concentrate control in the hands of more prosperous club members than a genuine attempt to deal with financial problems; the meeting to consider the change of rules was called for 10.30 on a Tuesday morning, and half an hour elapsed before enough members could arrive to form a quorum.

[11] ibid, 16 September 1895, p. 3.
[12] *Bradford Daily Telegraph*, 22 September 1950.

The meeting a fortnight later to ratify the change was at a time equally inconvenient to working members; one or two of those present described it as a 'hole-and-corner meeting' and asked for an evening meeting instead. Their request was ignored, but the vote confirming the change of thirty votes to twelve shows how few of the members could attend.

At the end of the 1895-6 season, in which Bradford finished in mid-table, well behind the champions, Manningham, the Northern Union clubs were 'conspicuously unsuccessful in a financial sense'.[13] Bradford were one of the main sufferers and were thought to be on the verge of bankruptcy, due not to playing losses but to the very substantial commitment to ground improvements. They owed £10,300 in 1896 (£C320,000), £4,500 on the ground purchase, £4,000 to the bank on overdraft and £1,800 for the construction of roads and extensions agreed to when the ground was bought.[14] At about the same time, electric trams started operating in Bradford, running to Park Avenue in 1898 and Manningham in 1900.[15]

Bradford's first two seasons in commercial rugby had been unimpressive on the field, but they continued to improve. In the following season 1897-8 they finished joint first in the Yorkshire Senior Competition, losing the play-off, and although association had been tried it seemed clear which game would pay. Association generated receipts of £130, which after expenses, including travel of £70, yielded a surplus of only £5 (£C160), so the experiment was abandoned.

Other rugby clubs in the district had tried association with similar results. Association began in Halifax in 1892 with some casual games on Savile Park, but the game did not flourish and a soccer ball could not even be obtained from any of the adjacent West Riding cities. In 1895 the activity was absorbed by the rugby club; matches were typically played in the early evening after rugby fixtures, but the experiment was abandoned in 1900 for lack of support. Association football was seen more as a source of supplementary income than as competition. Halifax loaned their Thrum Hall ground for Halifax FA Cup Finals, and Huddersfield were pleased to host the 1882 FA Cup semi-final between Sheffield Wednesday and Blackburn. It was unusual for the soccer authorities to use established rugby grounds, but on this occasion the venue met the need to provide a ground a similar distance from both towns.

Rugby had produced gate receipts of £2,370, and after expenses Bradford were able to announce profits of £710 (£C22,000), which helped to reduce capital commitments.

---

[13] E. Dunning and K. Sheard, op cit, p. 218.
[14] ibid, p. 219.
[15] C. Richardson, *Geography of Bradford*, (Bradford 1976), p. 118.

Bradford's side enjoyed a period of sustained success, third in 1899, and then champions of the Yorkshire Senior Competition in successive seasons 1899/1900 and 1900/01, winning in 1901 in spite of two points being deducted for a breach of professional rules. This contributed to reported profits of £960 (£C30,000) for the season and guaranteed their entry into the fourteen-strong Northern Union League of 1901-02, made up of the top seven teams in both Lancashire and Yorkshire. They came sixth, again declared profits (£400) and stayed in the more lucrative First Division the following season when two divisions were organised.

Thus while Manningham were leaving the Northern Union due to the financial losses caused by membership of rugby's Second Division, Bradford were an elite club, with a highly successful playing record which was helping, even in the financially strained Northern Union, to pay off the debts from laying out their stylish and well-appointed grounds.

1903-1915
EARLY SUCCESS

7. The Local Economy

The West Riding had replaced East Anglia during the eighteenth and nineteenth centuries as the most important region for woollen textiles, but after a period of great prosperity the trade declined during the last quarter of the nineteenth century, particularly during the 1890s.

The industry revived considerably between 1900 and 1915; the 'disastrous years of the 1890s were followed from 1901 by a notable export boom for woollen cloth. From the trough of 1901 to the peak of 1912 the value of wool textile cloth and yarn exports almost doubled and, apart from a relatively minor slump in 1908, the period was one of great prosperity for many branches of the trade.'[1]

The woollen textile industry consists of a number of different trades, each with its own local centre, and each experienced its own changes in fortune. The cloths that were produced ranged from the luxurious to the very basic. Huddersfield developed a reputation for the high-class worsted cloth used by quality tailors for morning coats or dress suits, and Halifax specialised in worsted coating, carpets and army cloths and blankets. The Yorkshire heavy woollen district made large quantities of cheap warm suits and coats during peacetime, and Dewsbury concentrated on shoddy or mungo, low-grade woollen manufacture using the rag-grinding machinery that was developed in the locality. Leeds was the most diversified of the textile towns. Its prosperity came initially from woollen cloth, flax yarn (from the great mills at Holbeck) and worsted cloth, but its engineering trade developed steadily, particularly in textile machinery, as did its clothing industry. The Hepworths, who were the first major clothiers to develop their own retail outlets (and who also put money into Leeds City FC), had over 140 retail outlets by 1905. In 1911 the clothing industry in Leeds was a larger employer than the textile trade.[2]

Bradford produced mostly worsted and wool-mix cloth, and fashion fabrics using new fibres such as silks and velvet plushes, particularly in the mills in the Manningham district. The volume of woollen imports,

---

[1] D. Jenkins and K. Ponting, op cit, p. 238.
[2] Joan Thomas, 'Later Developments in the Clothing Industry', *Leeds Journal*, September 1954, p. 338.

chiefly from Australia and New Zealand, and exports to Europe and America had a direct impact on the importance and prosperity of Bradford as the wool-dealing capital, and these consistently reached 'new levels' between 1907 and 1915. Also in 1911, the year City won the FA Cup, 'never had combs put through more wool'[3] in Bradford as demand reached its highest level. Profits naturally improved.

This did not lead, however, to prosperity for all. The number of employees in the woollen industry was still lower in 1907 than thirty years before, although this was largely due to a substantial fall in the number of children under fourteen, who had been working half days. The employment of men remained static and well below the level of female employment. (In 1907 male employees, of all ages, totalled 109,000 out of 261,000.)[4]

1904 was a poor year for employment, and in nearby Leeds distress was so acute that the council voted £10,000 that year for relief work.[5] Profits in Bradford were certainly far better than in the 1890s, but in the five years to 1907 were still low enough to trigger an arrangement to reduce some wages by ten per cent.

In the country as a whole, money wages rose 40% between 1880 and 1914; when changes in the cost of living are allowed for, real wages rose about 30% during the 1880s, less than 10% through to 1905, and then changed very little.[6]

Although wages in the West Riding were lower than in the country as a whole, there was a little more money around for a variety of leisure activities; in 1907 a series of chamber music concerts was proposed to 'limit the excesses of local courting habits which were particularly noticeable in Manningham Lane'.[7]

The most important leisure development was, however, the cinema, which had started in Bradford in the last years of the nineteenth century with intermittent showings at St. George's Hall. Screenings became more regular, and led to the opening of an extraordinary number of cinemas in the town in the period 1909-14. Of the sixty cinemas that have operated in Bradford, thirty-three were opened during this period and only one closed before the First World War. Several were in the Manningham Lane area and some had names that sound slightly incongruous in so industrial a setting; the Elysian Palace, the Electric

[3] D. Jenkins and K. Ponting, op cit, p. 240.

[4] B. Mitchell and P. Deane, *Abstract of British Historical Statistics*, (Cambridge 1962), p. 199.

[5] *The Times*, 28 September 1908, p. 8.

[6] B. Mitchell and P. Deane, p. 344.

[7] D. Russell, 'Popular Musical Culture and Popular Politics in the Yorkshire Textile Districts, 1880 – 1914' in J. Walton and J. Walvin (eds), *Leisure in Britain, 1780-1939*, (Manchester 1986), p. 100.

Palace, the Scala and the Olympic Picture Palace.[8]

The extent to which improved prosperity in the area was translated into attendances at, and entrepreneurial support for, professional sport depended ultimately on personal factors. Firms in the West Riding textile industry tended to be small, specialised and short lived. Only 10% of firms in existence in 1870 were still operational in 1912. Woollen textile manufacturers were 'very loathe to incorporate', generally reluctant to get involved in national issues, and half-hearted in their response to local issues and problems not directly connected with their trade, for 'most entrepreneurs in wool textiles seem to have made the business their whole life'.[9]

---

[8] G. J. Mellor, *The Cinemas of Bradford*, (Bradford 1983).
[9] D. Jenkins and K. Ponting, op cit, pp. 182, 303.

8. The Football Business

Most commercial football clubs were formed in the late nineteenth century. Of the 117 clubs that have ever played in the Football League, 85 were formed before Queen Victoria's death in 1901, and another 20 were established before 1914.

One of the main objectives of the Football League was to build upon its early start and establish itself as the undisputed national league, superior to the other leagues which had been quickly set up such as the Football Alliance, the Midland League and the Southern League.

This was partly a matter of simple prestige, partly an appreciation that the fluidity of arrangements implied a likelihood of 'absorb or be absorbed', and also a method of extending the ambit of controls on players' wages and mobility so as to strengthen the position of member clubs in dealing with their employees. This policy could not, however, be unduly hurried, for the entry of too many marginal clubs would weaken the quality upon which the Football League's reputation depended and also reduce the revenue of members by facing them with fixtures against inferior sides.

The League therefore needed to carry out their policy with some care; dangers were apparent in the first extension of the League from twelve clubs to fourteen in 1891-2 when the two newly admitted sides finished last, with Darwen conceding 112 goals in 26 matches. The absorption of the Football Alliance the following year increased membership suddenly to 28 in two divisions, and the quality of the twelve Second Division sides was poor. Only three clubs, Small Heath (Birmingham City), Sheffield United and Ardwick (Manchester City) have enjoyed continuous membership since then, although Grimsby missed only one season, 1910-11, when they were voted out so as to make way for Huddersfield Town.

A Third Division was discussed in 1908, and Huddersfield's formation that year was thought to have been nicely timed,[1] but the scheme was deferred and did not take place until after the Great War.

By 1903 the Football League was almost exclusively northern. Only two out of the 36 sides were from the South, Woolwich Arsenal (formerly

[1] *Huddersfield Daily Examiner*, 25 August 1908, p. 3.

Royal Arsenal) who were the first professional southern side, and Bristol City, and there were no teams to represent the Yorkshire textile district, where rugby was dominant.

The Southern League had been formed in 1894. Its original members included Millwall, Southampton St. Marys, Luton, Clapton Orient, Swindon and Reading, and Tottenham Hotspur joined in 1896. The standard of play was high and in three successive seasons from 1899-1900 Southern League sides reached the FA Cup Final. Southampton lost both times, but Tottenham won in 1901 to bring the cup south for the first time since the Old Etonians' victory in 1882, and for the first time since the Football League had been formed.

In 1902 the Football League Division Two was in need of strengthening, for it included clubs like Glossop North End, Burton United and Gainsborough Trinity, while the Northern Union was in a state of crisis. The rugby authorities also wanted to extend their membership by offering commercially attractive competition to marginal areas and clubs, but without reducing the gate revenues of its senior sides. With no floodlights to permit midweek fixtures the Northern Union faced a dilemma, and tried several different structures. In 1902 the fourteen-member single-division arrangement was roundly criticised by clubs left to play in their county competitions and for 1902-03 36 clubs were admitted in two divisions. The economics of the Northern Union Second Division were fragile, and the scheme only lasted until 1905, after which a single large division of about 26 clubs was formed. (This was still not ideal as it was too large for all clubs to play each other.)

Only six Northern Union clubs have changed codes and formed Football League sides, and five of them, Manningham, Holbeck (Leeds City), Birkenhead (Tranmere), South Shields and Stockport were in the Northern Union Division Two in 1902-03, while the sixth, Bradford (PA) was in the Northern Union Division One.

In 1905 the Football League expanded its membership slightly to forty (in two divisions) and this enabled it to attract more London sides, Chelsea, Fulham, Clapton Orient and Tottenham, and to accommodate several clubs from Yorkshire's rugby territory. The League had clearly made encouraging noises, for two clubs, Chelsea and Hull (a noted rugby town) were formed, incorporated, turned professional and voted into the Second Division within twelve months in 1904-05.

Attendances gradually improved. In 1908-09 First Division average attendances were about 16,000,[2] and by 1913-14 they averaged 23,115, ranging from 39,700 at Chelsea, who finished eighth to 10,600 at Derby County who finished twentieth. (Bradford City who finished ninth were

[2] S. G. Jones, 'The Economic Aspects of Association Football in England, 1918-39', *British Journal of Sports History* 1,3, 1984, p. 289.

only sixteenth best-supported, with an average home attendance of 18,800.)[3] Crowds by now were better behaved than during the 1890s, access onto the pitch was certainly more restricted, and the number of clubs punished for crowd misbehaviour declined quite notably between 1895 and 1912.[4]

Football may have been highly popular with those who came to watch, but its image in more respectable society was not entirely secure. *The Times*, in a special article on professional football in 1910 attributed this to its tainted business ethics, and ascribed the inferior status of professional footballers (relative to professional cricketers) to the fact that football employers, to whom 'money making has always been paramount' compelled players to indulge in discreditable tactics for League points.[5]

Professional footballers were also poorly paid in comparison with other public entertainers, although often better paid than semi-skilled workmen. Wages and transfer fees varied between about 30% and 60% of club incomes and in 1910 the maximum wage was raised to £5 per week, with some additional talent money for good performance in competitions. In that year, however, less than 10% of registered professionals received the maximum.[6]

Professional footballers' lack of status was in any case probably more of a middle-class than a working-class perception. Cricket professionals were required to play for their counties on the basis of birth or residence, and this virtually eliminated competitive bidding.[7] Cricket had a more leisurely and less industrial ambiance, and the employer-employee relationship was very different; cricket professionals had once been hired by the gentry, officially to work on their estates but in reality to play cricket, and teams of gentlemen and players mixed with a freedom that has been attributed to the social confidence of the gentlemen. In the Football League the employers were middle-men who provided organisation, rather than patrons who provided money, and their less assured social position may have led them to depress the social standing of their employees.

Some directors were openly paternalistic. Mr. S. Yates, an iron founder and financial backer of Blackburn Olympic, told his players that 'although they were merely working lads they might, if they could stick,

[3] Stephen Tischler, op cit, p. 84.

[4] See W. Vamplew, 'Ungentlemanly Conduct: The Control of Soccer Crowd Behaviour in England, 1888-1914' in T.C. Smout, op cit.

[5] *The Times*, 3 September 1910, p. 16.

[6] W. Vamplew, 'Playing for Pay: The Earnings of Professional Sportsmen in England 1870-1914' in R. L. Cashman and M. McKenna, *Sport: Money, Morality and the Media*, University Press, (Sydney 1980), p. 123.

[7] J. A. Schofield, op cit, p. 343.

together in the future, and with the assistance of people of influence, soon be able to reach the top of the tree.'[8] Other directors no doubt had different motives, or at least were more restrained in their public statements. The middle classes were used to participating in organisations devoted to political, religious, educational or charitable ends, and football clubs provided a natural extension. The director's role was clearly useful, and prestigious for both their towns and themselves. In 1905 the President of the Football League said, 'In most towns it is considered a distinct privilege to be on the board of the local club directorate, and the position is as eagerly sought after as a seat in the council chamber.'[9]

There were indirect pecuniary benefits through contracts placed by the clubs for catering and building work, but the direct financial benefits were slight. Few clubs paid dividends, none did so every year, and none were allowed to remunerate directors. *The Times*, again in 1910, found that more league clubs were financially strained than at any previous time, and thought or hoped that 'the syndicates are beginning to see that football is not really a money-making business'.[10]

If the financial benefits were modest there were the pleasures of untrammelled control of an interesting and locally prestigious business. Secretary-managers had little influence in the early part of the twentieth century, with team captains often deciding tactics, and the board controlled selection and pay[11] as well as watching other players and negotiating their transfer.[12] In consequence directors took charge of 'all weighty or important matters' and managers were often 'merely the mouthpiece of the board'.[13]

Although dividends were not all that common, this was in part because clubs chose, in good years, to retain profits and invest in ground development; Manchester United, Blackburn Rovers and Everton each spent about £35,000 (£C1,000,000) on new stands around 1909.

When the 1914-15 season ended, the Football League had partially achieved several of its long-term objectives. The retain and transfer system and maximum wage were both well-established, and the Players' Union was not; in 1914 sixteen clubs including Leeds City, Bradford and Huddersfield apparently had no Union membership.[14]

Of the forty members in the two divisions, only one, Glossop North

[8] Tony Mason, op cit, p. 33.
[9] See Tony Mason, op cit, p. 49.
[10] *The Times*, 3 September 1910, p. 16.
[11] M. G. Wilders, 'The Football Club Manager – A Precarious Occupation', *Journal of Management Studies* 1976, p. 161.
[12] Confirmed by reference to Huddersfield Town's Directors' Minute Books, 1908-15.
[13] Gibson and Pickford, op cit, Vol. II, p. 128.
[14] Tony Mason, op cit, p. 116.

End, would not be strong enough to remain in the League until 1986. The solution to competition from the Southern League would not be forthcoming until after the war but the League now contained six southern sides, and five from the Yorkshire rugby areas. As the League's founder W. McGregor had said in 1906, 'there was a time when the Second League was not so strong as it might be, but now that professional teams have been founded in Hull, Leeds and Bradford, and two Second Division teams are located in London, it is only reasonable to suppose that the Second League will, in another five years, be a competition infinitely more important than it is today'.[15]

---

[15] Gibson and Pickford, op cit, Vol. II, p. 6.

9. The Rise of Bradford City

Bradford City's election to the Football League in May 1903 meant an unusually busy summer. The eagerness of the Football League to introduce their game to the rugby-dominated West Riding placed City in the somewhat uncomfortable position of needing to assemble, organise and train an entire playing staff to a sufficient standard to compete in the Football League and the West Yorkshire League without having previously organised a soccer match of any kind.

By the start of the new season, players had been signed from non-League clubs together with fifteen more experienced men obtained cheaply from other League teams. The directors and new secretary-manager Campbell were so unfamiliar with the players they had signed that they adopted the unusual course of allowing the team to elect its own captain. The rugby posts had to be replaced with soccer goals, and even the new playing strip selected; Bradford City decided to retain the Manningham colours of claret and amber, with white shorts.

The facilities at Valley Parade were basic, even by the standards of the early years of the century, but there was too little time or money for major changes. To help accommodate the extra crowds, a number of lorries were borrowed to stand on the plateaus at the top of the banking behind the goals, but other covered accommodation at the ground was very limited.

There were no proper changing rooms on site, so for a while the City players dressed in a shed at the Burlington Terrace end of the ground, and the visitors in the old Manningham dressing-rooms at the back of the nearby Belle Vue Hotel. (Later on terraced houses in a nearby street would be taken over as dressing-rooms.) The club offices were for several years housed in an artillery barracks across the street from the ground.

There was great excitement at the first Football League match in Bradford in September 1903. The game was watched by the Mayor and Mayoress, the sun shone, balloons floated overhead and the enclosure was decorated with bunting and flags. The 11,000 crowd, who had paid £250, greeted Bradford, in claret and amber, with an enthusiasm that contrasted with the muted reception for Gainsborough Trinity, in royal blue. Only the result was out of keeping; City lost 1-3.[1]

The extent of the Football League's encouragement of soccer in the West Riding textile district was shown by their decision to play the English League v Irish League match at Valley Parade in October 1903, the first inter-league fixture not played at a major football centre.

An estimated 25,000, including senior officials of the Football League, paid £515 to watch, and the gates were shut fifteen minutes before kick off on the largest attendance at any type of football match in Bradford. This caused quite a stir in the town for 'never before had money been turned away from the Manningham ground'.[2]

City had a quiet season, finishing just below halfway in Division Two, but for an entirely new organisation this was a competent and promising beginning. Their achievement had not been gained by reckless expenditure either, for a small profit was reported at the first Annual General Meeting.

This progress certainly seemed to confirm the wisdom of the club's 'bold step' away from the losses of rugby. A year before it had been resolved that the club play the association game for at least one year; now the resolution carried with 'great enthusiasm' at a well attended meeting was that the club play association until it was thought necessary to make a change.[3]

The first three seasons of soccer were not, however, a very easy transition from the Northern Union. In each season City finished in mid-table, and attributed their lack of success to 'misfortune and ill-luck', particularly with players' injuries. They also had to spend money on new players, and on small ground improvements, and this raised their overdraft to £1,075, a level that caused some concern.

A particular difficulty was the difference in standard between reserve team players good enough to win the West Yorkshire League and Cup, and first team players; when the latter were injured the former could not cope and expensive replacements were needed.

The new line of business was bound to be highly competitive, particularly the market for players' services, and it would take time to develop the new expertise. The club was impatient for success, however, and the first secretary-manager, Campbell, resigned after two years of indifferent results.

Certainly there was far more interest in soccer, although in 1906 it was somewhat excessive when Manchester United were the visitors. The crowd were alienated by the visiting side's tackling and United players were violently attacked as they left the ground, stones were

[1] *Bradford Daily Telegraph*, 5 September 1903.
[2] ibid, 12 October 1903, p. 5.
[3] ibid, 28 May 1904, p. 3.

thrown and the referee was roughly handled. Valley Parade was closed for two weeks by the FA.[4]

In spite of this, gate receipts were five times as large as annual receipts during the last three years of rugby. Moreover the First Division and success in cup matches would bring even more lucrative returns; as much money had been taken at the gate for one cup match against Wolverhampton as in the whole of the last season in the Northern Union.

To pursue such success meant that substantial payments had to be made to players, and player costs were over six times as large as those needed for competitive rugby. This still left larger surpluses from match revenues to cover the relatively fixed costs of administration, but it also exposed the club to the higher travel costs of a national rather than purely northern competition (travel costs were four times their previous level).

A new club, with limited facilities, no existing expertise in player development, and no permanent capital would also have to generate large profits if they were to fund investments in ground facilities and player acquisitions via the transfer market. This was bound to be difficult.

The fourth season, 1906-07, was more promising; the club finished fifth, there were record gate receipts and a surplus on transfer dealings and this enabled the club to announce its highest profit to date and halve the overdraft. Although the soccer club's founder, J. T. Whyte, had to retire through poor health, there was a new optimism; the committee were publicly confident that 'they were not always going to be in the Second Division'. At the same time the committee made it clear that Valley Parade was unsuitable for a First Division club,[5] although it was three months before the implications of this statement were fully explored in public.

It seems likely that at least some of City's committee had anticipated the likely course of events two years before; at the football club's second Annual General Meeting in May 1905 there was an attempt to centralise influence when it was proposed that only members with at least £100 (£C3,100) invested in the club could sit on the committee, but the well-attended meeting of over a thousand members decisively rejected the proposal.

Now that Bradford City had serious expectations of promotion to the 'First League' the financial and organisational implications would have to be faced. Valley Parade, although acceptable as a Northern Union ground was inadequate for the crowds that success in the First Division would bring, and the only alternatives were to place the club's finances

[4] *Bradford Telegraph and Argus*, 10 January 1951.
[5] *Bradford Daily Telegraph*, 27 February 1907, p. 3.

on a sounder footing through full incorporation, so that investment finance could be attracted, or to amalgamate with the city's other senior sport's club, Park Avenue.

Amalgamation in 1907 would have brought together the developing expertise of Bradford City in the Football League and the superior facilities at Park Avenue, a combination that would have enabled Bradford to compete effectively against teams from other large cities. Such a move would also have left any Northern Union opposition in the town in a state of temporary disarray, although with potential access to Valley Parade.

Active discussions had taken place between the two clubs and an amalgamation proposal was put before the Annual General Meeting of Bradford City on 27th May 1907.

There were a number of specific points put in its favour:

Valley Parade was on a three month tenancy at the whim of the Midland Railway Company's directors;

The Midland Railway would not be able to let City know the position on fixity of tenure until the following March, and this would inhibit ground development;

Park Avenue could already accommodate 25,000 which was 6,000 more than City's largest attendance to date;

Park Avenue was worth £24,000 as building land, and the mortgage was down to £7,000;

The City club would retain their name, and would take over the whole of football management at Park Avenue so that membership of the all-powerful General (Finance and Property) Committee would be evenly shared.

Against this it was argued that Valley Parade could be extended to hold 48,000, whereas the natural maximum at Park Avenue was about 41,000.

In the discussion that took place it became clear that the strategic or real estate aspects counted for less with the membership than matters of identity and control. There was an acute awareness of Manningham and Horton Park as different districts within the city, and of the differences in the social class composition of the membership of the two clubs, and several speakers urged the City club to 'stick to their own heritage'. In the end 'there was no withstanding the fiery eloquence of several of the old Manninghamites' and the meeting voted decisively, 1,031 to 487, against amalgamation.

The Bradford historian Reynolds noted that Horton, Bowling and

Manningham 'retained their conscious separateness and continued to provide special focuses of community' long after Bradford itself had been swamped by immigrant workers in the nineteenth century and that their residents thought of themselves as men and women of their local township and referred to themselves that way in local documents. (By 1870 Bradford's growth had slowed and in 1901 it was one of the towns in England which had the highest proportion of native inhabitants.)[6]

An examination of the addresses of the early founders, shareholders and directors of the two Bradford football clubs indicates that residents of Manningham until the Great War generally gave their address as 'Manningham', whereas people in Little and Great Horton, close to Park Avenue's ground, identified their township as a district of Bradford.

Only one of the initial directors did not live in Bradford (A. H. Briggs who lived in Harrogate but had business interests in the city) and half of them lived within three-quarters of a mile of their club's ground.

Although such local identifications and loyalties did not necessarily prevent success being achieved in the Northen Union, they were to prove decisive in the world of soccer, where the ability to pay players depended on large audiences and better facilities, and where competition was national and principally between towns and cities, rather than between districts. The largest cities did support more than one successful club but their populations were greater than Bradford and they did not face the same local enthusiasm for commercial rugby.

Moreover, although the objections to amalgamation included a desire on the part of City's members to retain control of their club, the only alternative, full incorporation, rapidly concentrated power into the hands of a small number of entrepreneurial or middle-class professional people who were prepared to make the financial commitments, and were thought to possess the managerial skills suitable for the development of professional soccer.

Certainly the size of the majority against amalgamation made the position clear for the foreseeable future, and Bradford City set about securing their own future.

The optimism based on last season's results was justified when City immediately won Division Two and promotion to the First Division, winning twenty-four out of thirty-eight matches. After the home win over Lincoln a large crowd gathered round the pavilion and the players and directors were repeatedly cheered until they left in a char-à-banc drawn by four horses to go to a private reception.[7] Gate receipts were far higher than ever before, and the resulting profit more than covered further investments in new players. £1,635 (£C50,000) was spent, thus

[6] J. Reynolds, op cit, pp. 113, 163.
[7] *Bradford Daily Telegraph*, 27 April 1908, p. 5.

doubling previous expenditures on the stands and terracing, to provide new turnstiles, a system to check gate receipts, and increased seating accommodation. Extensive alterations were also made to the existing stands.

A more permanent leasing agreement was made with the Midland Railway for the use of Valley Parade, and it was announced that the club intended to make considerable ground improvements out of the finance obtained from a share issue in a new limited liability company.

In June 1908 Bradford City AFC (1908) Ltd issued their prospectus which sought to raise £7,000 in £1 shares with 5/- payable on allotment and the remaining 15/- over the following nine months.

This finance was needed to enable the ground to be developed to an extent compatible with their newly achieved First Division status, and to relieve the strain on the committee, who had individually guaranteed the substantial bank overdraft. Ownership of a hundred shares would entitle the holder to a free season ticket for the one guinea seats, with proportional reductions for smaller holdings.

An attempt was made to offset the risks of a small number of shareholders dominating the club's affairs; one share gave a shareholder a vote and every five more shares earned only one further vote. The directors could not be paid, had to have at least £10 invested in the club, but could decline transfers of shares between members as they saw fit.

Moreover the board's social composition was quite different from that of the committee that ran the club's affairs before 1908; each of the directors between 1908 and 1915 was either a merchant, professional person or gentleman.

The directors viewed the fact that only 3,600 shares were taken up as an 'unsatisfactory response', although this was twice the minimum level for the share issue to have been viable. It certainly did not go very far towards the £10,000 (£C310,000) that City spent on stands, terraces and equipment in 1908-09 under the direction of the country's best-known football ground architect, Alex Leitch. The main stand accommodated 5,300 seated spectators and 7,000 standing; the Midland Road stand opposite was smaller but more elegant, with pointed gables and room for 8,000 standing customers. At the same time the pitch was relaid and 'presented such a surface as no football team has ever played on in Bradford before'. The large terrace at the Manningham end was extended and the ground capacity was almost doubled to nearly 50,000; the club now had 'one of the finest appointed enclosures in Great Britain'.[8]

To have reached the First Division after five seasons in the Second

---

[8] ibid, 17 August 1908, p. 6.

Division was an impressive achievement for a new club and in their first season in Division One City were well supported, although they were always under threat of relegation. This was only avoided in the final home match of the season, when the tension was such that the Chairman, W. N. Pollack, spent the second half of the match in the privacy of the club's offices until the game was over. City's goal average, thanks to a defence that was the third tightest in the division was just good enough to keep them up and put Manchester City down. The opening First Division fixture at Valley Parade had been watched by a crowd of 30,000, and 35,000 came to the league match on Boxing Day. The first match in the new division would have drawn a far larger attendance had the Midland Road stand been complete; instead it was only occupied by (some) spectators to relieve congestion at the Manningham end after a barrier had given way, and the gates were shut at 3.20 on the largest crowd at any football match in the district.

In 1909-10 City improved considerably to finish seventh. Their defence was again one of the best in the division but the forwards scored more freely. Public interest declined towards the end of the season, however, when City were out of the FA Cup and had no chance of catching champions Aston Villa, and the directors hoped that the recent decision by the football authorities to allow bonus payments to be made to players would help to maintain incentives and thus spectator interest throughout the season.

The following season, 1910-11, was to bring unprecedented, and never to be repeated, success. In the league Bradford City finished fifth, and only goal difference cost them third place; indeed they seemed to have joined the traditional elite, for the top six read: Manchester United, Aston Villa, Sunderland, Everton, Bradford City and Sheffield Wednesday.

The FA put up a new challenge cup for competition that season. The first had been stolen from a shop window in Birmingham in 1895, and the second had just been presented by the Council of the Football Association to Lord Kinnaird to mark the completion of twenty-one years as President. Kinnaird was more familiar with the first FA Cup than the second one, for he won five cup winner's medals in the early years of the competition with the Wanderers and Old Etonians. The FA put the design for the third version of the cup out to tender, and commissioned the Bradford firm of Fattorini and Sons. (One of the Fattorini family had been in the delegation that secured the entry of Bradford City into the Football League eight years before.) Despite such omens Bradford's progress was at first unspectacular; 1-0 away to New Brompton (Gillingham), 2-1 at home to another 'non-league' side, Norwich City, and a 1-0 home win against Grimsby Town (in their only season outside the League) preceded the visit of Burnley in the fourth round.

The fourth round was in effect the quarter-final and public interest in Bradford had been stimulated by the club's sound performances in league and cup. The match on 11th March, 1911, drew a record crowd of 39,146, a record that still stands, and the only club attendance record that dates back to before the Great War. The crowd paid £1,640 (£C51,000), the gates were closed forty-five minutes before kick off, and the intrepid Burnley mascot who ran round the pitch was pelted with orange peel, banana skins and clods of earth pulled from the primitive terracing. City won a close contest 1-0.

Although Bradford beat Blackburn decisively 3-0 in the semi-final at Sheffield they were not expected to prevent Newcastle United from achieving an easy victory in the final. Newcastle had finished just below City in the First Division but their pedigree was quite different; First Division champions in 1904-05, 1906-07, 1908-09, FA Cup winners the year before in 1910, and runners-up in 1905, 1906 and 1908, they were the most scientific team of the era and included such renowned internationals as Veitch and McCracken.

Bradford's supporters were undeterred and eleven special trains took them down to London for the game at the old Crystal Palace ground at Sydenham. The match was spoiled by a gusty wind which interfered with combination play; Newcastle were dominant but a disappointing, featureless match finished 0-0.

Ten thousand Bradford supporters paid the 2/9 excursion fare to Manchester for the replay. The gates were locked at Old Trafford with thousands denied entry, but the 66,000 inside was a record for the provinces. Once again a strong wind was a levelling factor and many promising moves by Newcastle were hindered. Bradford City were resolute rather than polished, but a mistake by the Newcastle goalkeeper after fifteen minutes enabled City's Spiers to score the only goal of the match.

When the City train arrived home from Manchester at 9.00 pm the clamour was so great the Idle and Thackley Brass Band blew in vain, and the 'teeming populace seemed almost frantic with joy'.[9] The centre of Bradford was so congested that the team's char-à-banc only reached their hotel with difficulty.

The following season was bound to be something of an anticlimax, but City finished in mid-table in the First Division and reached the quarter-final of the Cup by winning 'away' to Park Avenue 1-0, before losing a third replay to the eventual winners, Barnsley, after three 0-0 draws. One of the replays was at Elland Road, Leeds where 35,000

[9] *Yorkshire Observer*, 27 April 1911.

paying spectators were joined by many more who broke in; the inadequacy of the ground's facilities became highly public when the match had to be abandoned in the second half since even mounted police could not keep the playing area clear.

The three seasons 1912-15 were, however, disappointing. City won a number of local competitions but receipts declined sharply, due to rapid exits from the FA Cup, some waning of local enthusiasm (particularly amongst season ticket holders) and increasing competition from Park Avenue.

Bradford City had made profits in every season since their adoption of the association code and promotion to the First Division had trebled their profits, although it had also increased the need to invest in players and ground facilities. Improved performance in the FA Cup had been lucrative, particularly in the triumphant 1910-11 season; the semi-final and final ties earned City a cheque from the FA for £4,750 (£C147,000), which dwarfed the related bonus and travel costs of £275 and £425 respectively.

The losses of 1912-15, which totalled £3,265 (£C100,000) represented a new and disturbing trend since Bradford City were a tolerably successful First Division side. This was the more serious because the receipts from the share issue in 1908 funded only one third of the ground development costs and the club were unusually dependent on profit flows. (See Table 1.)

City were particularly unfortunate or unwise to invest heavily in attacking players in 1914-15. The new players were intended to complement the First Division's most efficient defence, but the outbreak of war caused a decline in public support and led eventually to the suspension of official competition and player contracts.

Table 1 Bradford City Cash Flows 1903-1915

	£	£C
Cash generated by operations	11,545	356,000
Donations	380	12,000
Share issues	3,610	111,000
Bank overdraft	6,940	214,000
	22,475	693,000
Investment in transfer fees	6,585	203,000
Investment in stands, terraces, equipment	14,410	445,000
Investment in (players') houses	800	24,000
Repayment of loans	680	21,000
	22,475	693,000

At the end of the 1914-15 season Bradford City were heavily committed to the bank, who were providing twice as much financial support as had the shareholders through share purchases; it was therefore important that the club had directors who could guarantee the club's overdraft of £6,900 (£C213,000).

None the less Bradford had developed considerably since their entry into commercial soccer in 1903. Their search for players had produced a team with few local men; the 1911 side contained eight Scots, an Irishman and two men from Nottinghamshire. They were ambitious enough to take intelligent gambles; in 1910 they paid Notts County £1,000 to transfer the venue for their cup tie to Bradford, and although they lost money on the tie their victory enabled them to recoup the losses in the next round. They had acquired professional cunning; in the week before the Crystal Palace final they arrived early for a league fixture in London and persuaded the groundsman to 'take a rest' so that they could practise on the Cup Final pitch.[10]

Their fame had spread abroad, leading to tours of Scandinavia, and in 1914, Germany. Eight of their players had played for their country, three for England, one for Wales and four for Ireland, and having faced no relegation threat since their inaugural season in the First Division they appeared to have joined soccer's elite clubs in spite of a limited financial base.

The hostilities of 1914 had been expected to provide only a brief interruption to civilian life, but when the Great War ended English society and commercial football in Bradford had both been irrevocably altered.

[10] *Bradford Telegraph and Argus*, 16 July 1968.

10. Park Avenue turn to Association

As Bradford City finished their first season in the Football League in the Spring of 1904, Bradford FC had just won the championship of the Northern Union. Wakefield Trinity, with the best defence in professional rugby that season, were clear winners of the Northern Union Second Division, but the second promotion place lay between Holbeck and St Helens. On April 30th, a 0-10 defeat for Holbeck by Barrow, a mid-table side, enabled St Helens to equal Holbeck's points total by winning at home to South Shields.

The play-off took place two weeks later at Huddersfield; a 7-0 win for St Helens took them out of the financially unrewarding Second Division and back to the First Division, and left Holbeck where they were.

Later that summer Leeds City Association Club, which had previously been known as the Hunslet Association Club, decided to turn professional and try to enter the Second Division of the English League. A meeting took place of potential backers, including Norris Hepworth the wholesale clothier, to consider the ways and means of achieving this and in particular to look for a more suitable ground. It was understood that the ground of the Holbeck FC in Elland Road had been offered to the promoters[1] although Holbeck were still in the Northern Union. As the new season approached Holbeck steadily sold off their players even though they were due to play at Castleford in early September. Bradford City came to play a friendly match against Leeds City before the season started but found their old ground isolated, small and unsuitable. This seemed finally to convince the Leeds backers that they would have to make arrangements to take over Elland Road from Holbeck and to form a Limited Liability Company.

The Yorkshire Post felt that the newly formed Leeds City Club should be 'congratulated upon the enterprise they had shown' as the city could hardly support four professional rugby clubs (Leeds, Hunslet, Bramley and Holbeck) and Holbeck had found that 'Second League Northern Union football will not pay'.[2]

In April, 1905, the Leeds City Association Football Club Company

[1] *Yorkshire Post*, 30 August 1904, p. 12.
[2] ibid, 5 September 1904, p. 4

Limited was formed, with an authorised capital of £10,000. The prospectus made clear the intention to apply for admission to the English League, and added intriguingly that the 'directors have every reason to believe the application will be successful'.[3] Their confidence was well placed, for Leeds were elected to the Football League that summer, and on 4th September, 1905, attracted 15,000 to Valley Parade for the first association match between the representatives of the two cities. Bradford celebrated the 'new era' with a 1-0 win.

Two years later Bradford City and Leeds City were both only moderate Second Division sides, but while Bradford were able to report small profits, Leeds were making heavy losses. Although Leeds had spent £7,000 (£C215,000) on ground improvements, attendances were poor and they were already heavily in debt.

Bradford FC were by now an even more successful rugby side. They followed up the Championship win of 1903-04 by finishing second the following season and winning the Challenge Cup in 1905-06. In 1906-07, however, Bradford had their worst season to date, finishing eighteenth in the new large single Northern Union division, and, reflecting a general fall in public interest in the game, their financial results were the worst in their long history.

A meeting was accordingly held in April 1907 to consider whether the club should remain in professional rugby, revert to amateur rugby union or adopt association on a professional basis.

The meeting on 15th April was chaired by the Mayor of Bradford, Alderman (later Sir) Arthur Godwin. The first vote gave the verdict by just one vote to professional rugby, but when a recount was demanded a narrow majority was then in favour of amateur rugby.

A. H. Briggs, a woollen manufacturer from Harrogate, had a large financial interest in the club, and he consulted his solicitor and the committee, before announcing that the members' meeting was *ultra vires* and its decision null and void. Within a month the announcement was made that Park Avenue were to adopt soccer.

The local press was highly critical of these manoeuvres: 'According to the constitution of the club, it is stated, the Finance and Property Committee have absolute powers so the legality of their action cannot be questioned, but in the circumstances the meeting a few weeks ago looks all the more farcical.'[4]

Park Avenue's committee were so determined to adopt association because they had already arranged an amalgamation with the committee of Bradford City; detailed discussions had taken place over

[3] Leeds City Association Football Club Company Limited Prospectus dated 12 April 1905, Public Records Office BT 31-17428/84163.
[4] *Bradford Daily Telegraph*, 7 May 1907, p. 3.

several months, and although the exact terms had not been finalised there was agreement on both sides that the combined organisation would be based at Park Avenue. Although they also applied to the Football League for entry into the Second Division this was almost certainly a means of improving their bargaining position with Bradford City, rather than an attempt to go it alone; they had received no encouragement from the football authorities, for the Football League's policy was to penetrate new areas and they had recently admitted clubs from Bradford and Leeds.

Park Avenue's rejection by the general membership of Bradford City, and by the Football League (Fulham were elected with twenty-eight votes and Park Avenue with eleven votes came only fifth out of the nine applicants) faced the club with a difficult and unexpected problem.

The facilities at Park Avenue were excellent for cricket, rugby and the club's other more minor sports, but the capital expenditure had been considerable, the mortgage was £7,000 and profits were needed to reduce the level of debt. The club had lost £770 on all sports that season, an unprecedented if hardly ruinous deficit, but the committee took a serious view of the long-term implications. Cricket was prestigious but gave low returns; the club's gate receipts did not cover their costs, including professionals and groundsmen, and it was only the £425 commission on staging county matches that enabled cricket to earn any profits. The club needed a lucrative winter sport, and had to take a hard look at rugby's long-term prospects.

In the absence of amalgamation with City (and this had been decisively rejected by City's members), the alternatives were to return to commercial rugby or to take such measures as would overcome the opposition of the members of the Football League and enable them actively to compete with Bradford City.

City's members had been mistrustful of the management structure at Park Avenue, where A. H. Briggs was highly influential. His father Edward had been a leading supporter of the rugby club when they played at Apperley Bridge, and had been instrumental in their move to Park Avenue in 1879. A. H. Briggs had played for the rugby club and later travelled with them, but he was still in favour of the change to soccer as he thought it would help the club to improve its renown as a leading English sports organisation. He was very wealthy; his business interests included extensive textile mills in Russia and Bradford (including Briggella Mills at Little Horton), saw mills in Hull and a partnership in a 'gigantic establishment in Warsaw'. It was Briggs who first suggested that Rolls and Royce amalgamate, and who, when the minimum subscription was undersubscribed on flotation in 1906, produced the necessary £10,000, a service that earned him a place on the board of Rolls

Royce.[5] He was both determined (he was well able to dismantle and reassemble a Rolls Royce) and flamboyant (in Scotland he once accepted a train driver's signalled challenge and raced the Scots express; a 'splendid race' that was terminated by a police speed trap).

He was deeply involved in Park Avenue's affairs and took on few other public functions outside his business activities, active membership of his local Conservative Club and acting as a JP. He did not shrink from the logical, if rather startling and certainly potentially expensive, solution to Park Avenue's dilemma. Rugby would not generate sufficient profits, association would if the clubs were in the Football League, and the quickest way to convince the members of their case for admission was to join the strongest league outside the Football League, which was the Southern League! (A place was vacant due to the election of Fulham into the Football League.)

The chairman, Major Shepherd claimed that in seeking entry into the Southern League the club had 'taken the only course open to save the club from bankruptcy',[6] but this must have seemed an exaggeration at the time.

There were obvious risks because Bradford had no experience of commercial soccer, the cost of travelling 10,000 miles in a season would be very high, and they were required to guarantee the cost of opposing sides' long trips to Yorkshire. On the other hand Briggs and the committee were shrewd enough to see that such a spectacular measure would clearly demonstrate their commitment, and given only moderate playing success would provide a better platform for quick entry into the Football League than a season of worthy endeavour in a more local league.

The strategy was to prove highly successful. Bradford's match results were indifferent, and the financial cost was heavy; losses were £1,360, £6,800 was spent on the football ground, bringing the total spent to £30,000 (£C925,000), and further amounts had to be spent on the acquisition of new playing staff.

Bradford applied to the Football League, along with Tottenham Hotspur, also of the Southern League, and even this was risky. Their application was in breach of private undertakings to the Southern League to play for at least two seasons; the latter were incensed and would probably have refused Bradford a continued place in their league. The gamble paid off, however; Spurs and Bradford replaced Lincoln City and founder members Stoke City who had resigned for financial reasons, and this made Bradford the 55th side to enter the Football League (Bradford City were 48th, Leeds City 49th, Huddersfield 57th and

[5] D. J. Jeremy (ed), *Dictionary of Business Biography*, Vol. III, (London 1985), pp. 501-2.
[6] *Bradford Daily Telegraph*, 1 November 1907.

Halifax, who joined in 1921, 83rd). The woollen textile towns had been even slower to form clubs; 86 of the teams who have played in the Football League were formed before Bradford City, and 98 before Park Avenue.

The first season in the Football League Division Two saw Park Avenue finish low in the table, using 33 players in 38 League games, but they did not need to apply for re-election, and the losses dropped to £500 on the season. On the other hand the mortgage had increased to £19,000 (£C585,000). Soccer now had a financial importance quite out of proportion to the club's other activities, so in August 1909 the Bradford (Park Avenue) Association Football Club Ltd was established to manage the football side. The club leased the football ground, stands, dressing-rooms and offices to the company for twenty-one years, at an initial rent of £300 p.a.[7]

Every member was to have one vote for the first share held by him, and an additional vote for every five further shares, and directors could not be remunerated but had to have £10 invested in the company's shares. Every shareholder with £20 in shares was entitled to a one guinea season ticket, free each year, with proportional concessions for smaller holdings.

The prospectus sought the issue of £7,000 in shares, but only half were taken up. At the end of August 1909, 3,562 shares had been allotted to 60 applicants. 3,000 of these shares, or 84% were owned by the Briggs family, 2,000 in the name of A. H. Briggs, 500 in the name of Emma, his wife; the other 500 were held by A. E. Briggs, his son.

Apart from A. H. Briggs, the other eight original directors were each allotted 10 shares. The largest shareholding apart from the Briggs was 20 shares.

The full shareholding is set out in Table 2; even within the limitations of the data, the influence of the Briggs family with 84% of the shares, and the merchants, manufacturers and managerial and supervisory employees is apparent. The adoption of limited liability in the face of the greater expenditures needed to promote association football concentrated power both at board and shareholder level in the hands of the commercial middle classes at Bradford Park Avenue.

The football authorities were just as encouraging to Bradford Park Avenue now they were in the League as they had been to Bradford City; the England v Ireland international was played at Park Avenue during their first season and an attendance of 25,000 showed the level of support in Bradford for top-class soccer.

Association generated gate receipts and season ticket sales that were

[7] Bradford (Park Avenue) Association Football Club Ltd, Prospectus dated 26 July 1909, Companies House No 104075.

three times the level of those from rugby, but players' wages and travel costs were four times as large. Profits were being made, but Park Avenue could not afford to be patient with their high capital costs to justify and with little developed expertise they invested heavily in new players.

After two years they made their first managerial change and Gillies was replaced by Malley. The latter was more successful, in spite of

Table 2 Shareholdings in Bradford (Park Avenue) AFC Ltd. August 1909

Shares	Holdings	Total	Occupation
2,000	1	2,000	Spinner and manufacturer (Director)
500	2	1,000	Wife of spinner and manufacturer, Spinner and manufacturer
20	7	140	Manufacturer (2), Worsted spinner, Chartered Accountant, Confectioner, Woolsorter, Cashier
11	5	55	Manufacturer (2), Stuff and Woollen merchant, Newsagent, Baths Superintendent
10	8	80	Gentleman, Stuff merchant, Leather merchant, Wool and waste dealer, Timber merchant, Schoolmaster, Presser, Traveller (All Directors)
10	27	270	Gentleman, Chartered Accountant, Secretary, Jeweller, Wool buyer, Wholesale grocer, Mill furnisher, Printer, Ironmonger (2), Coal merchant (2), Bootmaker, Athletic Outfitter, Innkeeper, Fish dealer, Hairdresser, Fruit preserver, Manufacturer's agent, Insurance agent, Railway agent, Journalist, Foreman engineer, Weaving overlooker, Salesman, Dyers labourer, not given.
5	1	5	Hotel Manager
3	1	3	Accounts clerk
2	1	2	News editor
1	7	7	Warp twister, Weaving overlooker, Bookkeeper, Clerk, Traveller, not given (2)
—	60	3,562	

Note 1. The only female shareholder was the wife of the largest shareholder.
2. Every shareholder lived in Bradford, except for the three largest shareholders who lived in Harrogate.

having the temerity to change the red, amber and black colours traditional to Bradford in favour of a green and white outfit inspired by his own Glasgow Celtic connections.

The seasons preceding the Great War were proving very difficult for the commercial association clubs in the textile district. Bradford City were the most successful, although they started to make losses as gate receipts fell despite their comparative success at staying in an unthreatened position in the First Division. The sides that had followed them into the League were faring much worse.

The Leeds City club's achievements had not lived up to the expectations of 1905, and five years later all the directors were removed from office at an Extraordinary General Meeting, and a new board appointed. This made little difference to their results or attendances and in March 1912 the secretary-manager Mr. F. Scott-Walford, left the club due to ill health caused by the club's unsatisfactory finances. In an earlier letter to the directors he complained that he had personally been called upon to meet the club's liabilities and requested them to make proper financial arrangements or relieve him of his duties.

The total losses on the workings of the Leeds City club since its formation in 1905 were £11,320 and the deficiency of assets £8,365. The debenture holders appointed a receiver on 27th March 1912, and he was appointed liquidator in August under a voluntary winding-up as 'it had been proved to the satisfaction of the court that the company cannot by reason of its liabilities continue its business'. The receiver/liquidator ran the club as a continuing business and looked for a would-be purchaser, rather than close it down, because the club did not yet own their ground and if business had ceased the £7,000 spent on the ground would have been useless and the asset deficiency correspondingly larger.

The underlying weakness was the share issue that had only raised £5,500, which was totally inadequate to meet requirements, and this forced the directors to arrange an overdraft of £7,000. When the bank pressed their claims Mr. Norris Hepworth paid up and he was owed £10,300 (£C320,000) by the company. The club had to apply for re-election in 1912 but they appointed a new manager, Mr. Herbert Chapman, who was later with Huddersfield and Arsenal to achieve unparalleled success, and results began to improve. Gate revenues rose and season ticket sales were at a record level, but the financial position of the club came under further threat when Norris Hepworth died.

Huddersfield Town's formation in 1908 had been nicely timed for an application to a new Third Division of the Football League, but the scheme failed and the Midland League was full, so Huddersfield Town had to join the North Eastern League.

Competition against the reserve sides of Football League clubs in the

North East was rather severe and Town finished near the foot of the League. Travelling expenses were very high in spite of an arrangement whereby the North Eastern railway gave specially reduced rates for football teams,[8] so Town switched to the Midland League in 1909, finishing fifth. They made immediate application to the Second Division of the English League and were accepted in place of Grimsby Town in June 1910, but attendances, and thus gate receipts, were poor and the losses began to accumulate.

After only two seasons, in 1912, Huddersfield Town were reconstructed and a new company formed with creditors in the old company only receiving half of their due debts.[9]

At nearby Halifax, where rugby was now less popular, a company was formed in 1911 to promote 'high class soccer' in the town, for the promoters were aware of large numbers of people who journeyed from Halifax every Saturday to 'neighbouring towns where association is played'. They were also careful, however, to ensure by renting not buying a ground, that 'the club is not saddled with a large expense that might be disastrous in case of non-success'.[10] Only £575 was raised, and this comfortably covered the limited amounts spent on the ground, including a £50 grandstand purchased in 1911. Even so, losses began to mount and the club was forced to break up its promising Midland League team by transferring players to other clubs.

Against such an unpromising background the success of Bradford City, and of Bradford Park Avenue when they followed City into the First Division in 1914, should not be underestimated.

After five years of mediocre results in Division Two the investment seemed to have paid off when Park Avenue beat Blackpool on the last Saturday in May before 28,000 people to win promotion to Division One. The chase for promotion had increased gate receipts by 35% to £8,300, profits before investment were an unprecedented £2,210, and Park Avenue voted a full 5% dividend to the shareholders, although payment of this was postponed for at least six months at the discretion of the directors, since the effect of war on gate receipts and their bank overdraft were hard to foresee. A. H. Briggs, the majority shareholder, was happy to leave matters in the hands of the shareholders, but a proposal that the dividend be paid to the war fund was ruled out of order!

Park Avenue made a fairly successful entry into the First Division. Improved results in the second half of the season enabled them to finish ninth, five points behind the champions. Cup results were satisfactory,

---

[8] *Huddersfield Daily Examiner*, 25 August 1908, p. 3.

[9] *Yorkshire Post*, 5 July 1912, p. 12.

[10] Halifax Town FC Ltd, Prospectus dated 17 July 1911, p.2, Companies House No 116844.

for Bradford reached the last 16, losing narrowly to the eventual winners, but the war inevitably cast a shadow. Once war had been declared, takings in the Football League as a whole were only about half of their level the season before, and the only clubs in the country to take more at the gate were Arsenal, who had just moved to North London, and Bradford who had just been promoted. Surprisingly, in spite of the uncertainty that resulted from the war, Park Avenue invested a further £3,000 in transfer fees for new players.

By the time official competition was suspended Park Avenue had built a promising First Division side, but the bank overdraft was at its highest level since the club had been incorporated.

THE GREAT WAR

11. Political Pressures on Professional Sport

When Britain went to war with Germany in August 1914, the football authorities met to consider what their response should be. At the time there was little expectation that the conflict would be protracted and the Football Association at first proposed only a muted response from the world of professional football.

Clubs were asked to organise collections for the Prince of Wales fund, and to follow the FA in making their own contribution to war relief funds if their financial circumstances permitted. The football authorities also suggested that clubs send footballs to units at home and abroad 'so that, circumstances permitting, our brave defenders may enjoy the popular winter pastime',[1] but they saw no need to suspend the official competitions.

By November 1914, however, there was considerable opposition to the continuation of professional football. One MP called, in vain, for the Chancellor to put a special tax on gate money at football matches where professionals were playing,[2] and Asquith came under pressure to introduce legislation that would ban professional football. He declined, preferring to trust in informal communications and 'in the general good sense of football players'.[3]

The FA for their part thought that matches should continue, for they could be used to promote enlistment; the War Office and Football Association had agreed on a programme of appeals by prominent speakers at half-time with bands to march those willing to enlist to the nearest recruiting office at the end of play.

The actual response to these appeals was, however, 'grievously disappointing', particularly since the general level of recruitment was around 30,000 a week. At Chelsea no one in the 15,000 crowd joined up, in spite of an eloquent half-time speech by Colonel Burns MP, who had lost his son in the war (although a third of the audience were already in khaki). *The Times* drew unflattering comparisons with the patriotic

---

[1] *Yorkshire Post*, 2 August 1914, p. 8.
[2] *The Times*, 19 November 1914, p. 22.
[3] ibid, 27 November 1914, p. 12.

response of those who played more middle-class sports like rugby union, cricket and rowing.

The football authorities were so concerned at the change in public opinion that they publicised certain aspects of the relationship between clubs and the war effort; all professional players underwent military drill and rifle practice every week, 40% of all players registered with the FA were serving in the forces, no club had stopped any player from enlisting even where this involved breaking his contract, players contributed 2½% – 12½% of their wages to relief funds, recruitment was 'encouraging at every match' and collections had been taken for the Belgian Relief Fund.

The Council of Newspaper Proprietors Federation, representing London daily papers, was not impressed, however, and decided to publish (except in the sporting newspapers) only the bare results of matches.[4]

At first the only change made to players' contracts involved the pooling of between 5% and 15% of wages for the benefit of players at clubs in financial difficulty, but towards the end of the 1914-15 season the Football League placed a temporary ban on any agreements to pay close season wages and on the signing of new players.

The West Riding FA met in May. There was some feeling that the suspension of players' contracts would help clubs to continue playing, and that there would be little effect on enlistment, but the chairman pointed out that the North East Coast Armaments Committee had put a stop to racing in the area and might well do the same to football.

The Northern Union decided by a large majority to stop all competitive or professional matches until the end of the war, and when the FA met in July the prohibition of racing, the voluntary cessation of lawn tennis and several other sports, and the general tide of public opinion were factors that could not be disregarded.

The FA put an immediate ban on their own competitions, Internationals, the FA Cup and the Amateur Cup, and gave permission to leagues to arrange matches only where they did not interfere with war work. In addition all players' agreements were suspended until further notice and no players were to be registered or remunerated.

The Football League held their Annual General Meeting straight afterwards and were aware of both the political realities and the fact that attendances in 1914-15 were less than half their level of the previous season. A resolution was passed, *without discussion*, that in the interests of the country the League competition be suspended.

Several clubs, notably Newcastle, Middlesbrough, Sunderland,

[4] ibid, 28 November 1914, p. 5.

Blackburn, Aston Villa and West Bromwich Albion decided to close down for the duration of the war rather than play unofficial, amateur fixtures, but most clubs decided to play on in regional groupings that minimised travel costs and difficulties.

Football was not the only sport whose patriotism had been suspect; Bradford League cricket continued in spite of the cessation of County cricket, and clubs actively recruited star players in an effort to provide 'spectacular cricket'. The *Yorkshire Post*, in an article written the day after the frontal attack at Gallipoli, denounced this as 'out of harmony with the spirit of the times, directly opposed to the serious interests of the nation, and a melancholy response to the dominating and inexorable call'.[5]

The action of the football authorities in ending official competitions and professional contracts mollified public opinion, and any lingering debate was ended by the introduction of conscription in March 1916.

When the war ended in November 1918, society, and the local clubs, were left to count their costs. Some losses were trivial, as when the returning Headingley players found their ground in good condition but their two small stands carted away for firewood,[6] but other losses were permanent; 47 of the 190 Headingley members who had joined up were dead.

In September 1919, when official competition resumed, the football authorities attempted to rehabilitate the public image of soccer, and an article in *The Times* emphasised the contribution of football to success in the war. After weeks of fighting 'it was just a round ball that did more than anything else to revive tired limbs and weary minds', for 'everyone knows that association football is the game that soldiers and sailors love best'. With an eye to the future they also called on military institutions and public and other schools to 'devote special attention to the training of the officers of the future in the game that their men will play'.[7] None the less the response of the football authorities to the war had not been completely successful in a public relations sense; the loss of life was felt everywhere and there was a lingering suspicion, at least in some sectors of society, that professional soccer's commitment to the war effort had been somewhat tardy and reluctant.

[5] *Yorkshire Post*, 17 June 1915, p. 10.
[6] *Headingley Football Club 1878-1978*, (Leeds 1979).
[7] *The Times*, 25 September 1919, p. 5.

12. City and Avenue in the Midland Section

The 'heavy woollen towns' in the West Riding had generally benefited from armed conflicts involving European powers, particularly as West Riding manufacturers usually supplied cloth to both sides. Traders in Dewsbury, Batley and Ossett were well aware that war meant more blankets, rugs and army cloths, and some firms were thought to regard 'the rumours of war with a feeling approaching complacency'.[1]

This upturn in business was often at the expense of the worsted and better woollen trade,[2] but in the Great War the size and duration of the conflict, and the national interest, led to the adaptation of machinery used for fine and fancy cloths to the manufacture of heavy army material so that the whole of the textile district could share the new work. Factory Act regulations were relaxed to allow women and children to work overtime, many mills worked non-stop and Saturday afternoon work was 'almost universal'.

The largest orders were inevitably for khaki cloth for the War Office, green-grey for the Russian army, dark blue-grey for the Belgians and a lighter shade for the French. *The Times* described nearby Huddersfield as the 'Valley of Khaki', for in the town there was 'a nightlong glare of green and golden light and the murmur of looms without number'.[3]

The two senior association clubs in Bradford continued during the war, playing in a Midland Section, composed for the most part of fourteen teams from Yorkshire, Lincolnshire and the Midlands. The competition was of no particular importance, for national priorities lay elsewhere, but it did give clubs the opportunity to keep going and provide some distraction from the labours of war work. Clearly a balance had to be struck by the authorities between maintaining civilian morale and controlling activities that might hinder important work. Public houses were closed during the afternoon, and the FA decided to avoid public criticism by requiring the Bradford City v Norwich City FA Cup Third Round replay at Lincoln in early 1915 to be played behind closed doors as

[1] D. Jenkins and K. Ponting, op cit, p. 224.
[2] ibid, p. 223.
[3] *The Times*, 28 January 1915, p. 6.

the ground was close to a munitions factory.[4]

Huddersfield also played in the same Midland Section, without outstanding success. They continued to make losses, although smaller than before the war, while Halifax played in an informal competition called the Midland Combination only until 1916 and then closed down; their Sandhall ground was taken over for extensions to a munitions factory. Leeds City, on the other hand, achieved success for the first time in their history, although the full consequences were not to be felt until 1919. In 1915 a small syndicate reached an agreement to buy the club's assets from the liquidator. They immediately re-appointed Herbert Chapman as secretary-manager[5] and results improved, although Chapman later took over as manager of a munitions factory in the city and became less involved with the club's affairs.

In May 1916 Leeds won the Midland Section subsidiary tournament and declared a profit, largely due to gate receipts which were nearly half their pre-war level. A year later Leeds won the principal tournament in the Midland Section, but the doubling of railway fares caused them to consider withdrawal. The Football League's chairman successfully appealed to them for a change of heart, as their withdrawal would have set back the association game in Leeds for some years and given 'fresh life to the rival professional code',[6] an indication that even during the Great War the Football League were concerned with the long-term prospects of association in the district. In May 1918 Leeds City won the Midland Section again, with 23 wins in 28 games and beat Stoke, winners of the Lancashire Section's principal tournament home and away to become 'League Champions'. The League Chairman, Mr. J. McKenna congratulated the directors and players on their 'crowning achievement',[7] but within eighteen months he was to view their success in a very different light.

The two Bradford clubs were far less ambitious. With players' contracts suspended, and public interest sharply reduced, Bradford City sought merely to continue and minimise losses; every effort was made to operate as economically as possible. By the end of the war City were one of the weakest clubs in the Midland Section and gate receipts had fallen to a sixth of their pre-war level. The four seasons in wartime competition cost the club £2,400 (£C75,000) in operating losses, and there were other less obvious costs; the £2,675 spent in 1914-15 on transfer fees earned the club nothing and the ground steadily deteriorated. Naturally there had been no improvements, and only £600 was spent on maintenance

[4] Simon Inglis, op cit, p. 136.
[5] *Yorkshire Post*, 12 August 1915, p. 10.
[6] ibid, 10 August 1917, p. 10.
[7] ibid, 6 May 1918, p. 8.

between 1915 and 1919. All the operating losses were funded by the bank overdraft, which stood at £9,350 in April 1919. The club was totally dependent for its existence on the support of the bank, for it had only £500 in money owed and £3 in cash to set against trade debts of £2,250, and one of the directors' most important functions was to provide personal collateral to the club's bankers.

The loyalty of Arthur Lancaster was important during the Great War. Born in 1867 he had played rugby for Manningham before the switch to association; after the change he served on the committee until the limited company was established in 1908, whereupon he joined the board. He was well-known in Football League circles and succeeded W. N. Pollack as Bradford City chairman in 1917. Arthur Lancaster was one of the leading wool merchants in Bradford, and his business interests minimised his public commitments; the demands of business life gradually increased, and he resigned from City's board in 1921 after the club had survived the worst of the financial problems caused by the Great War.

The Annual Directors' Reports were brief and focused mainly on the number of players serving with His Majesty's forces (11 in 1917), engaged in war work, or killed in action (8).

Bradford Park Avenue were a little more successful than their neighbours in the wartime competitions, generally finishing in the top third of their section and twice winning the subsidiary competitions.

Attendances were still low, and in spite of reduced expenses, losses were sustained, until the 'marked increase in gate receipts after Armistice Day'.[8] The club was sufficiently concerned to reduce the reported accumulated losses by carrying transfer fees for players (notwithstanding the suspension of contracts) as assets, and to depreciate only office furniture, and not the more substantial alterations and improvements to stands and ground, practices which led the auditors to qualify their report.

During the 1914-18 war the Bradford Cricket League introduced international stars into their ranks and 'grounds were frequently packed'.[9] Bradford Park Avenue, in common with most Football League clubs were more concerned to be seen to be patriotic; in the 1914-15 season £215 was contributed to the League Relief Fund, and fifty balls and several parcels of football outfits were sent to various military headquarters at home and in France. The generosity of players and supporters enabled regular contributions of 'cigars, cigarettes, pipes and chocolates' to be sent, and over £100 was contributed to the Lord Mayor's War Relief Fund and the local Army Veterans Association. The

[8] Bradford (Park Avenue) Directors' Report, 5 September 1919.
[9] *Bradford Cricket Club*, (Bradford 1973), p. 9.

competition the club had entered in 1915-16 was said to have 'a healthy object', and the directors felt that 'the response of the players to the call of the hour must be a source of great satisfaction to the shareholders, as there were a dozen now in the King's service and wearing khaki, several being in the firing line at that time'.[10]

The shareholders presumably obtained less satisfaction from the news that Donald Bell, who had played for Park Avenue before 1914, became the only professional footballer to be awarded the Victoria Cross, for five days later he was killed by a shell splinter. Five Bradford City players, Torrance, Spiers, Lintoff, Draycott and Goodwin had also been killed in the fighting.

When the war ended both of Bradford's professional football clubs had survived without great loss, although the inability of either club before the war to attract shareholder finance of remotely similar size to their ground expenditures left their financial position unusually dependent on operating profits and bank support. All clubs had found the war trying, but the suspension of players' contracts had come at an unfortunate time for the city's clubs, and their substantial transfer payments had merely put them further into debt. They were, however, both still in the First Division.

[10] *Yorkshire Post*, 4 September 1915, p. 14.

BETWEEN THE WARS

13. The Decline Begins

The woollen textile trades enjoyed a short-lived boom in the years immediately after the Great War. Imports of wool more than doubled between 1918 and 1919 and exports increased even more. Foreign trade peaked in 1921-2 and then declined sharply, with severe effects on employment particularly in Huddersfield.[1] None the less the volume of foreign trade was 50% above the levels of the immediate pre-war period.[2] Woollen prices fell even more sharply than the level of trade; in 1939 prices were only 20% of the inflated level of 1920 and in 1932 they were even lower.[3] In the country as a whole, manual wages fell nearly 40% between 1920 and 1923,[4] so that wage rates were 10% lower than in 1914.[5]

The 25% fall in prices between 1920 and 1923 reduced the impact of falling wage rates and by 1938 real incomes in the UK as a whole were 20% higher than in 1920, although in textiles the improvement was only 7%.

UK unemployment was far worse than before the Great War, averaging 12.2% between 1919 and 1939 as against 4.6% between 1900 and 1914. Unemployment was worse in the heavy and traditional industrial areas, and male textile employment fell 22% between 1923 and 1939.

Working hours declined slowly, from 54 per week in 1900 to 46 in 1938, but investment in leisure activities increased, notably in dance halls, cinemas, holiday facilities at seaside resorts and, to a lesser extent, in commercial sport. Market demand for leisure was relatively high during the inter-war years[6] and speedway and greyhound racing were both introduced in the mid 1920s. Cinema was the dominant form of entertainment, with weekly audiences of about 25,000,000 by 1927,[7] but

[1] Ian Dewhurst, *Yorkshire through the Years*, (London 1975) p. 180.
[2] B. Mitchell and P. Deane, op cit, p. 194.
[3] K. V. Pankhurst, 'Fluctuations in Wool Prices 1870-1953', *Yorkshire Bulletin of Economic and Social Research*, 1955, p. 27.
[4] A. Howkins and J. Lowerson, 'Trends in Leisure 1919-39', *State of the Art Review*, Sports' Council/SSRC, (London 1979), p. 5.
[5] B. Mitchell and P. Deane, op cit, p. 351.
[6] S. G. Jones, 'The Leisure Industry in Britain 1918-39', *Service Industries Journal*, 5,1, 1985, p. 95.
[7] A. Howkins and J. Lowerson, op cit, p. 25.

the demand for leisure was considerably affected by regional wealth imbalances; in the South the middle classes bought increasing numbers of motor cars, golf clubs and holiday cruises despite the depression, whereas in the North the most popular pastimes were walking on the moors, cycling and watching football.

The immediate post-war period was an eventful one for the Football League. The minimum admission charges were doubled from 6d to 1/- and players' in-season wages were raised by about 50% compared with the pre-war scales although in 1921, a year of high unemployment, the maximum wage was reduced by £1. Bonuses of £2 for a win and £1 for a draw were also payable. Footballers thus remained poorly paid compared with entertainers and some cricketers, but were still paid considerably above the average industrial wage.

The League formalised the gate-sharing arrangements that had been helpful to poorer clubs during the war and required teams to pay 20% of their admission money (based on minimum admission prices net of certain costs) to visiting clubs.

The start of peacetime football was nearly disrupted by a rail strike, but the government gave permission for clubs to use petrol, which was in short supply, so that fixtures, including Clapton Orient's trip to distant South Shields, could go ahead. The rugby union authorities rather smugly expressed their confidence that rugby clubs would cancel matches rather than use petrol unnecessarily.[8]

The football industry grew considerably between the wars. Attendances rose from an average of 16,000 at First Division matches in 1908-09 to 30,000 in 1937-8,[9] although the enthusiasm of spectators did not meet with universal approval; in March 1919 the executive committee of the Shipbuilders' Employers Federation wrote to the FA and Scottish FA to ask for important cup ties to be played only on Saturdays as 'the midweek games have involved a very large loss of production due to workmen attending the game'.[10] The Birmingham Chamber of Commerce in conjunction with other Chambers also asked the football authorities in 1920 to end midweek football as it interfered too much with trade.[11]

The most notable change in the industry was the number of members; clubs in the League increased from 40 in 1915 to 88 in 1923. In March 1919 a special meeting of the Football League voted to increase both Divisions One and Two from 20 clubs to 22. Chelsea and Tottenham had

[8] *The Times*, 3 October 1919, p. 8.
[9] S. G. Jones, 'The Economic Aspects of Association Football in England 1918-39', *British Journal of Sports History*, 1,3, p. 289.
[10] *The Times*, 1 March 1920, p. 16.
[11] *Yorkshire Post*, 27 January 1920, p. 4.

finished in the Division One relegation positions in 1915, Derby and Preston had been promoted with Barnsley, Wolverhampton, Birmingham and Arsenal in the other leading positions in Division Two. The two extra places were assigned amid much indignation and accusation to Chelsea, who had been relegated, and Arsenal, who had finished sixth in Division Two. This began the longest unbroken run of any club in the First Division for Arsenal, although neighbours Tottenham were not too inconvenienced as they immediately won the Second Division.

The main expansion came in the following two seasons; in 1920 the Southern League First Division was elected *en bloc* into the new Division Three (South) although only as associate members with restricted voting powers at League meetings, and in 1921 apparent regional equity was restored with the inauguration of a parallel Division Three (North). The regional balance was more apparent than real. Of the original members of Division Three (South) more than half subsequently played in the First Division, including Portsmouth who have twice been champions, and only Merthyr Tydfil have since left the League. The northern clubs were already disproportionately represented in the Football League and their new entrants were highly marginal clubs, none of whom ever reached the First Division. (Grimsby Town were in Division Three (North) in 1921-2 but they had transferred from Division Three (South) the previous season!) Eight of the original Division Three (North) clubs have dropped out of the League.

One of the new clubs, Halifax Town, was a close neighbour of Bradford. Halifax had been a moderate Midland League side for three seasons before the war. Their ground was taken over during the war for extensions to a munitions factory, and they then played at the Exley Ground, which was not only difficult of access but generally ankle-deep in clay in wet weather and 'frightfully bleak' in wild weather.[12] In 1921 they beat Bradford (Park Avenue) 1-0 in the West Riding Cup semi-final at Exley, but a better ground was essential. At a public meeting on 9th July, 1920, their chairman, Dr. A. H. Muir, said: 'Speaking from inside information, I know that if, in February 1921, we can produce a ground that will meet League requirements, and we can show financial backing that is worthy of a town of this size, our position as members of the English League, with all that means, is absolutely secure.'[13]

Unfortunately the returns from League membership never lived up to expectations. The City Fathers were persuaded to lease the Shay to the club, although fears were expressed that the change would spoil the

---

[12] F. T. Dickinson, *Milestones 1911-37: History and Records of Halifax Town AFC*, (Halifax 1937), p. 25.

[13] ibid, p. 31.

views[14] and one council member preferred that the area be used for tennis courts and bowling greens. Volunteers then set to work to level the vacant land. Additional finance was obtained, £1,500 coming from a share issue, so that the Shay was able to open in September 1921 with dressing-rooms, embankments and the foundations for a modest stand. 10,000 'perched on the rough embankments' to see Halifax score five, but it was not to last, Town finishing one from the bottom of the division and having to apply for re-election in their inaugural season. Although attendances were quite good for such a noted rugby town, the losses were frightening and soon threatened the club's survival. It was all a far cry from the hopes of the *Halifax Courier* when Town's admission to the League had been announced, that this would be of 'considerable benefit to the town', 'invaluable as a provider of Saturday and holiday occupation for the masses of our menfolk' and 'strikingly promising to tradesmen'.[15] Football was even cited by 'highly intelligent authorities' as the 'safeguard of the nation against revolutionary disaster'. The Football League may have brought a little prestige to the town, but financial success could be elusive even for large clubs, and was probably unattainable for a team from so small a city. Halifax struggled on through financial crises, and on a meagre budget managed to achieve a respectable level of performance in the Third Division (North), but their true success was to survive at all.

It was Bradford's other neighbouring cities, Huddersfield and Leeds, that provided the real competition and the most sensational events in the Football League in the immediate post-war years.

On 26th September a joint commission of the Football Association and the Football League met in Manchester to enquire into allegations that Leeds City had paid players during the war, contrary to both League regulations and public expectation, but their investigation was hampered by the refusal of the club to produce certain papers. Leeds were suspended on October 6th and could not play their match the following Saturday pending a further meeting of the commission on 13th October.

It was hoped that the replacement of the former controlling syndicate by a new board would appease the football authorities, and the *Yorkshire Post* was 'confident'. Their confidence was misplaced. Leeds City were expelled from the Football League and Burslem Port Vale took over their fixtures (and inherited the results of the eight matches played by Leeds), while Messrs. J. Connor, J. C. Whiteman, S. Glover and G. Sykes, syndicate members, and Herbert Chapman and G. H. Cripps, former officials, were suspended sine die and not allowed to attend   .

[14] *Halifax Courier*, 7 August 1920, p. 4.
[15] ibid, 12 March 1921, p. 31.

football matches or take part in football management.[16] These were drastic measures. The local press was critical that the League had shown 'unseemly haste' in defending their own public position, but the football authorities, and League President J. McKenna, were clearly concerned to reassure the public that the 'game would be kept clean' and that the measures adopted during the war to ensure that professional football clubs acted in a manner consistent with the national interest were sincere.

During the Great War Leeds had certainly been unusually successful in attracting a number of quality players to work in the city and had achieved unprecedented success in the wartime competitions, a success that had left the clubs financial affairs in a 'very satisfactory condition'.[17]

The football authorities did not delay; a sub-committee of the League were in Leeds on October 17th to arrange the transfer of the Leeds City players whose transfer rights were now vested in the League. It was a 'melancholy spectacle' when representatives of over thirty league clubs gathered at the Hotel Metropole. Transfer fees of between £100 and £1,000 were placed on twenty-two players, valuing the squad at £12,150. The club's representatives felt that the fees were too high and arranged instead to make sealed offers. Although the players were told that no one would be required to go where he would not feel comfortable, the whole business seemed not unlike a refined cattle auction.

An auctioneer was then instructed by the only club director exonerated by the commission, to sell the club's effects, including the 'shower baths, billiard tables, jerseys, shirts, vests, knickers, spare goal posts, footballs, nets and boots'.[18] The ground and stands were not for immediate sale and there was speculation that football would never be played at Elland Road again as an offer had been made to convert the ground into a brick works to utilise the valuable clay deposits under the surface.[19] The Yorkshire Amateur Association offered instead to rent the ground, and steps were already in hand to form a new club, Leeds United, when a further extraordinary development took place. On 30th October the new club was in active discussions with the Yorkshire Amateurs and hoped to play their first match on the Elland Road ground on November 8th, a Midland League fixture against Sheffield United Reserves. The match was postponed, however, because of a proposal[20] that Huddersfield Town be moved to Elland Road, Leeds and then be

[16] *Yorkshire Post*, 14 October 1919, p. 14.
[17] ibid.
[18] ibid, 18 October 1919, p. 18.
[19] ibid, 16 October 1919, p. 16.
[20] See the *Huddersfield Examiner*, 8 November 1919.

renamed Leeds United. The Huddersfield club had found playing in the
Football League a financial disaster. Money had been lost in every
season, the club had been reconstructed in 1912 but to no avail.
Huddersfield was a middle-of-the-table Second Division side in a town
whose Northern Union rugby side was perhaps the finest of all time,
champions in 1911-12, 1912-13, runners up in 1913-14, champions in
1914-15 and runners up again in 1919-20. In these seasons Huddersfield's rugby side won 85% or more of the league points it contested,
and had similar success in the Yorkshire League, the Challenge Cup and
the Yorkshire Cup.

In contrast the soccer club's results were indifferent, their attendances poor and their losses severe. By April 1919 £21,000 (£C345,000)
had been invested in the ground, accumulated losses were £6,650 and
the club owed the Crowthers, David Stoner and Joseph Hilton more than
£25,000 (£C410,000). The Crowther brothers owned a large textile
business in nearby Milnsbridge, which was to make history in 1931
when the firm accepted a challenge made by Sir Malcolm Campbell to
British manufacturers to make a suit from sheep to wearer more quickly
than the six hours achieved by a Pennsylvania company. Ninety-four
employees and forty men from a tailor's firm worked with great
enthusiasm, and in an atmosphere of considerable excitement achieved
their task in the startling time of two hours ten minutes.[21]

Although the family business was prosperous the Crowthers could not
provide unlimited financial support, and by 1919 their pocket and
patience were exhausted; attendances of only 4,000 early in the season
convinced them finally that association football had no future in the
town, and they wished to move to Leeds unless the club could settle its
debts forthwith.

Huddersfield appealed for a little time, and Leeds United played their
first match at Elland Road against Yorkshire Amateurs in a blinding
snowstorm and then went ahead with their Midland League fixtures.
The Management Committee of the Football League decided that,
unless £25,000 be paid to the Crowthers by 31st December 1919, consent
would be given for the removal of the club to Leeds. A 'very vigorous and
organised canvas of the town' raised £8,000, and the publicity doubled
gate receipts, but even so £320 a match was too little to cover expenses,[22]
and unless 'the employers and business people came forward there was
no prospect of saving the club'.[23]

Legal niceties were used to buy more time, whereupon salvation
appeared from an unlikely direction; Huddersfield started to win match
after match. By April they had won promotion to the First Division and

[21] E. Lockwood, *Colne Valley Folk*, (London 1936), pp. 20-1.
[22] *Yorkshire Post*, 9 December 1919, p. 16.
[23] ibid, 20 December 1919, p. 16.

reached the FA Cup Final, losing ironically to an Aston Villa goal scored by one of the players, Kirton, who had been sold by the League at the Hotel Metropole, Leeds, in October 1919. This unprecedented success enabled the club to settle with the Crowthers, and by 1926 they had won the League three years in succession to become, under Herbert Chapman (whose ban had been lifted by the FA), the most successful club in England.

Hilton Crowther's preference for Leeds over Huddersfield as an association football centre was not mere opportunism; in October 1920 when Leeds United Association FC were incorporated he became their first chairman, and he carried the financial burdens at Elland Road to the tune of £35,000 until Leeds gained promotion to the First Division in 1924 and a debenture issue raised the funds to repay him. He served on the Leeds board for over thirty years.

Huddersfield were on the way up as Bradford's clubs were on their way down and out of the First Division for good. In Huddersfield's first two seasons in Division One, Bradford (PA) and then Bradford City occupied the relegation positions.

The weakening position of the Bradford clubs was not due to competition from commercial rugby. The city had only one club in the Northern Union, which became the Rugby League in 1922: Bradford Northern, who were formed in May 1907, after Park Avenue had adopted association. The club's facilities were very poor. They started at Greenfield, Dudley Hill, in September 1907 and moved to Birch Lane a year later. Conditions at this ground were so discouraging that the club were thought to have lost revenue due to people going away from Bradford to see rugby under more pleasant and comfortable conditions. After the Great War Bradford Northern 'financially were in a very bad position'[24] and they were not a successful club. The fact that they survived at all was probably due to Bradford Council's Director of Cleansing, Mr. Call, who had the idea of creating Odsal Stadium out of a refuse-tipping area. Years of controlled tipping preceded its opening as a ground in September 1934. Although it was an improvement it was far from ideal. The ground was a long way from the city centre, which affected attendances in the days before cars were widely owned, and its enormous size (102,000) was inappropriate for league crowds and did not help to create any atmosphere. It was also very bleak, and had only a tiny stand of 1,250 seats.

With the resumption of competition after the Great War, Football League clubs ceased to be 'shadow businesses'. Bradford City's gate receipts for the first three seasons, partly because of increases in admission charges announced by the Football League, were twelve

[24] Bradford Northern Rugby League FC, *Souvenir History of Odsal Stadium*, (Bradford 1981), p. 18.

times the wartime levels and three times the level of the three seasons before 1915, also spent in Division One. All season tickets were sold in 1920, although this only represented 6% of receipts as most of the ground was for standing spectators.

Players' contracts were restored, and wages and other costs were much higher than in 1914. The new wage agreement meant a substantial increase in the wage bill in 1920 in spite of a reduction in the playing staff from 41 to 33. Referees' fees had doubled, and increases in the minimum required for a police constable for three hours to 10/- meant that the standard requirement for twelve constables had to be reduced.[25] Even outfit costs, with footballs costing 30/-, and shorts £5 per dozen, were three times pre-war levels. A more serious increase was in the cost of travel, but there was little alternative as char-à-banc firms were charging at least as much as the railways.

Bradford City were financially vulnerable. Success had been achieved quickly before the war, but the lateness of their entry into professional football had made it impossible to accumulate reserves that would have seen them comfortably through the Great War.

They had the smallest share capital in Division One and half the modest ground expenditures had been financed by bank overdraft, as had the wartime losses.

The ground and equipment had 'fallen into disrepair during the war period'[26] and some ground expenditures were inevitable; in the first three seasons £4,750 (£C72,000) was spent on re-covering the South Parade Stand, on encircling the pitch with a cinder track for training, and in reconstructing the Back Burlington Terrace entrances 'in a manner which will enable the spectators to pass through the turnstiles with greater rapidity and comfort'.[27]

The increase in gate receipts was sufficient, however, to more than cover higher costs, particularly if the club were successful. This was well appreciated by the directors, who in 1920 'realising the vital importance of maintaining their position in the First Division decided on a course of specialist training which proved very costly'.[28]

At the end of the 1920-1 season the operating profit, combined with a surplus of nearly £7,000 (£C90,000) on transfer deals, had funded the ground repairs, eliminated accumulated losses and reduced the bank overdraft to under £1,000.

The risks were recognised by the directors,[29] for they saw the need to

---

[25] *Yorkshire Post*, 27 August 1920, p. 12.
[26] Directors' Report Bradford City AFC (1908) Ltd., 26 August 1920.
[27] ibid.
[28] ibid.
[29] ibid, 11 August 1921.

1. Tyrrel Street, Central Bradford, c 1910

2. Bradford City, Champions of Division Two 1907-08

3. First Division football at Valley Parade in 1908, crowds on the Spion Kop end and in the newly constructed Midland Road stand.

4. Bradford City, FA Cup Winners in 1911

5. The Manningham district of Bradford, c 1950

6. Former Park Avenue Chairman S. Waddilove (left) makes a presentation to Alderman and Mrs H.J. White in 1955

7. Aerial view of the Park Avenue
grounds, summer 1957

8. A snow-bound Valley Parade

9. The Park Avenue team meet their new manager, W. Galbraith, in November 1958

10. Bradford City's players and officials about to travel to Arsenal for the 1962 Cup tie

11. A sparse crowd at Park Avenue

12. Park Avenue Board at the Annual General Meeting in January 1970. Herbert Metcalfe is in the centre.

13. Promotion: a player's celebration. R. Campbell in 1982.

14. The main stand at Park Avenue in 1980

15. Abbot scores from the penalty spot v. Millwall on 28th November 1984, to put City top of Division Three

16. Bradford City, Division Three Champions 1984-5

17. The fire at Valley Parade, 11th May 1985

18. Rebuilding the main stand at Valley Parade, August 1986

bring the team to a 'satisfactory standard of efficiency' as even more urgent than the need for further accommodation extensions. In 1921-2 they were relegated in spite of spending an unprecedented £9,000 (£C160,000) on player acquisitions; the club lost their last five matches when only three points were needed for survival.

This reversed the financial progress of the previous seasons for the bank overdraft was back to £8,400. The club did make renewed efforts to increase their share capital, but the timing so soon after relegation was unfortunate and the public response was slight.

Although there were obvious benefits if City could quickly return to the First Division, the directors were at the limits of the company's funds and were unable or unwilling to commit substantial personal capital. The directors saw the 'absolute and primary necessity as putting the finances on a sounder basis' by reducing costs, and in 1923 'practically every item of controllable expenditure' showed a decrease.[30]

From 1922, when Bradford City were relegated to Divison Two, until 1927 when they were relegated to Division Three (North), they lost money on playing in every season except 1924-5, when they reached the last sixteen of the FA Cup. Although economies were made in all cost areas this did not compensate for the far steeper decline in revenues. Consistent surpluses on transfers recovered just over half the deficit on operations but naturally did nothing to strengthen the playing staff, and the side was always in the lowest third of the league table.

Bradford Park Avenue had a fairly successful first season after the war, finishing half-way up the First Division and reaching the quarter final of the FA Cup, losing 1-4 at Chelsea. The attendance of nearly 62,000 provided some monetary compensation for defeat and contributed to a profit for the year of £7,000 (£C108,000).

Towards the end of the season in March 1920, A. H. Briggs, who now owned the Park Avenue site, offered to sell the cricket area at a price of £10,000 (£C150,000), well below its commercial value, on condition that it was used for all time as a cricket arena for the city of Bradford. He died the same month. This was a serious blow to the soccer club, for it removed both a sense of direction and the wealth to support it, and it contributed to the rapid descent of Park Avenue into the Third Division (North). They finished bottom of Division One and one from the bottom of Division Two in successive seasons, 1920-1 and 1921-2, the latter season being the one in which Bradford City were relegated from the First Division.

When Avenue were relegated from the First Division they finished six points away from safety, and their 26 defeats in 42 games was the worst

30 ibid, 16 August 1923.

record in the whole Football League; yet the club made a small profit and even a small surplus on transfer dealings! It seems likely that had Briggs been alive more money would have been spent on new players to try to stave off relegation.

In the Second Division gate receipts slumped by 40% and in spite of net transfer expenditures of £4,200 (£C75,000) Avenue were relegated again. In the Third Division (North) Park Avenue's results improved and they lost only six times at home in their next seven seasons. In the six years in the Third Division they finished in the top five each time, but in spite of this McCluggage and Turnbull had to be sold in 1925 to relieve pressing financial difficulties, and later Peel was sold to Arsenal for £1,750.

In 1927-8 for the third season in succession they scored 101 league goals, but their defence was tighter and 66 points won them the division. Attendances were improved, averaging 14,000, and matches against Bradford City and Doncaster each drew 23,500 to Park Avenue. In September 1927 the local derby at Valley Parade was watched by 38,440, the second largest soccer attendance ever in Bradford. Bradford City for their part finished sixth and spent heavily on new players. This took the bank overdraft to its limit and provoked a financial crisis in the summer of 1928. Most of the board resigned and a new directorate was elected under the promptings of Tom Paton, a Bradford accountant who exerted considerable influence behind the scenes.

The new board also appointed former manager P. O'Rourke, who had been manager when City won Division Two in 1908 and the FA Cup in 1911, and he achieved immediate success. Gate receipts were 60% higher as City won the division and promotion; and although transfer expenditures were high, the club had sufficient money to make much needed alterations to the club premises in Burlington Terrace, adjoining the ground. The trainer's house was taken over to provide for the players' needs, and the old billiard room was converted into the club's first gymnasium. Two great teak baths were installed for the two teams, and a tea room was provided for the joint use of players and directors after matches. Adjoining this was a kitchen and washing-room for kit. At the same time the cinder running-track round the pitch was replaced by a new track and many of the terraces were improved.[31]

By 1929, ten years after the resumption of peacetime football, the West Riding textile district was well established in soccer, although the balance of power had swung towards Huddersfield and Leeds rather than Bradford. Huddersfield had recently won the League Championship three times in succession and played at Wembley in an FA Cup Final. Leeds were too strong for the Second Division, although they were

[31] *Bradford Telegraph and Argus*, 24 July 1928.

not very successful in the First. Park Avenue were third in Division Two, and Bradford City were Champions of a Division Three (North), in which even Halifax were safely placed in mid-table.

The Bradford City board was stable and respectable but not particularly wealthy and were forced to be patient in pursuit of success. The club's finances improved, with profits in seven successive seasons from 1927 to 1934, and this enabled some expenditure on new players, although the board's refusal to strengthen the team when they were top of Division Two in January 1933 was thought locally to have cost the club promotion to the First Division. The club was, however, able to accept an invitation from the LMS Railway Company in August 1931 to buy the remainder of the land at Valley Parade, at a further cost of just under £4,000 (£C95,000).

This gave City greater scope and security for ground improvements, but the intended roofing-over of the Spion Kop end, which would have increased cover at the ground to a very reasonable 28,000, was not carried out when results deteriorated after 1934. Relegation followed, and gate receipts declined continuously to less than half the 1933 level. The club lost money heavily in each of the five seasons before World War II, totalling £1,700 (£C390,000), and without wealthy patronage were forced to sell players regularly. This covered three-quarters of the losses. The bank overdraft was only two-thirds of the modest share capital, but the club's inability to keep its better players led to relegation to the Third Division (North) and disillusionment for their supporters. In spite of finishing in a promising third place in 1938-9, their gate receipts in the two seasons before World War II were the lowest in peacetime since 1907; average home league attendances of 7,115 in 1939 compared poorly with 18,450 in the promotion season of 1928-9.

Table 3 Bradford Park Avenue: Home League Attendances 1925-6 to 1938-9

	Total	Per match
1925-26	278,000	13260
1926-27	217,000	10340
1927-28	297,000	14130
1928-29	373,000	17740
1929-30	312,000	14860
1930-31	239,000	11380
1931-32	277,000	13200
1932-33	223,000	10640
1933-34	239,000	11375
1934-35	189,000	8985
1935-36	206,000	9830
1936-37	219,000	10425
1937-38	233,000	11115
1938-39	210,000	9995

At Park Avenue home attendances were less variable than at Valley Parade (see Table 3). After promotion to the Second Division in 1928 they finished quite near to the promotion places in the six seasons 1928-9 to 1933-4, in spite of continuing player sales and a lack of continuity at board level.

In March 1930, for example, the sale of Millership to Sheffield Wednesday provoked public protests, and in November 1932 Geldard, the youngest person to play in the Football League, was sold to Everton for £4,000 (£C97,000); the following year, aged 19, he was in the Everton side that won the FA Cup.

The board was subject to considerable change in the period between the death of A. H. Briggs in 1920 and the takeover by the Waddiloves in 1935; in all 23 people were directors of Park Avenue during this fifteen-year period.

In May 1935 the financial problems were sizeable enough to test the resolve and pockets of the board of directors. Ernest Waddilove, a major shareholder and bank guarantor, requested an extraordinary meeting to consider the financial position and in particular to relieve him of a small part, £1,000, of his bank guarantee. He felt that player sales should be avoided, and that 'directors should function and accept financial responsibilities or make room for others who would'. The meeting eventually resolved, with 'cordial unanimity' that Ernest and his cousin Stanley Waddilove, who had been a director from 1923-31, be 'co-opted to the board of directors as soon as any vacancies occur'.[32] Vacancies were not long in coming. At a board meeting the following day Messrs C. H. Turner, Brearley, Copley, Ambler and Ward resigned, leaving three directors to manage the club until a new board was elected.

The next day, 3rd May, as Bradford was being decorated for the weekend Silver Jubilee celebrations, the two Waddiloves agreed to co-option on condition that the position of the new board was secured by a reallocation of shareholdings by way of purchase.

The conditions asked for were ostensibly 'agreed unanimously, in a spirit of magnanimity and good fellowship',[33] an impression marred only by the resignation of two more of the old board, leaving Councillor H. J. White and the two Waddiloves in control.

Bradford P.A's future was 'now secure', and the appointment of four more directors later that month brought together a settled and notable board, whose members were to average a further fifteen years' service as directors.

The money behind Park Avenue came from the Waddilove's family business, the Provident Clothing and Supply Company. The firm was

[32] ibid, 1 May 1935.
[33] ibid, 8 May 1935.

started in 1880 by Joshua Waddilove (who was knighted in 1919). He was deeply religious, founding a Waddilove training college for Wesleyan Methodist ministers in Nairobi, and his business was based initially on the concept of 'Christian service to the needy' whereby payment for clothing was made in small weekly amounts (minimum 6d). The firm became more commercial, used collection agents and grew into the 'world's biggest check-trading organisation'.

The family was certainly wealthy, Sir Joshua leaving an estate of £1,250,000 in 1920 (£C19,000,000), and his grandson Stanley lived for many years in 'Heathcote' at Ilkley, a house designed by Sir Edwin Lutyens and built in 1908 for £40,000 (£C1,250,000). On his death in 1962 he left £465,000 (£C3,400,000).

Stanley Waddilove had been on the board of Park Avenue from 1923 to 1931 and was a director for a further twenty years until 1955; his length of tenure was matched only by W. E. (Willie) Collins, who was also passionately attached to the club. Willie Collins' background was, however, very different. He moved to Bradford from Halifax as a clerk to a firm of spinners and manufacturers but made rapid progress and was made secretary-director when the firm was incorporated. 1920 was for him an eventful year; he joined Park Avenue's board and left the textile trade to found his own firm of radio and electrical wholesalers. He was involved in local affairs, as Liberal Councillor for the Great Horton ward from 1934 to 1946, and in his local congregational church, golf and bowling club. He was a director at Park Avenue from 1920 to 1934 and 1935 to 1949.

Another prominent local businessman who joined the board in 1935 was John Turner. He was a director for twenty-one years, until he resigned aged 72. A prominent local businessman, with his own firm specialising in reed manufacture, he acted as secretary to the Bradford Worsted Spinners Federation for thirty-three years until 1960. His origins were modest, starting work as an office boy in a Bradford textile company, but he was successful in business, receiving an MBE in 1953 and leaving £53,000 in 1965 (£C360,000). Turner was very active in local matters, in politics predictably as a Liberal member of Bradford City Council, in local business circles, and as a JP for thirty years. He also found time to act as Chairman of the British Amateur Athletics Board, and for twenty-five years from 1930 he attended in his official capacity every major international athletics event, being chief judge for the sprint races at the 1932 Los Angeles Olympics.

Henry Hudson also joined the Park Avenue board in 1935. He was the archetypal 'mill lad' who became Lord Mayor of Bradford. Born at Kirkheaton in 1870 he came to Bradford aged 3 and found work at Odsal Mills at the age of 10.

In 1885 he went into business with his father, who combined hand loom weaving with poultry farming, and they made carpets in the evening. This gave him a working day of 6 am to 10 pm, and a belief that 'the only way to get on in life is to work hard'.[34] This helped him to build up two flourishing wool and waste companies, but he was no autocrat and was active in local affairs. For sixteen years he was chairman of Bradford Mental Welfare Committee, a freemason, an officer in the Methodist Church, and for seventeen years he represented Great Horton as a Liberal Councillor. In 1937 he became Mayor.

He was interested in sport, playing cricket for thirty years and rugby for local clubs, including Manningham, but his weight of under ten stone limited his success. He later became a life member of Bradford RUFC and president of Great Horton Cricket Club.

His health in later life deteriorated, but he was on Avenue's board until the age of 80 and visited his firm's office daily until a week before his death at 87 in 1957, when he left an estate of £26,000 (£C470,000).

The Park Avenue board was stable, cohesive, wealthy and dedicated to the club's success; Stanley Waddilove spoke of making Avenue the 'Arsenal of the North' and was prepared to bear the cost for a time of reversing the previous policy of selling off promising players. He had an almost fanatical desire to see Park Avenue succeed and on one occasion even paid a transfer fee out of his own pocket. Willie Collins was also one of Park Avenue's most ardent supporters; in 1935 his greatest desire was 'to see the Bradford Football Club in the first flight of League clubs'.[35]

In spite of this support at board level Park Avenue's results did not improve. In the four seasons before the war they finished 16th, 20th, 7th and 17th, and twice went out of the FA Cup in their first match.

The 1936-7 season, in which they narrowly avoided relegation, was the worst financial year in the club's history; they lost over £5,000 (£C115,000) and made further losses in the next two seasons, although the effects were ameliorated by money received from transfer sales. £1,500 was spent in 1936-7 on painting the whole of the stands, and improving the changing rooms, and in 1938-9 a supporters' bazaar raised £1,800 which was to be the nucleus of a ground purchase fund.

In February 1937 Park Avenue were approached by a syndicate asociated with a 'well-known London stadium', almost certainly the White City, to transfer the club lock, stock and barrel so that First Division football could eventually be brought to a thickly populated part of London. The offer was declined!

In 1936-7, although Avenue just stayed up in Division Two, neighbours City finished immediately below them and went back down to

[34] ibid, 9 July 1937.
[35] ibid, 5 June 1935.

Division Three (North). Neither club was in a sound condition, and further amalgamation talks were announced in December 1937. Park Avenue director H. J. White said there was insufficient support for two senior association clubs in Bradford and that Park Avenue were losing £100 a week, City probably twice that amount. There were major difficulties, however. Any combined club would start with a very large debt chiefly from Park Avenue, and the existing lease at Avenue was due to expire in August 1940. Their balance sheet was most unusual; by commercial criteria they were totally insolvent, with assets totalling less than £1,000 and debts £19,000 and thus depended entirely on Stanley Waddilove for their continued existence. The ground (being leased not owned) provided no security for the bank overdraft, so the bank looked to the directors and chairman for personal guarantees.

In October 1938 the talks were concluded. Park Avenue were still in favour of amalgamation, because the city of Bradford would not support two soccer clubs, and because both grounds were too small, with Park Avenue uncomfortable if crowds exceeded 24,000. Park Avenue Chairman Waddilove called for a continental type of stadium, with municipal support, offering soccer and rugby on alternate Saturdays, possibly at Odsal Stadium. Bradford Northern, who had fifteen years left on their Odsal lease, were doing quite well and were not in favour and, decisively, Bradford City did not want to amalgamate as 'their debts could be wiped out by one transfer'.[36]

Within a year Avenue had managed to stay up, coming seventeenth in Division Two, City had promised much but failed to deliver, coming third in Division Three (North) but missing promotion by fifteen points. Far more importantly, Europe was at war and the chance had once again been missed.

[36] ibid, 29 October 1938.

WORLD WAR II

14. Wartime Arrangements

During the Great War the football authorities had been slow to suspend official competition and professionalism, and until the introduction of conscription the industry was roundly accused of a lack of patriotism. In World War II the football authorities showed greater awareness of the public mood; on 8th September 1939 the FA 'entirely suspended' all football, except that arranged by HM Forces, until official notice was given to the contrary.[1] Thus within a week of Britain and France declaring war on Germany the FA had taken immediate control of football, a control which could then be relaxed in line with judgements of the public mood.

In early October eight regional competitions were announced. The five West Riding textile district clubs were part of an eleven-team North Eastern League, and there were also leagues for the North-West, East Midlands, Western, Midlands, South West and Southern regions. Only six clubs did not take part, Aston Villa, Sunderland, Derby, Exeter, Ipswich and Gateshead, although Birmingham City did not play at home and Arsenal shared Tottenham Hotspur's ground.

League tables were compiled, but no trophies were to be awarded, and thirty-three playing days were defined, with provision made for friendlies to be played on these dates in the absence of league matches.

In November the Football League arranged a knockout competition between representative teams from each of the eight regional groups. Some of these games were to be played on midweek evenings so as not to interfere with league games, and all proceeds were to go to the Red Cross.

In March 1940 the FA extended the season by five weeks to June 8th, but matches were 'not to interfere with counter-attractions like cricket and lawn tennis'.[2]

The 1941-2 season was run on a different basis. There were to be competitions for North and South on a points basis, ending on Boxing Day, with a League and Cup competition for the second half of the season; the top thirty-two clubs after ten games qualified for the Cup competition proper.

[1] *The Times*, 9 September 1939, p. 3.
[2] ibid, 5 March 1940, p. 13.

When the season started there were difficulties with playing kits, but the Board of Trade said that the supply position did not permit clubs to be given licences to purchase football kit without coupons, and suggested that club supporters each give a coupon to their club.

Correspondence in *The Times* about football pools was mixed, regarding it as a 'clog on the war effort', 'an unrivalled means of amusement' and, more analytically, as 'a likely stimulant to war savings'.[3]

The prompt action of the Football Association and the early introduction of conscription helped a more tolerant attitude to football to prevail in World War II than in the Great War, and in June 1943 the Football League increased players' match fees from £1 10/- to £2, without any great public outcry.

Rugby League reorganised itself slightly and formed a war Emergency League, initially in two county sections, with the winners playing each other for the championship. After two seasons the declining number of Lancashire clubs caused the formation of a reorganised single league of seventeen clubs, fourteen of them from Yorkshire.

The pattern of wartime football was subject to frequent changes. In the 1944-5 season, clubs were allocated to one of three sections, North, South and West, so as to reduce travel, and the re-emergence of Preston, Accrington, Hull and Port Vale increased the Northern League to 54! There were only 18 clubs in the South and 6 in the West.

The regional league and cup competitions were run independently until Christmas, after which they joined forces 'in the same complicated mixture of league and cup games which make war-time football so difficult for many people to follow'.[4]

Official acceptance of football may have been helped by the contribution it made to Entertainment Tax; £280,000 was paid over in the 1943-4 season alone.

The football authorities had reacted promptly when war broke out in 1939; they moved with equal speed when enemy forces surrendered in 1945. The German army in Italy surrendered on 2nd May, and as enemy troops in Holland and North West Germany joined them on 4th May the FA War Emergency Committee announced the resumption of the FA Cup for the following season.

On 6th May all German fighting forces surrendered; the following day the Football League decided that professional football would be run in the next season in four regional groups. The forty-four Division One and Two clubs would play in North and South Divisions, and the Third Divisions would resume their pre-war North and South basis but without

3 ibid, 14 January 1942, p. 5.
4 ibid, 25 August 1944, p. 8.

any right of promotion.

In July 1945 further modifications were made; the Third Divisions were to be split up, with the Northern Division divided into a North-West and North-East section. Bradford City and Halifax were to play in the latter. FA Cup ties were played over two legs and the Third Divisions ran their own cup competition in the second half of the season.

The first post-war season was notable for a threatened players' strike, a major ground disaster and a reduction in admission prices.

The Players' Union was determined to strike in pursuit of a pay claim, but they called it off when the Football League decided to raise the maximum wage from £8 to £9 a week.

On 9th March 1946, at a cup tie at Burnden Park, Bolton against Stoke City, thirty-three died when an excessive concentration of people built up in one section of the ground before the crush barriers broke; crowd control had clearly been inadequate and the Inquiry was told that there was no legal requirement for ground inspection, although plans to erect buildings had to be approved by the local authority.

The maximum wage was then raised to £10 per week in season, £7 10/- in the close season with maximum benefits up from £650 to £750. The Football League also decided to resume full competition in 1946, with normal promotion and relegation taking place, as it was felt that clubs had been given sufficient time to readjust to peacetime and reassemble their playing staffs. The population had been deprived of entertainment during the war years and the resumption of full competition would lead to sudden prosperity for many clubs. Bradford's two sides were not to be among them.

15. Improved Finances at City and Avenue!

The football authorities organised regional competitions during the war. Their format was frequently changed and the confusing fixture lists offered no prestige to clubs but some entertainment for the civilian population. Settled sides were an impossibility, and guest appearances by ex-professional players working or stationed in the locality were common occurences. Football kept going after a fashion and provided no conflict with national priorities.

Bradford City were most unsuccessful in the unofficial competitions, finishing near the foot of the large northern division in 1942-3 and the two following seasons. In 1945-6 after the war had ended but, before normal competition resumed, they finished seventh out of ten clubs in the 'Football League Division Three North: East' and eighteenth out of twenty sides in the Division Three North Second Championship, although they were more successful in the Division Three North (East) Cup Qualifying competition. Gate receipts had fallen to only £1,000 in 1940-1, but, in common with most clubs, attendances improved thereafter. Costs fell even more, with local matches and no professional players to pay. The club made some money on playing operations during the war, and some quick profits on the transfer market in 1945-6. This, allied to the generosity of some of the loan creditors, meant that in May 1946 the club's liabilities were lower than for many years, and a long standing bank overdraft had been converted to a small credit balance. The ground had, however, deteriorated considerably during the war.

The composition of City's board of directors was virtually unchanged during the war years. Councillor Sharp's personal contribution was probably crucial to the continuation of the club's activities, and he acted as honorary manager and then secretary between 1942 and 1947. The board of seven included three other councillors or aldermen, indicating the extent to which the club's management now attracted the city's more civic-minded inhabitants. Alderman Barnett had been a councillor since 1926 and acted as a director between 1939 and 1952, when he died aged 72. He was Lord Mayor of Bradford in 1944-5, had interests in the grocery and wine trade, managed a local cinema chain, and also found time to lead the Conservative Council.

John Russell Rose was also an alderman of the city, and was Deputy Lord Mayor of Bradford in 1947, towards the end of his eighteen years as a director of the football club. He was head of one of the largest motor distributors in the provinces, leaving £71,000 (£C650,000) on his death in 1953, but he was equally interested in competitive walking and held high office in the national walking and athletics associations. In 1914, many years before his election to Bradford City's board, he had helped to found the Sportsmen's Battalion to prepare men for the Regular Army and at one time had over a thousand men enlisted. The first meeting was at Manningham Lane Skating Rink, close to the ground at Valley Parade, and Rose asked a famous footballer, Laurie Hickson, to address the meeting.

Although City's board clearly included men with considerable civic consciousness there was still no enthusiasm for amalgamation with Park Avenue; in January 1940 there was a meeting at board level to discuss the possibility of wartime amalgamation between the two clubs, but no agreement was reached.[1]

The threat to Park Avenue's continued existence became public the following month when one of the club's directors, Alderman Hudson, said that if the club was to survive 'all the club's guarantors should pay up with a smile'.[2]

The underlying problem was the expiry of the lease at the end of August. In April the ground trustees indicated that the tenancy might be extended 'in a spirit of compromise' if Avenue's directors made an offer that was reasonable in the context of the reduced revenues of wartime football.[3]

In August 1940 the club announced further losses of £1,765 (£C27,500). These losses were far smaller than they had been hitherto, but the directors took a serious view of matters, perhaps to influence the lease negotiations. Certainly the accumulated losses of £30,150 (£C470,000) were disturbing enough, and the bank overdraft had reached its limit of £17,000 (£C270,000). This led the directors to announce publicly both their unwillingness to commit the company to an annual lease obligation and their intention to suspend operations unless the supporters rallied round.[4]

The directors' tactics proved successful. Avenue's board was a cohesive group, and the Waddilove's business wealth meant that any bank limit was at a level they judged appropriate, rather than at the

[1] *Bradford Telegraph and Argus*, 10 January 1940.
[2] ibid, 6 February 1940.
[3] ibid, 25 April 1940.
[4] ibid, 6 August 1940.

limit the directors could actually guarantee, but equally clearly there were limits to their subsidy of the club's activities. The ground trustees accordingly modified their demands and an accommodation was reached which enabled the club to continue.

After these difficulties had been overcome matters improved, both on the field and financially. From 1941 until the end of the war Avenue were generally in the top half of their league, finishing ninth out of the fifty-four clubs in the Football League North First Championship, of 1944-5. Attendances improved considerably after the very low levels of 1940-1 and gate receipts in 1943-4 and 1944-5 were slightly more than half the immediate pre-war figures, and 50% above those at Valley Parade. With no professional players to pay, Avenue were able to declare profits in each season, for the first time since 1930, and this reduced the accumulated losses and bank overdraft by a quarter.

During the Second World War county cricket was suspended, but many county players signed up for Bradford League sides. In 1943, for example, eighty were employed by Bradford clubs. The Park Avenue cricket ground was used by the army during the later war years, however, so Bradford Cricket Club was inactive during this period.[5]

In 1944 Valley Parade was also under special requisition, and was only available to the club for first team fixtures on Saturdays. All City's regular players were in the services, but there were occasional indications of better things to come; in April 1944 Avenue attracted one of Bradford's largest ever football crowds, and record receipts, when 32,865 spectators paid £2,870 to see a holiday League (North) Cup Third Round tie against Blackpool. In the first leg Bradford had drawn 2 − 2 at Blackpool, but the return of Matthews strengthened the Lancashire side and Bradford's Scottish fullback, Stephen, turned a cross from Matthews into his own net for the only goal, a score that put Blackpool into the semi-finals. An estimated 30,000 were locked out, thousands walked miles to the ground and some travelled to the game from as far away as Nottingham and Liverpool.

In the transitional season of 1945-6 Bradford City's results and attendances in the Football League Division Three North (East) were poor, but Park Avenue, in the Football League (North), were playing some of the strongest sides in the country and their attendances went up immediately. Gate receipts were now as high as at any time in the club's history and their profit for 1945-6 was the best the club had ever made.

Since the Great War Bradford's two clubs had found, and would continue to find, it difficult to make professional football pay. It is salutory that both clubs were able to improve their financial position

[5] *Bradford Cricket Club*, (Bradford 1973).

despite the restrictions of the wartime period; for Park Avenue World War II was to prove financially the most successful period in their history.

1946-1958
THE POST-WAR PERIOD

16. Post-war Prosperity

In the post-war period, as reconstruction work got under way, the level of unemployment was very much lower than before the war and wage rates and inflation were much higher. Wage rates were 60% higher in 1946 than pre-war, and in the twelve years to 1958 wages rose a further 90%[1] and prices 65%. Wool textile production was relatively static until 1952, and then increased by 25% in six years. Wool prices trebled, employment in woollen textiles, reversing the pre-war trend, increased by 40%,[2] and even textile industry wages increased, by a notable 75% in twelve years.[3]

Once the war was over the leisure industries boomed, including the cinema, cricket, speedway and greyhound racing. In Bradford there were still forty cinemas, but the arrival of television in northern England in the mid 1950s caused many picture houses to close down.

County cricket audiences were up, and the most immediate competition to professional soccer in the West Riding, rugby league, also attracted record attendances. Bradford Northern were handicapped by their remote and uninviting stadium and for economic reasons built a speedway track round the pitch and a new stand to increase the number of seats. They attracted their best crowds during the period 1948-54 in which they at last achieved some success. They had won the Wartime Emergency League Championship three times during the war and now in peacetime won the Challenge Cup in 1946-7 and 1948-9 (finishing runners up in 1947-8), were beaten Championship finalists in 1947-8 and 1951-2, Yorkshire League Champions in 1947-8 and Yorkshire Cup winners in 1945-6, 1948-9, 1949-50 and 1953-4. Their dominating play increased average home attendances to 15,000 (three times the level to come in 1956 and 1957) and the club's record attendance of 69,000 was established by the visit of Huddersfield in March 1953.

The Rugby League Cup Final replay a year later at their Odsal ground between Warrington and Halifax was watched by an audience of 102,569, one of the largest crowds ever drawn to any English stadium.

In the Football League attendances also reached record levels in the

---

[1] B. Mitchell and P. Deane, op cit, p. 144.
[2] ibid, p. 98.
[3] ibid, pp. 145-6.

early post-war period. Attendances totalled more than 40,000,000 in 1947-8, 1948-9 and 1949-50 and throughout the period to 1958 average match attendances in the Football League were above 15,000, although in the Third Division (North) they varied between 7,000 and 9,000. Total attendances were 30% higher than pre-war, and in 1951 it seemed that the Third Division clubs were 'getting slightly more than proportionate shares of the increased attendances since the war'.[4]

In 1946 Entertainment Duty, first levied in 1916, was reduced for the live theatre and spectator sports, including football. In two years the duty fell from 7½d per spectator to 1d, and the football clubs at the Chancellor's specific request reluctantly reduced their minimum admission prices from 1/6 to 1/3, still 3d above the pre-war norm. Average net takings per club in 1948-9 were twice as high as in 1937-8;[5] in Division Three (South) the average increased from £12,000 to £26,000, in Division Three (North) from £7,000 to £16,000.

This was an almost 'golden age' for smaller clubs, and the League soon acted to marginally increase their numbers, although not their influence. In 1956 the League was extended from 88 to 92 clubs, but only the 44 in Divisions One and Two each had a vote at meetings; the other 48 associate members in the Third Divisions shared just four votes.

Although clubs in the Third Divisions had limited influence on Football League policy, they did have direct and automatic entry into the upper divisions; the champion club in both Third Divisions was promoted each season into Division Two. Of the clubs in the Third Division when its membership was extended to 48 clubs in 1950 nine of the southern clubs have since reached the First Division; in the Northern section, which now included the two Bradford clubs, only Carlisle in season 1974-5 were to reach the First Division.

Although the post-war period was for professional football prosperous and untroubled, it saw the beginnings of the changes that would have profound effects on the shape and character of the industry over the next thirty years.

The maximum wage system was a long-established and distinctive feature of the football business. It lowered player costs and reduced the bargaining power of the more wealthy clubs and thus helped to promote more equal competition, but it was a unique restraint on the 'freedom to trade' of employees. In May 1949 the League AGM bought off discontent by approving a provident scheme that would provide retiring professional players with a lump sum equal to 10% of their earnings from the game. This was financed by an increase in the levy on receipts from

[4] Political and Economic Planning, *Planning* Volume XVII No 324, *The Football Industry*, p. 168.
[5] ibid.

League matches and cup-ties involving League clubs from 1% to 4%.[6]

In 1953 a dispute with the players was concluded when the Industrial Disputes Tribunal announced in July that the maximum wage for professional footballers aged 20 and over would go up from £14 to £15 during the season, and £10 to £12 out of season; the following year the Association Football Players and Trainers Union with 2,300 members was accepted for affiliation to the TUC.

In May 1947 the FA removed their ban on midweek football and announced that midweek games would be allowed at the start and end of the season, when matches could be played in the evening, and on national and local holidays, although no additional competitions were launched at this time. Instead the FA began to promote an increasing number of floodlit and representative matches, particularly towards the end of the period when they also decided to allow the televising of selected games.

The advent of television dated from July 1952 when the football authorities announced that the following season's Cup Final was to be both broadcast and televised. The FA were also willing to allow the second half of two international matches to be televised provided that all match tickets had already been sold; a year later the League clubs announced that they were not against television in principle, but wanted 'a measure of control so that their own fixtures would not suffer financially'.[7]

By 1956 the Football League Management Committee were concerned at the decline in attendances, which were 20% down on the peak figure of 1949.

Although the League talked of 'football indigestion' as a cause of declining attendances it seems clear that in 1956 their concern was mainly that any additional fixtures should be under their control and for their financial benefit rather than the FA's.

The League was, of course, entitled to be concerned at the fall in attendances, but in public they gave far less publicity to the fact that industry revenues were rising not falling, as the increase in minimum admission prices from 1/3 to 2/- was greater than the fall in attendances, even when inflation is taken into account.[8] Professional football instead gave, and has continued to give, an impression that it expects to be above the most basic relationship in economics, that demand falls as prices rise; it seemed almost as if the League had come to take spectator loyalties for granted.

[6] *The Times*, 31 May 1949, p. 6.

[7] ibid, 15 June 1953, p. 10.

[8] P. Bird, 'The Demand for League Football', *Applied Economics*, 1982, Vol. 14, pp. 637-49, Fig. 1.

Football in the post-war era was facing real growth in leisure industry competition, particularly from television, and social changes that were to weaken local identification and loyalties. As yet, however, the decline in attendances that accompanied price increases was almost constant between divisions; there were no signs of the increasingly selective approach of spectators that in the next twenty-five years would transform the rewards for success, and the penalties for failure, in professional football.

17. Third Division Bradford

Bradford's two professional association football clubs had entered the Football League in the early years of the century, City as a newly formed club in 1903 and Park Avenue after one not very successful season in the Southern League. City took five seasons to reach the First Division, Avenue six, and when official competition was suspended in 1915 Avenue and City were ninth and tenth respectively in the First Division.

After the Great War Avenue and City were soon relegated. Both had periods in the Third Division (North) but both spent most of the interwar period in the Second Division. Avenue were well placed in each season 1928-9 to 1933-4, but as the war approached they struggled to stay up; City were relegated in 1937 after several undistinguished seasons in Division Two.

The post-World War II period marked Bradford's two clubs as Third Division sides. City's results in the Third Division (North) were mediocrity itself; their average position over twelve consecutive seasons was twelfth out of twenty-four, they were bottom once and their highest position was third once. They finished in the top six in three seasons, but never really challenged for promotion, finishing 22 points (1946-7), 16 points (1953-4) and 9 points (1957-8) behind the promoted team. They did no better in the FA Cup; only twice in twelve years did they reach the potentially lucrative Third Round, and on each occasion they lost 0-1 to Third Division opponents.

Park Avenue began the post-war period in the Second Division. This lasted four seasons. At first, in the Third Division, they were moderately successful, but in the three seasons 1955-6, 1956-7 and 1957-8 they finished near the foot of the league, and had to apply for re-election in 1955-6. Twice in the last six years of the period they reached the FA Cup Third Round but lost heavily to teams from higher divisions.

The decline of Bradford's soccer clubs was particularly disappointing as the large crowds of the post-war period offered the prospect of good commercial returns for success and because both clubs had improved their financial position during World War II, even if their grounds were deteriorating.

If gate receipts were much higher after the war, wages, travelling and other expenses had also risen considerably.[1] Wages were the major cost; for First Division clubs they were 30-40% of total expenses, in the Second Division 40-60% and up to 80% for Third Division clubs.[2] Transfer fees were also much higher than pre-war; there were about thirty transfers between 1947 and 1950 of £15,000 or more, and the highest fee rose to £30,000.

The Third Division (North) was not a strong league. None of the clubs in the Division in the first season after the war ever reached Division One, and promoted clubs generally found it hard to survive even in the Second Division. Of the twelve clubs promoted between 1946 and 1958 three were immediately relegated and another three lasted only three or four years in Division Two. Third Division (North) clubs were generally marginal to the Football League, faced considerable local competition from successful northern sides, attracted crowds that were about 25% lower than in Division Three (South) and had small, poorly developed grounds.

In 1946 Bradford City were, however, in better shape financially than for many years, with no bank overdraft and accumulated losses of less than £2,000.

Secretary-manager Steele, who was with the club from 1947 until 1952, was able to spend money; unlike most Third Division (North) sides, City were even prepared to spend on new players in spite of the difficulties of competing 'in these days of £25,000 transfers',[3] but the club achieved nothing. They were generally well supported for a Third Division club, with league attendances 30% above the divisional average, but they earned little from cup matches. Wage bills took over 75% of gate receipts and they lost £17,000 (£C185,000) in five years in which their average league position was fifteenth.

Changes were made at board level in March 1948. Two directors resigned and were replaced by Herbert Munro, Herbert Holden and O. S. Wain, who were to stay on the board into the 1960s. The nucleus of the new directorate was completed by the appointment of Albert Harris a year later. All four were local businessmen, but none of them had any particular civic involvement and none were conspicuously wealthy nor able or willing to heavily subsidise the club's activities. Wain was director of a clothing firm with a prominent city centre retail outlet, Munro managed a local furnishing fabric manufacturers and was involved in freemasonry and his local golf club, Holden was director of a cinema group and a prestigious local club and was active in his local conservative, golf and bowling clubs and Harris ran a timber merchants

---

[1] *Political and Economic Planning*, op cit, p. 173.
[2] ibid, p.177.
[3] *Bradford Telegraph and Argus*, 18 January 1949.

and joined City's board after a period as treasurer of their supporter's association.

Their first major problem was to deal with the Midland Road Stand which by early 1949 was viewed, in the aftermath of the Burden Park disaster, as a bad risk. The stand ran along the lower side of the terrace that had been cut into the hillside in 1886 to provide the playing area, and its foundations were never as stable as those built into level ground; indeed Bradford City is still the only Football League club with a ground cut out of a distinct slope. (The Main Stand on the opposed, higher side of the slope had secure foundations, but all spectators had to leave by climbing steps against the slope until they reached the street level outside, a circumstance that was to have horrible consequences in 1985.) Shareholders at the Annual General Meeting in October 1949 were told that reconstruction of the Midland Road Stand would have to be deferred as the club had just made a substantial loss and it would cost £12-16,000 (£C150,000) to make it usable.[4]

In 1951 Bradford Corporation ordered the club to dismantle the stand as its foundations were now seen as unsafe, and in April 1952 the club accepted a bid from Berwick Rangers for the stand. Berwick's ground building plans had been held up due to national shortages of steel and concrete, and they were prepared to pay Bradford £450 and bear the dismantling and transport costs. They did not want the old timbers which City kept for their planned new cover 'in solid ground'.

The Midland Road side was therefore open as a 'temporary expedient' for the start of the 1952-3 season, as it had been in September 1908 for the opening match in the First Division.[5]

In 1952 secretary-manager Steele left the club, and after one of the directors, Albert Harris, had briefly acted as a stand-in manager the club appointed Ivor Powell, who 'cut expenses to the bone'.[6] The wage bill fell 40% in one season, travel costs by 15% and the club actually declared a small profit in spite of a 10% drop in match receipts.

A public appeal in December 1952 for £20,000 for new players was not very successful; City instead made some money on player sales, which covered ground improvement costs that year. Construction began on the new Midland Road stand, with some of the finance coming from a Football Association loan subsequently repaid by the Supporters' Club. In 1954 floodlights were installed on telegraph poles along each side of the ground. Results were variable in Powell's three seasons, but a bottom four position in 1955 seemed too high a price to pay for austerity and the new manager P. Jackson was given the security of a five-year

[4] ibid, 14 October 1949.
[5] ibid, 22 November 1952.
[6] ibid, 29 September 1953.

contract and told to make the development of home produced players the priority. By 1956 City were not willing to sign any players aged over 30 and had the youngest side in Division Three. They also had their lowest wage bill since 1948.

In 1950 under Steele, Bradford employed thirty-two professionals in the last half of the 1949-50 season, paid as follows:

Under £5 pw	(under £C55 pw)	4
£6-7 pw	(£C65-75 pw)	5
£8-9 pw	(£C85-100 pw)	19
£10-11 pw	(£C110-120 pw)	3
£12 pw	(£C130 pw)	1
		32[7]

In the latter half of the 1955-6 season there were twenty-five professionals of whom eight were paid under £5 per week and only four received over £12 per week.

In 1957-8, the last season before the introduction of new national Third and Fourth Divisions, Bradford City finished third, their highest position in the post-war period. They had made moderate profits in five of the last six seasons and gate receipts were at their highest level since the war.

The increase in the bank overdraft since 1946 was quite small in spite of losses in the period under Steele, and in spite of the money spent on the ground, chiefly the Midland Road stand, and this was almost entirely due to the growth of donations from the Supporters' Club. The donors obtained little influence for their money; the shareholders who ultimately controlled the club had contributed only £2,100 for new shares since the war.

At Park Avenue it was difficult to criticise the scale of financial support provided by the shareholders and directors; the club had become chairman Waddilove's 'life's hobby'. Even his patience was not inexhaustible, however, and in the post-war period every effort was made to reduce his financial commitment.

Waddilove was disappointed by the lack of crowd support and he viewed the city of Bradford as 'not sufficiently football-minded'. Crowd support was certainly lacking while they were in the Second Division; their average gates of 15,000 were almost 40% below the divisional average of 25,000, partly due to the ground capacity, and this left the club with little alternative but to sell players.

The 1946-7 season started with the sale of England international Shackleton to Newcastle for £13,000 to reduce the bank overdraft; he

[7] Private papers.

later said that with a little persuasion he would have stayed, as they had the makings of a First Division side and had they gone up 'things would have been different'. The Ministry of Food refused permission for Park Avenue's supporters' club to supply spectators with light refreshments, but in spite of such privations attendances were well up on the previous year.

The club bought five more houses to meet difficulties in accommodating players and staff, and in June 1947 negotiations led by Henry Hudson enabled them to purchase the ground, after forty years of paying an annual rental of about £600.

The club felt they could now entertain large schemes of improvement and extension and that this marked the end of proposals to merge Park Avenue and City.[8]

In August two nursery teams were established to 'improve the playing staff without recourse to fantastic transfer fees'.[9] Bradford started the 1947-8 season with six straight wins that put them top of Division Two, but later results were less impressive and they finished in the bottom half of the table. Among their team was Ron Greenwood, who later wrote that manager Emery only saw players before kick-off on Saturday. 'No one talked tactics and we worked things out as the game went along.'[10] The season was notable only for the cup win at Arsenal, the winning goal being scored by Elliott, later to be sold to Burnley and to play for England.

In 1948-9 playing operations cost Park Avenue nearly £8,000. Gate receipts were up 15%, entirely due to cup ties against Newcastle and Manchester United, but players wages and benefits were double the level of two years before, and playing expenses at £32,000 almost entirely absorbed gate receipts. For the third year in succession, gains on transfers more than covered operating losses and reduced accumulated losses to £8,500, but the reserve team was failing to produce senior players, and the directors saw themselves as 'constantly handicapped by inadequate support'.[11] By the summer of 1949 the bank overdraft was down to £1,035, losses accumulated over a long period had been cleared, the football ground bought and the Horton Park End concreted over, but these achievements were largely due to a concerted policy of *utilising* 'fantastic transfer fees' by selling players.

In 1949-50 Stanley Waddilove met public criticisms head-on: 'more players would be transferred unless gates improved.'[12] He pointed out

[8] *Bradford Telegraph and Argus*, 14 June 1947.
[9] Bradford (Park Avenue) AFC Directors' Report 1948.
[10] R. Greenwood, *Yours Sincerely*, (London 1981).
[11] Bradford (Park Avenue) AFC Directors' Report 1949.
[12] *Bradford Telegraph and Argus*, 1 December 1949.

that wages were 65% of gate receipts and asked if there was any other business in which 'workers took so huge a share of receipts'.

Near the end of the season the local press[13] carried a front-page article on the Bradford City and Park Avenue 'doldrums'. Their struggles among the game's 'lowly' was contrasted with the large gates being attracted elsewhere in Yorkshire, and was attributed to a willingness to sell their best players.

At the end of the season City were nineteenth in Third Division (North), and Park Avenue were bottom of Division Two, and went down. They did not play in Division Two again.

The unavailing attempt to avoid relegation had a severe financial impact, with operating losses reinforcing transfer-fee expenditures. Chairman Waddilove, who was said to be dominating and 'never slow to criticise', indicated where responsibility lay by stating at the AGM that the board, not the manager, decided which players should be signed. 'Weaknesses in the relegated team were known, but the club could not pay £20,000 for another team's reserve player ... instead they would need to find a young, strong player at £5,000-£6,000.' Derek Kevan was at Avenue at this time and was young and strong enough for West Bromwich Albion to purchase and turn into an England international.

Avenue were quite well supported for a Third Division (North) side although gates were slightly lower than those at Valley Parade, but they did not take steps to reduce their heavy wage bill.

Horton Park was closed as a passenger station in September 1952[14] although this probably had only a limited effect on attendances as by now most spectators came by road.

In 1953 the club lost £10,700, the second heavy loss in succession, and appointed Kirkman as the new manager under an agreement that he would manage while the board dealt with financial matters. Interestingly Kirkman was preferred to the other short-listed candidate, who subsequently achieved considerable managerial success elsewhere, Bill Shankly. Shankly may of course have been less prepared to accept board control.

By 1955 the financial position was even worse; Kirkman was sacked as an economy measure and complained that a director had undermined his authority. The club was now £35,000 in the red and Stanley Waddilove ended an era by resigning to make way for a new chairman, and new financial arrangements.

Reginald Kellett, who had been a director at Park Avenue since 1949, succeeded Waddilove as Chairman. His father Jonas had played Rugby Union at Park Avenue before the switch to association, and he played

---

[13] ibid, 20 March 1950.
[14] H. Hird, *Bradford in History*, (Bradford 1968), p. 176.

soccer, representing his battalion during the 1914-18 war, and turning out for Blackpool and Chelsea.

Kellett had had a varied life: he was working in Alaska when war broke out, so he joined the Canadian Army. After the end of the war he travelled to North America, mining for lead, silver, zinc and copper, and working on the railroads, before returning to the family mill in Tong Street. He was managing director of the two family firms, which specialised in furnishing fabric weaving, and cotton and rayon manufacture, and stood as a local councillor for the Conservative and National Liberal Association.

He and his wife were interested in youth work, and he had been a vicar's warden and a school manager. Before joining the board he took a regular interest in Park Avenue's third team, and while on the board he often attended games played by the second, third and fourth teams. For six months in 1955-6 he acted as honorary manager and 'without his ceaseless efforts the club might have gone out of existence',[15] but by now he was 65.

Avenue finished 23rd out of 24 in Division Three (North) and made their first, but not their last, application for re-election to the League. Their 122 goals conceded was the worst defensive record in the entire League since 1947. Young became the club's fifth manager in six years, and the club reverted to green and white shirts. Red, amber and black had been the colours of the original rugby club, and the first association colours, but T. E. Malley who was manager from 1911 to 1924 had adopted Celtic colours. On his departure various designs based on red, amber and black had been worn.

Park Avenue, like Bradford City, did not raise much money from share issues and the bank overdraft increased enormously to help fund the club's investments in the ground and players' houses.

By 1957-8 the post-war soccer boom was over and crowds and local interest would never be as large again, particularly for Third Division clubs. While local attachments were still high the admission fee offered community involvement as well as mere entertainment; twenty years before, J. B. Priestley had written that the shilling admission fee, even when ill-afforded, enabled you, like half the town, to push your way 'through a turnstile into another and altogether more splendid kind of life, hurtling with conflict' and also conferred benefits of social inclusion through the rest of the week as 'a man who had missed the last home match of t'United had to enter the social life on tiptoe in Bruddersford'.

Although the social outlook had changed in twenty years, and although Bruddersford is no doubt an idealised view of Huddersfield

---

[15] *Bradford Telegraph and Argus*, 3 February 1960.

during their time as the outstanding side in England, none the less the early post-war period offered clubs at least as good a chance as at any time in the history of the Football League to provide a major social focus for their town, and reap the financial rewards for doing so.

In 1950 there were nine cities, apart from London, with more than one football club and only two had a population smaller than Bradford's 292,000. The smallest was Birkenhead, but New Brighton finished bottom of Division Three (North) and left the League in 1951, leaving the city to Tranmere Rovers. The other was Stoke with 275,000 people and two clubs, Stoke City and Port Vale. Port Vale have never reached Division One. Stoke City despite being founder members of the Football League in 1888, won no major honours until 1972, and they faced no rugby league competition.

In Bradford 'half the town' did not push through the turnstiles of Valley Parade or Park Avenue after the war because the city had two football clubs and a successful rugby league club and because the period of football's greatest prosperity had seen Bradford's soccer clubs sink, almost permanently, into the comparative obscurity of the Third Division (North).

1958-1985

THE OLD ORDER CHANGES

18. Textiles in Decline

The woollen textile industry revived briefly after the war, but by the 1960s it was in irreversible decline. Raw wool imports peaked in 1953; by 1965 they were a third lower and falling. Woollen exports (including re-exports) were highest in 1947; in the next twenty years they fell by more than half.[1]

In the 1960s profits in the wool textile industry were 'low and declining',[2] and between 1963 and 1973 the woollen and worsted sectors' share of total textile output fell from 29% to 20% and its share of net capital investment from 22% to 12%.[3]

Most of the difficulties stemmed from obsolete machinery, old premises and traditional working practices. Firms were typically small family businesses and generally lacked the access to capital that might have transformed their position in a declining industry. In 1969 less than one in six woollen and worsted firms were integrated;[4] instead they specialised in one aspect of manufacture and were situated in a close geographical proximity that was made necessary by this functional interdependence.

The number of employees was highest in 1950; employment had fallen 9% by 1961 and by a further 11% in the next four years. During the 1960s and 70s an extensive programme of rationalisation and mill closure was carried out; the reduction in woollen and worsted employment was concentrated on Bradford and Huddersfield. Bradford absorbed 45%[5] of the total reduction and migration out of the city was considerable.[6]

The textile district by now was anything but the prosperous area it had been in the years before the Great War. Between 1947 and 1965 UK weekly wages rose 230%, but textile wages as a whole rose by slightly less (210%) and the woollen and worsted industry was already one of the

---

[1] B. R. Mitchell and H. G. Jones, *Second Abstract of British Historical Statistics*, (Cambridge 1971), p. 93.

[2] G. H. Oxtoby, 'The Wool Textile Industry', *Yorkshire Bulletin of Economic and Social Research*, 1970, p. 208.

[3] West Yorkshire Metropolitan County Council (WYMCC), *Structure Plan Survey Report*, (Wakefield 1983), p.98.

[4] C. Richardson, op cit, pp. 127-8.

[5] YMCC, op cit, p. 101.

[6] ibid, p. 27.

lowest paid in the country; the industry had one of the worst incidences of lowest quantile earnings (51%), along with clothing and footwear (67%).[7] During the same period inflation amounted to 190%.

West Yorkshire had the lowest earnings of the seven metropolitan counties (7% below the average).[8] In 1972, 33% of the working population was considered low paid, as against 25% nationally.[9] 21% of employees earned under £1,000 pa (England and Wales 18%) and only 32% earned £2,000 or more (England and Wales 38%).[10] There were also fewer car owners; 60% of households had no car (England and Wales 48%).[11]

By 1975 the traditional view of West Yorkshire as a highly industrial conurbation dominated by woollen and other manufacturing industry was out of date.

Table 4 Employment by Industrial Groups, 1961 and 1975

	1961		1975	
	West Yorks	Britain	West Yorks	Britain
Primary	5.3%	6.0%	3.3%	3.3%
Textiles	20.5%	3.8%	10.5%	2.2%
Manufacturing	33.1%	35.6%	29.7%	31.0%
Construction	5.0%	6.6%	4.7%	5.7%
Services	36.1%	48.0%	51.8%	57.8%

The decline in textiles accelerated the decline in other manufacturing industry, much of which supplied the textile trade, and the only growth area was another low pay 'industry', services.

Bradford in particular was affected and suffered a 36% decline in manufacturing employment between 1961 and 1975 (Britain 12% decline) and a 14% fall in total employment (Britain 2%).[12] In 1971 Bradford had proportionately fewer managerial, professional and other non-manual inhabitants than England as a whole (30% as against 35%)[13] and, more ominously, was in a region with one of the worst records in the country for attracting new industry.

Since the 1950s the woollen and worsted trade on which Bradford was heavily dependent had permanently declined. The programme of rationalisation and mill closure caused net migration from Bradford and higher rates of unemployment than general to the UK. Migration had

[7] ibid, p. 159.
[8] ibid, p. 148.
[9] ibid, p. 160.
[10] ibid, p. 86.
[11] ibid, p. 36.
[12] ibid, p. 94.
[13] ibid, p. 35.

been offset by an increase in the proportion of families originating in the Indian subcontinent, particularly in the Manningham district that surrounds City's ground, but the new arrivals did not bring with them any developed tradition of support for the city's football teams.

The decline in textiles was compensated for by an increase in service employment, but this merely substituted one low wage industry for another and confirmed Bradford as a traditional, working-class city with a serious poverty problem, which had lost its traditional industrial base.

Bradford's soccer clubs were, by 1958, firmly entrenched in the Third Division. The structure of football club ownership and control precluded supporters and municipalities from exercising real influence; Bradford's clubs had looked in the past to charismatic, wealthy local entrepreneurs (Park Avenue) and local civic leaders and businessmen (Bradford City), but neither club now offered much prestige, and industrial decline would inevitably weaken both business support and grass roots support through the turnstiles.

19. The Football League Under Strain

The Football League arose in 1888 out of the desire of senior clubs to regularise fixtures and thus increase revenues. The League grew rapidly as new clubs of sufficient quality were attracted from other leagues, and after the absorption of the Southern League First Division into the Football League Division Three (South) soon after the Great War the Football League was the undisputed national league, with over sixty members drawn from all regions of the country.

Association football gradually increased in public importance through the inter-war period, and in the years after World War II it attracted unprecedented support from a population deprived of entertainments during the war period.

Football had become a world game with leagues in almost every country, but nowhere else was there a league consisting of as many as ninety full-time professional clubs.

After the peak attendances of the immediate post-war period in which comparatively good-humoured crowds packed onto the large terraces of grounds developed many years before, the football industry had to come to terms with a number of important social changes.

The volume of custom for a wide range of sporting events and other entertainments inevitably declined, partly as wartime deprivations receded and partly because of increased competition in the leisure industry, notably from television.

The working week was gradually shortened and Saturday morning work became the exception rather than the rule. This meant that large numbers of working men were no longer finishing at midday in the inner city areas in which football clubs were based. It also meant that they had more scope for alternatives uses of Saturday during an era of increased material prosperity and considerable change in roles within the family.

Television both increased the competition for football and also sought to show matches and excerpts to their viewing public. Increased affluence meant more cars, which provided more opportunities for families to escape from city areas and also gave soccer enthusiasts easier access to superior football in their general locality.

Improved housing standards during the age of 'you never had it so good' increased the time and money spent on home improvements, lowered the concentration of housing in urban areas and reduced public tolerance of the limited facilities at football grounds. They also brought with them increasingly anti-social crowd behaviour, which changed the public image of the professional game.

Many of these were gradual social shifts, more easily observed in retrospect than at the time, or in advance. The decline in soccer attendances was more tangible and unmistakable and provoked a reaction from the football authorities.

It is difficult to avoid the impression that the football industry was complacent during the boom years after the war and began belatedly to change only as a more pessimistic outlook emerged. The same could, of course, be said of many other organisations, and the football industry could justly point out that if it could have done better it has at least avoided the decline in outlets experienced by the cinema.

In Bradford the number of cinemas declined from forty shortly after the war to only nine in 1970. In the Football League there are still ninety-two member clubs, the same number as in 1950 when the League was last extended. The composition of the membership has not changed greatly in the post-war period; entry into the industry before 1987 has been restricted to clubs who can secure more votes than any existing member who has finished a season in the bottom four of the League. Since 1945 only six clubs have failed to secure re-election, and one has resigned, all of them from the north of England. The distribution of member clubs between divisions has changed far more, of course, partly due to general economic and demographic factors and partly due to changes within the Football League.

Much of the post-war period was a time of rising prosperity. Bird[1] found evidence during the period 1948-9 to 1979-80 that League football was an 'inferior good', with an income elasticity of -0.6, and that rising income would reduce the demand for League football, but other research has cast doubt on so direct a connection. Certainly rising incomes increased competition between leisure industries and also changed the class composition of support for the game; the growth of hooliganism as a national problem had a particular focus on and impact on football and helped to discourage the family audiences that might have justified further investments in new stands.

Demographic change has decreased the population concentration in the old urban areas, as people moved to smaller towns and southwards. The move out of the cities has not greatly affected the distribution of League honours, partly because of compensating changes within the industry, but the southward drift of population has led to the

[1] P. Bird, op cit, pp. 637-49.

replacement of Lancashire town sides like Burnley, Bolton and Blackburn in the First Division by teams such as Watford, Ipswich and Oxford, and to the replacement of six northern sides in the League by Peterborough (1960), Oxford (1962), Cambridge (1970), Hereford (1972), Wimbledon (1977) and one northern side, Wigan Athletic (1978).

There have also been considerable changes within football, which as a business is most unusual. The Football League from the outset acted as a cartel, controlling entry into the League and competition structures so as to avoid one-sided contests which would not attract the public, controlling players' wage levels and freedom of contract, so as to hold down the industry's main cost and maintain social controls on their working-class employees and controlling the level of financial return on capital and senior management time so as to prevent football being commercially exploited. For many years the League limited inter-club price competition by stipulating a minimum admission price, and operated complex schemes for sharing gate receipts.

The central purpose behind these arrangements was to restrict competition within the industry, thus preventing domination of the League by clubs in the large cities and, by achieving more even contests, to maintain public interest and maximise joint revenues. The main consequence was that football clubs had or developed unusual business objectives, in that clubs were motivated by playing success not by making or maximising profits. In many ways it is a very attractive notion, a business in which the quality of the product matters more than the size of the gains, but it is a position which fits uneasily with the need to make substantial long-term investments in a high risk industry.

Football is a very risky business because the gap between success and failure on the field is small, the mechanisms of team building and organisation intangible and elusive, and player abilities variable over time, yet the 'demand response', the willingness of people to attend matches, is highly affected by these variations in performance. In financial management 'risk' is equated with the variability of returns; in few other industries can firms shift their industry ranking so quickly or find their level of income so changeable. These effects are pronounced enough in League football and are compounded by cup results where each successive win or draw makes a substantial difference to the club's income and, given that many costs in football are relatively fixed and do not vary with the number of matches played, their profit or loss.

To increase incomes, clubs need to invest in stadium facilities, but these are often costly and are high risk investments, as the stadia have no alternative uses and cannot be readily resold and turned back into cash. Any other business faced with this situation would either adopt a cooperative structure utilising the enormous fund of available local goodwill and commitment or raise equity capital. In either case the business has to give something back: real influence to supporters or municipalities or effective voting rights and monetary returns to shareholders. Football has instead allowed power to concentrate into the hands of directors; shares rarely offer a monetary return and are thus only useful as a means of control.

Football clubs are as a result often grossly under-capitalised, with clubs financing ground improvements either through loan finance, usually on short-term bank overdrafts, or out of retained earnings from past successful seasons, a solution only available to clubs that are already achieving good results.

The decline in league attendances from the peak of 41,000,000 in 1948-9 had led the League in 1956 to attempt to set controls on matches using professional players but organised by the Football Association. This was far more a matter of establishing the scope of their own powers than any real objection to increasing the number of matches. In 1956-7 the decline in attendances was nearly 20% from 1948-9 although the minimum admission price was now 60% higher, and 10% higher in real terms; attendances still compared favourably with the 1919-39 period.

The League then decided on the largest structural change for over thirty years, although not a particularly central one; Divisions Three South and North were amalgamated in 1958 into Divisions Three and Four, with the top half of each regional division forming the new Division Three and the lower half the new Division Four. The logic of this change has always seemed a little obscure; more matches affecting promotion and relegation, which tend to enhance crowds, would now take place without affecting the First or Second Division clubs, and matches would tend to be slightly more equal but travel costs would be higher for the least wealthy clubs in the League and there would be fewer 'local derbies'. There was also a tendency over time for the weaker northern clubs to make up a disproportionate part of the Fourth Division, and the new arrangement probably did them no favours; the proportion of league attendances in the Third Division (North) in 1957-8 was 13%, in Division Four in 1979-80 it was 9.5%. (Division Three (South) in 1957-8 was 18% and Division Three in 1979-80 16%.)

At the same time, improved technology was to make possible a more important change, 'product extension' or new competitions. There had been some experimental night matches in the 1890s but the light generated was poor and the FA disapproving, so it was not until the post-war period that floodlit matches became more common. The lights were only likely to make economic sense, however, if they were used for more than cup replays and league games postponed by poor weather. Although there was an inevitable risk of market saturation the cost structure of professional football, with its heavy fixed costs, implied that additional matches were likely to raise revenues by more than costs. This coincided with an initiative within European football to hold cup competitions for city sides and then club sides from countries throughout Europe. The first Fairs Cup was held over the period 1955-8 and included sides from Birmingham and London, who lost the final to Barcelona. In the 1958-60 competition Chelsea represented London, and Birmingham lost the final, again to Barcelona. The European Cup started in 1955-6, with Hibernian as Britain's only representative, but Manchester United entered the following season, losing to Real Madrid in the semi-final.

League clubs had typically played forty-two to forty-six league matches and anything from one to about eight matches in the FA Cup. The European Cup competitions, with the Cup-Winners Cup starting in 1960, meant up to another ten midweek games for the top clubs. There had been an earlier proposal for a Football League Floodlight Cup, and in 1960 the idea was adopted under the name of the Football League Cup, offering additional midweek games for all League sides. Other often short-lived competitions proliferated to increase the number of matches being offered to the loyal, if not insatiable, customers.

At least as important were the less voluntary changes in players' conditions. When the Football League was founded in 1888, one of its official objects was to regulate the players' terms of employment, both by obtaining agreement on a maximum wage and by establishing the principle that no player would play for a club unless his previous employer had agreed to transfer his registration. These unique restrictions on freedom of employment persisted until a dispute in 1960 forced the abolition of the maximum wage, and until the Eastham v Newcastle United court ruling in 1963 caused the retain and transfer system to be modified. The retain and transfer system remained in existence until 1978, when it was finally replaced by freedom of contract subject to a transfer fee negotiated between clubs, or if they could not agree, by an independent tribunal, but the main restraints on players' contracts were lifted in the early 1960s and wages rose immediately, particularly in the First Division.

In 1957-8 the maximum wage was still in force, stipulating £20 per week in the playing season and £17 in the close season, and average wages in the league doubled to £1,560 p.a. in 1964, although prices generally rose only 15%. This was not just a once and for all adjustment; the bargaining position of players had been transformed, and players' average wages in 1982 rose to well over twice the level needed to have kept pace with inflation from 1964. On the other hand, as any comparison of team photographs will reveal, clubs chose to employ fewer players, nearly 40% less in 1982 than 1960. There were also considerable differentials between players in the different divisions in both pay and security; by 1973, 14% of First Division players were on a basic wage of over £100 a week, but only 1.5% in Division Four were on a basic rate of half that amount,[2] and six times as many First Division players as Fourth were on a two-year contract (with a two-year option attached) or longer.

Transfer fees rose to spectacular levels. They had long been a peculiarity of the football industry but were often misunderstood. The fee was for the transfer, not of the player, but of his registration form, without which he could be employed by but not play for his new club. Although transfer dealings were very important to individual clubs, at a collective level the funds were largely circulating, apart from the levy to the Players' Benefit Scheme and to the player and any 'leakage' to other leagues. The most important effects were probably the stimulus given by high transfer fees to wage levels, and the extent to which higher fees encouraged elite clubs to improve their own scouting and coaching systems and rely less on lower division clubs to carry out this function for them.

For many years the Football Association, under rule 45(a), required certain restrictions to be included in member clubs' articles of association. A maximum dividend was stipulated, originally 5% and recently raised to 15%, and until 1981 no directors could be remunerated, and since that date only one per club. Most clubs did not even pay the restricted dividends that were allowed, and investors came not to expect substantial income from their investments; inevitably the supply of share capital and directors' talents was heavily rationed.

Until 1981 a minimum admission price was laid down, although prices varied between different parts of a ground, and while this avoided prices being depressed it also tended to prevent the pricing differentials that might have been expected between top sides and those in the Fourth Division. It certainly supported the League's policy of raising prices in real terms; while League attendances fell 40% from 1957-8 to 1981-2 the minimum entry price was sixteen times higher and meant that aggregate League revenues, in spite of attendance decline, rose even after inflation is taken into account.

Indeed, the so-called financial crisis in soccer is, to the extent that it exists, due to failures of cost control, and to changes in the distribution of attendances and revenues between elite and unsuccessful clubs.

The differential effects of rising wages and the growth of new competitions, which tended to be more beneficial to large than small clubs, were offset to some extent by increases in the industry's

[2] Commission for Industrial Relations, *Professional Football*, Report No 87, 1974, paras 81-2.

income-sharing schemes. Since 1920, 20% of gate receipts net of certain costs were paid by home clubs to visiting League sides. In addition, FA Cup gate receipts were shared between opponents, after the deduction of a levy paid to a match pool which was subsequently divided between League entrants, and a 4% deduction was made to pay for League administration costs, and costs such as referees and linesmen common to all clubs.

These settled arrangements were supplemented by pooled and redistributed receipts from League Cup matches, and by the sharing of rapidly rising joint incomes from the pools promoters, the television companies and, more recently, from competition sponsors.

In 1959 the courts decided that the fixture lists were copyright, and payments by the Pools Promotors' Association grew from £170,000 in 1960 to £3,000,000 in 1981. Television fees were initially very small, but the amount received by each League club rose from £1,300 in 1967 to £24,000 in 1979.

The amount paid out of the various pools to each club thus increased considerably. In inflation-adjusted terms it rose tenfold from 1958 to 1985[3] and helped to insulate smaller clubs against the effects of cost increases and more discerning support, at least until the changes in the 1980s, which are designed to increase the differential between the successful and unsuccessful clubs. Thus in 1983 the arrangement whereby home clubs paid part of their receipts to visiting League opponents was abolished so that clubs instead retained their home gates. In 1986 far more major changes were made following the threat of the leading clubs to form their own breakaway 'Super League'; a lower percentage (10%) was to be paid into the FA Cup and League (Milk or Littlewoods) Cup Pools, and these and television monies were to be shared 50% to Division One clubs, 25% to Division Two clubs and 25% between Division Three and Four clubs. The majority required at League meetings was reduced from three-quarters to two-thirds with First Division clubs having 1½ votes each (total 33), Division Two one vote each (total 22) and the Third and Fourth Division clubs sharing 8 votes.

Sponsorship also increased in the 1980s, both of competitions and individual clubs; competition sponsorship was generally performance-related, while club sponsorship was weighted towards successful clubs that appeared on television. The Committee of Enquiry into Sports' Sponsorship estimated that the distribution of sponsorship and advertising in 1982-3 ranged from 56% to Division One clubs to just 8% to Division Four clubs.

[3] A. J. Arnold, I. Benveniste and A. Collier, *Cross-subsidisation in the English Football League*, Department of Economics, University of Essex, Discussion Paper No 302, November 1986, p. 57.

During the post-war period attendances briefly reached unprecedented levels; the aggregate attendances of 41,000,000 meant an average of 22,000 per league match in 1948. This compared favourably with total attendances of 28,000,000 in 1937-8. Even the much quoted decline in attendances to 1981-2 meant crowds per match in Divisions One and Two that were 15% higher than in 1906-07, when Bradford's two sides were starting out in the football business.

Soccer in fact lost far less of its audience than the cinema, which lost 90% of its custom and had to close innumerable outlets; county cricket, which lost three-quarters of its support between 1949 and 1966;[4] and rugby league, a closely competing activity in Lancashire and Yorkshire, which lost two-thirds of its paying customers between 1957-8 and 1981-2.

The soccer authorities also helped to cause reduced attendances at league games by raising admission prices far faster than inflation, and by providing clubs with new cup competitions that enabled them to play in midweek under floodlights.

The restrictions on financial competition between clubs, which took a number of forms, were either successfully challenged (in the case of players' contract restraints) or were progressively dismantled (in the case of income-sharing arrangements).

More mobile spectators were also more discriminating; although the total revenues of the industry rose rather than fell, costs, particularly players' wages, increased and the distribution of wealth, and honours, shifted towards the leading clubs. The League had gradually abandoned its preference for more equal competition through policies of restraint; increasingly the football business was to become one in which the rewards for success and the penalties for failure were ever more sharply defined.

---

[4] J. A. Schofield, op cit, p. 353.

20. Park Avenue: Down and Out

Until their relegation from the Second Division in 1950 Bradford Park Avenue had spent only six seasons out of the top two divisions; they were in Division Three (North) between 1922 and 1928 when their lowest position was fifth. After 1950 even fifth place was beyond them, and in the last three years of the Third Division (North) they finished 23rd, 20th and 22nd in consecutive seasons, out of 24 clubs.

Inevitably they were founder members of the new Fourth Division when it was formed out of the bottom halves of the two regional Third Divisions at the end of the 1957-8 season.

They appointed a new Scottish manager, W. Galbraith, in November 1958 and he brought with him a liking for the traditional Scottish short-passing game and Scots players. Three years before at Accrington he had selected a team of eleven Scots, the first time a Football League side had done so since 1902, and within eighteen months eight of Avenue's team were Scots.

Results were moderate and gates were somewhat below the divisional average, although an FA Cup second round tie at home to neighbours Bradford City in 1958 was watched by a crowd of 20,000; Avenue lost 0 – 2. In 1958-9 Avenue won 6 – 1 and 5 – 1 against non-League opposition to earn an away tie against Chelsea. The crowd of 32,000 made up a little for a 1 – 5 defeat.

In February 1960 Reginald Kellett died, ending a succession of three wealthy, charismatic chairmen; he left a board of two local businessmen, a garage owner, a retired builder, and a demolition contractor, as well as a bank overdraft at its limit of £30,000 (£C235,000).

The team's results were improving, but Galbraith moved on in January 1961 to Third Division Tranmere. The formidable Jimmy Scoular was appointed as player-manager. He had been a Scottish international in the early 1950s when with Portsmouth, and he transformed the playing style to a more open game that featured the long passes to the wing at which he excelled. His players coped well with the change, winning promotion in May by coming fourth, six points behind champions Peterborough who scored 134 goals in their first season in the Football League. Tranmere Rovers were one of the relegated sides they replaced in Division Three.

League attendances were 50% higher than the previous year, when they had finished in midtable and receipts were helped slightly by the new League Cup competition. Avenue declared a moderate profit which paid for some ground improvements but left the overdraft still at £30,000.

Park Avenue eventually obtained planning permission for their 95-foot-high floodlight pylons, even though the ground was close to a housing estate and Horton Park itself, and the lights were inaugurated at a friendly match against the Czech national side in October 1961; Bradford's enterprise was rewarded by a crowd of 17,500. This was not, however, the first floodlit game in Bradford; Bradford Zingalis had played rugby against Keighley at Frizinghall in November 1878 under rather more experimental lighting.

Gale-force winds the following February brought down the floodlights, a 'bitter blow'[1] so soon after they had been put up. The bulk of the loss was, however, recovered under their insurance policy and new flood-lights were installed for the 1962-3 season. After the midtable position in 1961-2, relegation the following season was a big disappointment, but their away record had been poor; defensive weaknesses left them with an inferior goal average which took them down.

Scoular said after the season that it was 'nobody's fault that we stood still – it was a matter of finance ... the money just wasn't there'.[2] Although the supporters had donated over £90,000 in six years, the club could not afford to spend on the transfer market to try to stay up and the wage level made it hard to attract new players; Scoular was reluctant to breach the club's wage policy and pay higher wages to new players because of the potentially divisive repercussions. Crowds had been no better in the middle of Division Three than when winning promotion from the Fourth; in their relegation season attendances were down by 20%.

In 1963-4 Park Avenue finished halfway down Division Four, and, following two resignations, the board of only three, Murphy, Jackson and Pickles dismissed Scoular. The only excitements in the season were a 7 – 3 win over Bradford City and the fact that Jim Fryatt's goal on 25th April 1964 against Tranmere was the fastest in the history of the Football League; the referee timed it at four seconds after the kick-off.

The following season, Park Avenue challenged for promotion, but finished seventh, six points behind the champions, Brighton. They were difficult to beat but drew as many matches as any club in the Football League. Attendances were 35% better than the year before and were well above the divisional average, but the club scarcely broke even

[1] Bradford (Park Avenue) AFC Ltd Directors' Report 1962.
[2] *Bradford Telegraph and Argus*, 25 July 1963.

financially. In the 1965-6 season Avenue finished in midtable, achieved nothing in either cup competition, and attendances fell back to the average for the division. The club lost £12,000 (£C75,000) which was partly covered by transfer fees received and partly by the directors' loans increasing to £15,000 (£C95,000). Their lack of success was particularly disturbing since they had scored 102 goals, the second best in the Football League. (Their defensive record of 92 goals was the worst in the League apart from York, bottom of Division Three, and Bradford City and Wrexham, the bottom two in Division Four.) Kevin Hector scored 34 goals, the top scorer in the Football League, which brought his total to over a hundred league goals before he was 22, a record beaten only by Jimmy Greaves and Dixie Dean.

That summer England won the World Cup; amid the general euphoria in September 1966 Avenue sold Hector for £40,000 to Derby County. The fee was the largest ever received by a Fourth Division side, but it was to cost Park Avenue far more.

In midseason persistent rumours of a divided board were confirmed; a vote of no confidence caused the resignation of Murphy, a demolition and haulage contractor, and Pickles, a 72-year-old retired builder. In early March the shareholders called an extraordinary meeting to force the remaining directors, Evans, Jackson and Brown, to resign. Three days before the meeting the manager, Buchanan, and the general manager, Galbraith, were persuaded to resign, and this was enough to defeat the resolutions to remove the directors. It did nothing, however, for the playing results; without Hector they scored only half as many goals as the year before and finished last but one in the Football League. This forced the second application for re-election in the club's history. The income from the sale of Hector had not even reduced the bank overdraft; the club merely doubled its investment in players' houses and extinguished all debts due to the board of directors.

The crowd had proved its loyalty; in spite of poor results, attendances still matched the average for the division, but even moderate success in the two cup competitions did not prevent operating losses, which were primarily due to rising wages.

The appointment to the board of Sutcliffe, a dairy owner, and Burkinshaw, a restaurateur, and a new manager, Rowley, brought no improvement in results, attendances or finances.

Former chairman Phillips was well aware of the club's reputation for living above its station and asked in December why a Fourth Division club needed two managers, two secretaries, a trainer, a physiotherapist, a full-time scout and other part-time trainers.

A month later Bradford announced staff reductions that would cut 15% from an administration salary charge of £10,000, but their playing staff of twenty-seven was still one of the largest in Division Four. Director Evans tried to provide consolation by stating that soccer was '60% luck'; Park Avenue were clearly unlucky as they finished bottom of Division Four with only 30 goals and 4 wins in 46 matches, the lowest number of wins in the entire Football League since 1932. They applied for re-election for the second year in succession. Attendances were down to 3,600, 40% below the divisional average; even the new economies left a loss of £17,000 (£C102,000) and with no more Kevin Hectors to sell, the bank overdraft rose to over £33,000.

Early in the 1968-9 season the manager, Rowley, resigned halfway through his three-year contract, and Don McCalman took over on a temporary basis, during 'the biggest financial crisis in the club's history'. Three days later, Evans resigned from the board, accepted responsibility for the worst time in the club's history, and acknowledged his own lack of understanding of the finer points of the game. An inability to sleep and his doctor's advice also contributed to his decision.

An article in *The Times*[3] made the salient point when it identified Bradford as the only city that had had two Division One sides that had both descended to Division Four. Avenue's decline in the post-war period from a Second Division side, with 15,000 crowds, no debt and a progressive young side was attributed to the sale of good players, poor administration and a failure to cut their coat according to their cloth by employing too many staff.

In October, Secretary George Brigg completed forty years at Park Avenue; the following day Leeds went to the top of Division One and Avenue to the bottom of Division Four. A public meeting of 500 people at St. George's Hall was told that the club was losing £500 a week and needed to raise £10,000 from the issue of new shares. Two weeks later only £1,365 had been raised, home attendances were down to 2,700, and the club had won only once in their first seventeen League matches.

On 17th November a board with limited personal wealth found a solution; Herbert Metcalf joined the board and promised to provide the necessary financial support. Three weeks later Laurie Brown came as player-manager to replace McCalman, but the position at the end of the season was little different.

Avenue were again bottom of the Football League with 5 wins in 46 games. They had tried 31 players in the first team and scored fewer goals and conceded more (106) than any other side in the League that season. They were now applying for re-election for the third year in a row, but the instinct of League clubs to 'support their own' protected them; they received 38 votes, 22 more than the best-supported outsider, Cambridge.

[3] *The Times*, 3 October 1968.

The following season was, however, to change the other clubs' views on Bradford's suitability to be a League side. In October, Metcalfe, the head of a Manchester-based National School of Salesmanship, had been on the board nearly a year. He had not, due to business commitments, seen the team play that season but he wrote to player-manager, Laurie Brown, to say that he would pick the team. He did; Brown resigned and nineteen professional players asked for a transfer. Metcalfe then told Brown to take a two-week holiday anywhere in Europe at the club's expense; Brown refused. The following day Metcalfe took over as chairman and appointed McCalman, who had been manager before Brown, as manager again; Metcalfe's price for providing the finance to save the club was 'a free hand'.[4]

At the end of October it was announced that McCalman and Metcalfe would pick the team, but five players still wanted a transfer; in mid-November the local press confirmed that in reality Metcalfe had the final say on team selection.[5]

Metcalfe then decided that the club should adopt a more businesslike approach; 14,000 circulars were issued offering cut-price season tickets for next season, but Ambler was not impressed and resigned from the board saying that the chairman was not informing the other directors on financial matters. Metcalfe's view was that he paid the wages so he had the right to pick the team,[6] but he promptly announced that he would stop selecting the side to 'see what McCalman can do'.

The Annual General Meeting in January 1970 was preceded by the announcement that the club's debt had been halved by the conversion of the directors' loans into shares, but the excess of creditors' claims (£97,000) over funds available to meet them (£4,350) was not viewed as alarming because the 'third team in two to three years will be producing some lads worth £50-100,000'.[7]

By now affairs were being handled in a manner that bordered on farce; on 20th February McCalman was sacked by Metcalfe, with the rest of the board publicly dissociating themselves from the decision. Metcalfe felt that one point from four games was not good enough, but McCalman said the chairman 'never gave me any real reason for being dismissed'. Director Sutcliffe added that McCalman had selected the team for the postponed game at Aldershot although Metcalfe had wanted to do so.

The chairman's conviction that his personal judgement would pay off in the seasoned world of professional football was shown by his approach

[4] *Bradford Telegraph and Argus*, 30 October 1969.

[5] ibid, 11 November 1969.

[6] P. Stepney, 'Towards a Politics of Football: The Case of Bradford Park Avenue' in Explorations in Football Culture, ed. A. Tomlinson (unpublished), (Brighton Polytechnic 1976).

[7] *Bradford Telegraph and Argus*, 6 January 1970.

to Frank Tomlinson who had been out of football since 1958(!) and was in charge of sports activities at Hawker Siddley, Manchester. He became Bradford's third manager that season. The unprofessional nature of the club's activities persisted to the end of the season when their latest signing failed to arrive for a match after attending a wedding; Avenue played without a substitute and were fined for handing in a late team sheet.

Bradford (PA) finished bottom of the League once more and sought re-election for the fourth successive season. A year before they had received far more votes than the non-League applicants, but the way the club had been run during the last year eroded their support. On 30th May 1970, as the opening matches in the 1970 World Cup in Mexico were being played, the main applicants for the League polled: Darlington 47, Hartlepool 41, Newport County 31, Cambridge United 31, Wigan 18 and Bradford 17. Bradford Park Avenue were out of the Football League.

With the loss of League status Avenue applied to and were accepted by the Northern Premier League and announced they would cut full-time playing staff to five or six. In the last three seasons in the Football League gate receipts had fallen to £25,000 p.a., £18,000 a year less than the club's wage bill; accumulated losses had risen from £18,000 to £89,000 in three years.

Herbert Metcalfe seemed undeterred. He had invested at least £57,000 (£C250,000) in Park Avenue, £25,000 being loans converted into shares and £32,000 on clearing the ground mortgage, which was more than anyone else in Britain had invested in a struggling club and a commitment which would have bought him a place on the board of almost any club in the country. He would not, however, have had such a free hand at a more successful club. In August 1970 he said that 'since the club has now a manager, a coach and a scouting system of my own choice I am very hopeful we are able to start on the road back – eventually I hope to the First Division'.[8]

On 24th October 1970 he died, however. Along with condolences, the club announced immediate staff cuts and asked players to take wage cuts, warning that liquidation could follow if they insisted on their contracts being honoured.

In November the players unanimously agreed to take a wage cut of £4 each to help the club, and a crisis meeting was again held at St. George's Hall; the audience of 800 nearly rivalled home league gates in the Northern Premier. In early December manager Tomlinson was sacked 'as an economy measure'. Unusually he made no complaints, and said he would probably go on the dole as 'it seems unlikely another club will seek

---

[8] ibid, 10 August 1970, p. 12.

my services'.[9] Player-coach Tony Leighton, who had come from Bradford City on a free transfer, was promoted to player-manager.

The club finished 14th out of 22 in their first season in the Northern Premier, and when they applied for election to the Football League they received only one vote, as did Romford and Boston United. It would have taken over thirty votes to have got back into the League, and Bradford (PA), with their recent history of mismanagement and their proximity to Bradford City were clearly not thought of as a side with any future in the Football League.

In 1971-2 Park Avenue slipped lower in the Northern Premier, 18th out of 24. Vaux Breweries lent £9,000 for the building of a social club at the Canterbury Avenue end, and the cricket pavilion was given a facelift, including a new lounge and bar, but in all it had been a dismal season, culminating in a home defeat by South Shields in the FA Cup Fourth Qualifying round. Home attendances by the end of the season were around 1,200, a third of the level in the last three seasons in the Football League. In May 1972 Avenue applied again for entry into the Football League, but the chairman, Sutcliffe, saw the chances as 'about nil'; the motive was to put up a marker with an eye towards a rumoured Fifth Division.

Financial matters were now more important and serious than even playing results. The wage bill had been heavily reduced, but the lower attendances and prices in the Northern Premier cut gate receipts; incomes fell even more because Avenue were no longer eligible for the

Assets	£
Ground and offices	14,000
Floodlights	2,000
Dwelling houses	2,200
Training ground	3,600
Equipment, Furniture, Fittings	2,400
Debtors, Cash	800
	25,000

They owed:	
Creditors	14,200
Bank overdraft	28,100
Building Society mortgage on houses	1,200
Directors' loan	700
Loans from former directors, including Metcalfe	45,800
	90,000

[9] ibid, 4 December 1970.

monies distributed round the Football League clubs under their income-sharing arrangements. This removed a third of their income overnight, and it was only the £12,000 a year raised by the Supporters' Club and the Development Association that kept the club afloat at all.

Despite this loyalty the financial position in May 1972 was almost hopeless. The club's assets and liabilities were listed as shown on p. 136.

Playing operations were losing money, and even success in finding promising players would not be very lucrative as non-League sides had little leverage in transfer negotiations with League clubs. Although the club existed to play football it had legal obligations to its creditors. There was now no alternative; they would have to sell the Park Avenue ground.

Sporting leagues exist in most countries, with differing emphases on local identity. In the American NFL, financial and playing objectives are both important and clubs are prepared to move their franchises in search of greater support, as for example when the Raiders left Oakland, near San Francisco, for Los Angeles. In Italy sides sometimes share one municipal stadium, as for example in Milan, but in England a strong sense of the past and an acute sense of place have combined to create a deeply territorial, almost tribal, association between club, ground, local district and supporters. Although many clubs have had more than one ground, few have moved during the twentieth century, once their identity and supporter loyalty have been established. Only Arsenal have moved districts, in their case with great success, but the intended transfer of Huddersfield Town to Elland Road, Leeds and more recent proposals to merge Reading and Oxford, or close Craven Cottage and amalgamate Fulham and Queens Park Rangers have all been greeted with outrage. In Bradford it was the perception of the two teams being rooted in particular city districts, and their identity being inseparable from their grounds, that discouraged any merger between City and Avenue; although the sale of Park Avenue was a commercial imperative, it would also threaten the club's very identity.

In February 1973 Avenue rejected a council offer of £80,000 (£20,000 an acre) for residential development of the football ground, which would have enabled the council to move Bradford Northern from Odsal, and use Odsal once again for tipping refuse (a facility reputedly worth about £2 million). Bradford Northern, who had been at Odsal since 1934, would however have lost representative match and speedway income.

At the same time the council were negotiating with a London property company to build a 'multimillion pound commercial sports complex at Odsal, not based on the football ground'.[10]

Park Avenue's Chairman, Sutcliffe, now accepted that the objective

---

[10] ibid, 19 February 1973.

was the survival of a non-League side with traditions, not a return to the Football League, and his preference was to sell Park Avenue (capacity 32,000) and acquire a 3,000-capacity ground better suited to the Northern Premier League. In March 1973, however, a plan was announced to move Park Avenue to Valley Parade, but with their identity retained, and an extraordinary shareholders' meeting voted 70-18 in favour of accepting any 'reasonable offer for the ground in excess of £80,000'.[11]

Chairman Sutcliffe saw it as 'a great gesture on the part of Bradford City',[12] for the sale enabled Park Avenue to remain in the Northern Premier, but the benefits were to prove short-lived. The rent at Valley Parade was £7,000 a year and crowd support dwindled in the new surroundings from 1,300 a game to 700. The match receipts were now less than the rent, even before wages and other expenses.

The last competitive match at Park Avenue was in late April against Great Harwood; player-manager Leighton scored a late goal to lift Bradford to fifth in the Northern Premier.

Bradford played two 'last games' at Park Avenue. In early May 1973 over 3,000 people, the best attendance since leaving the Football League, saw Bradford City beat them 1 – 0, and also in May a 'Former Park Avenue v Former City' charity match attracted under 1,000 people. The teams drew 2 – 2, and Avenue had the 64-year-old Farr in goal.

Before Park Avenue started the new season at Valley Parade, Titan Properties, a Leeds-based development company, paid the club £95,000 for the ground without planning permission. Bradford Corporation turned down Titan's plan to build old peoples' flats on the site, 'so as to keep the sports facilities which exist there'.[13]

In November the council tried to buy the ground from Titan Properties and in February 1974 agreed terms, believed to be £110,000, which gave the property group a quick profit and left Avenue with the feeling that they had been badly treated by their council.

Leighton had been sacked as manager in October 1973, but stayed on as a player; Roy Ambler who had guided the reserves to promotion in the Yorkshire League the previous year took over following six successive home defeats, including scores of 1 – 7 and 0 – 6, displays which were described as 'pathetic' and depressed attendances to under 600.

Results improved, particularly at home, but attendances increased only slightly, and the financial position became impossible when the club realised, belatedly, in April 1974 that they would have to pay capital gains tax on the ground sale profit.

[11] ibid, 31 March 1973.
[12] ibid, 27 March 1973.
[13] ibid, 14 August 1973.

The club played their last fixture, as at Park Avenue against Great Harwood; a last-minute goal by skipper Mick Fleming won the match for Avenue to provide the 'romance'; a farewell crowd of just 698 provided the bleak reality.

The following day, 3rd May 1974, just over fifty shareholders met at 2.30 pm at the Midland Hotel, Cheapside, Bradford. The club Chairman, George Sutcliffe, outlined the club's decline: how there had been many changes at board level, how each successive board had borrowed heavily in the hope that a 'profitable sale of a skilled player might save the day' and how this policy inevitably weakened the team and its public support.

The club had a substantial amount of cash, £37,000, left from the sale of the ground, but no other assets of any size at all, and they owed £47,000 to various investors as follows:

	£
Inland Revenue for capital gains tax and PAYE	11,000
Directors' loans	2,000
Loans from H. Metcalfe (now deceased)	15,000
Loans from other former directors	9,500
Trade creditors	9,500
	47,000

Although losses were smaller in the Northern Premier than in the Football League, Avenue had no assets to sell, no ground to play on except Valley Parade, which was costing them nearly twice as much as their gate receipts, and no reasonable prospects of avoiding further losses; the shareholders appointed a liquidator to wind up the club's affairs rather than run any more creditors' money into the ground.

The Inland Revenue, as preferential creditors, were paid in full; all the other creditors received 75p for every £ they were owed, and the holders of the 48,000 Ordinary Shares (mostly in the hands of Metcalfe's executors) received nothing.

The days of a Northern club that started in the Southern League, a club that reached the First Division of the Football League within seven years of deserting commercial rugby, a club that Stanley Waddilove tried to turn into the 'Arsenal of the North', were over; the ground where Shackleton and Greenwood had enlivened Bradford afternoons and Scoular had stamped his pugnacious authority on matches was now empty. While Bradford's council deliberated on its eventual fate, the neat Edwardian stands slowly deteriorated, vulnerable to the elements and hooligans alike, as the grass spread over the terraces, and elder bushes, sycamore saplings and a small forest of rosebay willow herb began to reclaim the stands, the club offices and the rusting turnstiles.

21. Decline, Recovery and Tragedy at Valley Parade

Bradford City were founder members of the new national Third Division, having finished third in the last of the Third Division (North) competitions in their best season since the war.

The new Third Division was bound to be a more difficult league, because it included the best half of both regional leagues, and because the Third Division (South) was thought to have been the stronger division. Southern sides took five of the top six places, and northern sides each of the bottom six, although two of these teams, Notts County and Doncaster, had just been relegated from Division Two the year before. City finished in midtable.

In January 1959 plans had been made to spend over £50,000 on the ground, but in October the urgency of the situation was made public when the Football League wrote to complain about the quality of the floodlights. In addition, the Midland Road stand, which had only recently been rebuilt, was again condemned as unsafe. Improved floodlights were expected to cost £10,000, and £12,000 was needed to make the Midland Road stand safe, with a further £13,000 for a second phase of development. In spite of supporters' club donations of £23,000 since 1949 this would force the sale of the more talented players unless new long-term finance could be attracted.

Receipts in 1959-60 were increased by a run in the FA Cup as far as the fifth round. The eight matches, three of them drawn, were watched by 172,000 people, and if the 3 – 0 home win over Everton was the highlight the 0 – 5 defeat in the fifth round replay before 53,000 people at Turf Moor, Burnley, was the most lucrative.

This compensated for a small decline in League attendances as City slipped to nineteenth; the result was a profit of £5,800 (£C45,000), the best financial return since City were in the Second Division in the 1930s.

In normal circumstances this profit could have been used to strengthen the team, but the need to improve the ground was imperative. Forwards McCole and Stokes were sold to Leeds and Huddersfield respectively and the 18-year-old Trevor Hockey was not picked for an FA Cup match, so as to maximise his availability for his new club and thus his sale value. The directors spent £14,000 on second-hand floodlights from West Ham United in March 1960, started work on covering the 3,500 capacity 'Bradford end' and built new club rooms, office accommodation and dressing-rooms in the south-west corner of the main stand. Prior to this they had used an old house at the back of the Kop at the north end of the ground. 'The players changed in the cellars which were often flooded and ridden with cockroaches and entered the playing area along a tunnel under the Kop, through a gap still visible in that corner of the ground'.[1]

Although this was progress, the season 1960-1 was most disappointing, and relegation to the Fourth Division came as a 'great blow to everyone concerned with Bradford City',[2] particularly the manager, Peter Jackson, who lost his job. Cup receipts were small in spite of the new League Cup competition which was, at first, not very popular; a home tie with Manchester United only attracted a crowd of 5,000, although this was partly because the lack of floodlights forced the game to be played on a Wednesday afternoon. The club had made money in the first two years in Division Three, but the poor results in 1960-1 cut attendances to their lowest level since the war and caused the deferment of the Midland Road rebuilding scheme, ostensibly so that 'team building could take priority'.[3] Although the club had accumulated profits of £15,000, and a credit balance at the bank of £5,500, the team was not strengthened.

Back in the Fourth Division crowds were only 10% below the previous season because City, after a poor start, played well in the second half of the year and missed promotion by only one point. This still meant a loss of £7,000 on playing operations, compensated for by transfer receipts.

In 1962 one of the new floodlight pylons blew down in a gale; on the field City had perhaps the worst season in their history, finishing one from the bottom of Division Four and having to apply for re-election. The average League attendance fell to 4,000, losses increased to £15,000 and the bank overdraft was up to £12,000, three times the level of the previous year despite the sale of two key players, Harland and Green. In the FA Cup a 5 – 2 win at Oldham raised hopes at the club, but in the Third Round only 14,000 saw the home defeat, 1 – 6, at the hands of Newcastle.

Crowds improved the following season when a late run by City saw them again narrowly miss promotion, this time by failing to win their last home match, but they went out of both cup competitions in the first round; in the League Cup they lost 3 – 7 at Park Avenue. The Fourth Division was proving a trap; City were losing money in every season and

[1] S. Inglis, op cit, p. 111.
[2] Bradford City AFC Directors' Report for 53rd AGM, 20 December 1961.
[3] *Bradford Telegraph and Argus*, 19 August 1961.

were selling players to keep the bank overdraft within tolerable limits, but this did nothing to help them build a side that could win promotion.

This situation was not unusual for Fourth Division clubs; Bradford could not complain of their level of support, which was average for the division, and they did not face particularly strong competition from rugby league at this time as Bradford Northern collapsed in 1963-4 after their attendances fell to 1,000 a game.

The 1964-5 season was one of change; the chairman A. V. Harris who had been on the board since 1949 was replaced by Stafford Heginbotham, a toy manufacturer in the city, who joined the board as chairman, and his friend, local solicitor George Ide, replaced J. Kelly as one of the four directors. The club dropped to nineteenth, only two points clear of the re-election zone, crowds fell 35% and even an extended run in the League Cup did little to help the finances, as the largest crowd was only 11,000; a 1 – 7 defeat at Villa Park did not help morale. In the FA Cup City were knocked out in the First Round by non-League Scarborough 0 – 1. W. Harris replaced R. Brocklebank as manager, Manningham was closed as a passenger station on 22nd March 1965,[4] nearly 100 years after it had been opened, and only the losses and the player sales were unchanging.

1965-6 was even worse; City finished 23rd and had to apply for re-election again, with a defensive record that was one of the worst in the entire Football League. They were put out of both Cups in the First Round by Fourth Division opponents, losing at Darlington despite leading 2 – 0 at half-time, and attendances were back to the level of their previous re-election season, three years before. Five years in the Fourth Division had overturned their financial position, with playing losses totalling £52,000 (£C375,000), debts of over £50,000 and readily disposable assets of only £16,000. The club expressed some gratitude that 'the number of votes recorded for us at the re-election ballot was at least a show of confidence by the Football League clubs in our ability to improve' but this was small consolation.[5]

In 1966 the club sent out five thousand letters to the local business community in connection with ground advertising, and offered life membership of the club for one hundred guineas, but there was a very poor response. Bradford is an unusual city in that it has no high-class housing district; those who run successful businesses in the city typically live outside it, resulting in a less developed 'social network' and an unwillingness to support local sporting activities, particularly in the absence of real success on the field. City decided they could only build a 'modest little cantilever stand' on a very narrow flat area along the Midland Road side to give some shelter to a maximum of 4,000 standing

[4] H. Hird, op cit, p. 176.
[5] Bradford City AFC Director's Report for 58th AGM, 12 January 1967.

spectators; a scheme to spend £60,000 to re-develop the Midland Road stand was to await 'real success on the field'.[6] It was to be a long wait. The redevelopment at least ended six years in which the ground had been three-sided and required the pitch to be moved closer to the main stand.

By December 1966 survival was in doubt following continued heavy losses that required the directors to make personal commitments to the club of £30,000, 'easily the highest in the club's history'.[7]

A crisis meeting in St. George's Hall in January 1967 was packed to capacity with 2,000 people (two-thirds of the previous home gate), but little resulted beyond some increase in ground advertising.

The threat to Bradford City's existence was very real, but the board decided to provide more finance and support the new manager Willie Watson, who had taken over from Harris in April, by reversing the policy of player sales in an attempt to get out of the Fourth Division. The club improved to midtable, then fifth, once again a point away from the fourth promotion place.

In January 1968 City increased their authorised share capital from £15,000 to £25,000, but attracted negative publicity when former Mayor Robinson objected to the club's refusal to allow a club supporter from the 1930s to transfer his 637 shares.

The chairman, Heginbotham, agreed that this was so but refused to give reasons, saying that 'the directors had the right to control who should and does hold the shares in the company'.[8]

The club's original articles of association, section six, did give the necessary powers as the shares 'shall be allotted by and at the discretion of the directors', who held only 16% of the issued shares (2,309 out of 14,266 shares). Their position was more secure than this implies, however, since most shareholdings were of less than ten shares and many were in the names of shareholders who had either died or moved out of the district and could not be traced. It didn't matter too much of course; the club had never paid its shareholders a dividend.

Also in 1968 the Chester Committee gave new publicity to an old issue when they identified Bradford as a city that might benefit from amalgamating its professional soccer clubs.

Bradford City appointed a new manager, J. Wheeler, in June 1968 to fill the vacancy that had resulted from the premature death of their previous manager, Grenville Hair, who had not long replaced Willie Watson. They maintained their three-year policy of not selling players, and victory at Darlington in May 1969 kept Darlington in Division Four but earned Bradford their first promotion for forty years. Park Avenue

---

[6] *Bradford Telegraph and Argus*, 14 October 1966.
[7] ibid, 21 December 1966.
[8] ibid, 23 January 1968.

did not share their celebrations, as they had again come bottom of the League, conceding over one hundred goals.

City's promotion was celebrated by a civic reception at City Hall, and a 'heroes' reception' from hundreds of supporters.[9]

The directors' policy had been vindicated, but at some considerable cost. Attendances had naturally improved and gate receipts were up 45% in two years, but in common with many other clubs City were finding it difficult to control wage costs, which had risen 60% in two years and now exceeded gate receipts by nearly £8,000. In spite of the 'magnificent efforts' of the pools agents, the supporters' association and the ladies' committee, the playing loss on the season was over £10,000 and net transfer payments were nearly £4,000. None the less the club had escaped from the Fourth Division and success in the Third Division would improve their strained finances.

The club offered Wheeler a five-year contract, announced increased prices for the new season and reduced their professional staff to sixteen, which the manager expected would enable them to hold a 'reasonable place in Division Three'.[10]

This was an accurate forecast. An added bonus was the progress made in both cup competitions. In the Football League Cup City reached Round Four, beating Sunderland away before losing at West Bromwich. In the FA Cup they reached the Third Round and managed a 2 – 2 draw at home to Tottenham Hotspur (a match for which prices were raised by between 20% and 50%) before losing the replay decisively 0 – 5. Cup attendances totalling 135,000 and league attendances that were 25% above the divisional average combined to give City their best profit for many years; the policy of reducing the playing staff had contributed to this by reducing the wage bill.

The accumulated losses were now below £7,000, but with over £70,000 in long term assets and only £14,000 of this funded by share capital, the company was still faced with sizeable debts and an overdraft of over £28,000 (£C160,000).

The club therefore decided on an innovative source of finance; the corporation were asked to buy Valley Parade and lease it back to the club at an annual rental of 10% of the purchase price. The corporation agreed to the proposal but would only pay £35,000. The agreement stipulated a maximum period of ninety-nine years and gave the club 'certain rights to reacquire', so they agreed to the offer. Park Avenue had that summer failed to secure enough votes to stay in the Football League, so City were offered Park Avenue's ground but they declined, officially because it

[9] ibid, 14 May 1969.
[10] ibid, 21 May 1969.

would have 'cost £60,000 to bring it up to Valley Parade standard'.[11]

The first season in the Third Division had shown City the way forward, but the slide to nineteenth in 1970-1 and the inability to progress in cup competitions against Third and Fourth Division opposition cut gate receipts by 30% and led to a loss of £15,000 that wiped out the previous year's gains.

The following season began badly with only two points from a five-game sequence that ended in a 1 – 7 defeat. The board reacted nervously; the manager, Wheeler, was promptly sacked, only two years into his five-year contract.

The new manager, Edwards, emphasised discipline and literally instructed some players to 'get their hair cut'. He also banned Wednesdays off until earned.[12]

On April 1st for the start of the Easter matches Bradford were fourth from the bottom of the division with hopes of escaping the drop; by April 22nd City were bottom for the visit of the leaders, Aston Villa, whose lordly playing style and victory provoked running battles on the thinly populated terraces. City won only one of their last ten matches and remained at the foot of the division.

Mercifully the financial losses were quite small, due to a combination of greater economy, particularly with ground repairs, player sales and the continuing success of the development fund and the club's other promotions.

Facilities at Valley Parade were certainly not lavish; the manager's office in July 1972 was equipped with a desk, chair, filing cabinet and bookcase with a combined value of £30, and the boardroom furniture, including twenty-two armchairs was valued at £240. The directors' box was probably the most basic in the League[13] but Heginbotham, in December 1972, rejected a move to Odsal as 'Valley Parade was the start of League football in the city'.[14]

Return to the Fourth Division posed problems that were no easier to resolve for being familiar. Football just did not pay in the Fourth Division. Home wins over Grantham, Tranmere and Second Division Blackpool in the FA Cup brought an attractive tie away to Arsenal in the Fourth Round. The 0 – 2 score was entirely respectable, but in spite of sharing the proceeds of a 40,000 attendance losses for the season of nearly £19,000 were punishing.

In April 1973 a merger scheme was announced whereby Park Avenue would become a nursery side to City with players interchanged between

---

[11] ibid, 1 June 1970.
[12] ibid, 17 November 1971.
[13] S. Inglis, op cit, p. 112.
[14] *Bradford Telegraph and Argus*, 13 December 1972.

City's reserve team in the North Midlands League and Park Avenue in the Northern Premier. City were to drop their third team, Park Avenue their second team, and administration of both clubs was to be under the control of the City general manager, Mellor, with Avenue's player-manager and secretary losing their jobs. Bobby Kennedy, City youth team coach, was to take charge of the Avenue team.[15]

Avenue's ground was sold to a Leeds development company, but the merger scheme was abandoned when the Northern Premier League refused to accept Park Avenue as a nursery club, and Avenue instead retained their identity, manager and secretary but paid City a £7,000 pa rent for use of Valley Parade.

In October 1973 a takeover bid was mounted for City, which led to wholesale board changes on 25th January 1974. Heginbotham, Porter, Ide and Jones resigned, and Dunne, Morrison, Tordoff and Wilkinson joined the board. This gave City a 'fresh start' and the youngest board of directors in the Football League, with Bob Martin, who was soon to become Chairman, the dominant figure. He was from Shipley, close to the Manningham district of Bradford, a grammar school boy who went into a mill to become a weaving overlooker but left at 29 to start his own successful discount centre.

The new board were keen to buy back the ground from the council, but one aspect of the club's attempt to forge closer links with the munici-pality was resented by supporters; 800 signed a petition in April 1974 deploring a proposed change of name from Bradford City to Bradford Metro.

At the end of the season City had improved to eighth but were a long way from promotion. The losses were nearly as bad as the year before and an investment of over £10,000 in new players pushed the overdraft over £40,000, a large figure for a club that no longer owned their ground.

Park Avenue had gone into liquidation and would no longer be contributing rent for the ground, so a move to Odsal was considered. The playing staff had to be cut back to sixteen again and results were much the same as before. Crowds at just over 3,000 were the lowest ever, the team lost to Hartlepool in the First Round of the FA Cup and in January 1975, the manager, Edwards, was sacked. City considered a plan to go part-time and Mellor, who had been secretary for nineteen years, resigned in March because of disagreements with the board and because 'they have forgotten it is an entertainment business'.[16]

The club could perhaps be forgiven a rather grim attitude in view of the increasing financial pressures. Inside ten years retained profits of £20,000 had been turned into accumulated losses of £94,000. The club owed a total of £115,000 to creditors (£30,000), the bank (£44,000), the

[15] ibid, 11 April 1973.
[16] ibid, 24 March 1975.

directors (£26,000) and other lenders, yet had no ground and less than £40,000 in assets, a notable change from ten years before. The cash crisis was in spite of the proceeds from 'selling' the ground to the council, and in spite of development and other fund revenues that had averaged more than £15,000 pa, for the last ten years.

In June 1975 City had further talks on a switch to Park Avenue, but nothing was resolved. Bradford Metropolitan Council's chief executive said that without more money they would not be able to re-develop Park Avenue, but the ground was falling apart as they deliberated. There were plenty of schemes; Jim Streets who had promoted speedway at Odsal wanted to move there but the plan was rejected, partly on noise grounds. Other plans were devised for greyhound racing, a banked cycle velodrome and an athletics arena. None was apparently feasible and a plan to move Bradford Northern there from Odsal had to be scrapped due to the mounting cost of repairs.

At Valley Parade, the manager, Kennedy, had 'no money for new players' and the cash crisis led to a public appeal. Relief arrived in the form of higher receipts from the League pools and, more importantly, the income from reaching the Sixth Round of the FA Cup. Bradford were the first side from Division Four to reach the last eight in the competition and were drawn at home to Southampton. They decided to treble seat prices and raise standing prices from 65p to £1.50 with no reductions for children or pensioners; the city was generally critical and, despite urgent improvements to crush barriers to prevent the crowd limit being lowered, only 14,000 people came, 7,000 less than the crowd for the visit of non-League Tooting and Mitcham in the Fourth Round. Although the financial benefits were obvious this did not help to produce an atmosphere to unnerve their opponents, and Southampton won a dull game 1 – 0.

City finished seventeenth that season but made an unprecedented profit of £32,000 for the year. The manager, Kennedy, was therefore given nearly £30,000 to spend on new players for 1976-7. The new signings helped to increase the wage bill from £56,000 to £94,000, but playing losses (excluding transfer expenditures) were small as an exciting season ended with City winning promotion with only one point to spare.

Not all was well, however. A brick wall collapsed under crowd pressure for the second time that season, and the quality of the club's administration was brought into question by an auditor's report which stated that 'proper books of account were not maintained during the period but were written up subsequently on the basis of information then available',[17] leaving the auditors uncertain whether all transactions had been recorded.

[17] Auditor's Report, Bradford City AFC (1908) Ltd Accounts for 1976-7.

The board now faced a takeover bid and they issued new shares, mostly to themselves; this increased the share capital by 50% and increased their holdings from 25% to 40% of total shares issued. Terrace prices were raised from £1 to £1.50, a new secretary T. Newman was appointed, and a commercial manager, R. Fielding, who devised a new lottery that the chairman, Martin, rather grandly said could earn City £200,000 pa.

The Lotteries Act 1978 raised the maximum for prizes and for ticket prices and provided a considerable initial stimulus to lottery sales. City's lottery contributed over £90,000 to club revenues in its first season of operation, but attendances were lower than the previous year and salaries were 35% higher. City struggled in the League and made early exits from the two cup competitions. In January 1978, the manager, Kennedy was sacked. Two directors, Davidson and Tordoff resigned in protest and called on the chairman, Martin, to resign.

The new manager, Napier, described the youth policy as non-existent and the scouting system as diabolical,[18] and the club spent an unprecedented £63,000 in the five weeks up to the transfer deadline in an unavailing bid to avoid relegation.

The club decided to spend £20,000 on ground improvements including widening the pitch by three yards to give more room to wingers; the pitch was one of the narrowest in the League and managers said how easy it was to defend at Valley Parade.[19] This required the demolition of a brick wall in front of the main stand, and the first few rows of the 'paddock'. Other minor changes included adding to the one women's toilet in the ground.

Early results were poor; Napier resigned as manager in October 1978 and Mulhall was hired from First Division Bolton. The enormous growth in lottery funds could have quickly stabilised the financial situation or funded ground improvements; instead it provided the means for the board to gamble on buying 'name' players who were accustomed to high wages at First Division clubs. In the absence of any wage policy or resistance to players' demands, wages rose by 65% to £215,000, more than twice their level of two years before and nearly three times as large as gate receipts. The board's gamble on quick success did little to improve results, however, and City finished in the lower half of the division, losing £63,000. At the season's end the club bought the ground back from the council; apart from any emotive appeal this improved the company's ability to borrow on overdraft.

Over the summer of 1979 there were renewed discussions on a plan to move City to Park Avenue, to a complex built to provide football, squash

18 *Bradford Telegraph and Argus*, 9 February 1978.
19 ibid, 9 May 1978.

and gymnastics. The site of the former Horton Park railway station would have provided extensive car parking space, but the plans came to nothing. In 1979-80 the financial position improved. The League arranged a new contract with the television companies and this raised the sum received from the League pools to over £80,000. Attendances and gate receipts rose by 50% as City chased promotion, and the lottery scheme finally achieved Bob Martin's predictions by contributing over £200,000 to club revenues. Bradford started the season with seven wins and a draw, and in March the top four, Walsall, Huddersfield, Portsmouth and Bradford, appeared to have broken away from the other clubs, but Newport, who won ten games in a row from late February, were closing the gap. On the last Saturday of the season, May 3rd, Huddersfield and Walsall were already promoted; Bradford were at Peterborough having 60 points, Newport were at Walsall having 59 points and Portsmouth were at Northampton on 58 points and the best goal difference. Bradford needed just a draw for promotion; even defeat would have sufficed unless Portsmouth won and Newport drew or won, but City lost and Newport and Portsmouth both won to go up instead of Bradford.

At least the club had made a profit, but £38,000 did not even fund the £45,000 spent on transfer fees and seemed a small return given the club's income, particularly from lotteries.

In the close season Bradford's prices, among the lowest in the League, were increased by a third, but City did not fulfil the promise of the previous season, and never challenged for promotion. Attendances halved, and ominously the national decline in lottery income cut City's promotions money by over 30%. The only high point was a 1 – 0 win over Liverpool in the First Leg of the Football League Cup Round Two, even though Bradford lost 0 – 4 in the Second Leg.

There was a formidable gap between the plans for Park Avenue and the reality; a sports and conference centre costing £5,000,000 was the next proposal, but due to indecision and unwillingness to spend far more modest sums on repairs the dilapidated stands and floodlights had to be demolished in November 1980 due to the threat to public safety. The prompt announcement of a £500,000 re-development scheme for Valley Parade[20] had an air of bravado, more than conviction, about it. With City in the lower half of Division Four, manager Mulhall returned to Bolton and the bank overdraft reached £120,000, its highest recorded level and over three times its size three years before.

The chairman, Bob Martin, welcomed shareholders to the club's seventieth Annual Shareholders' Meeting by expressing the board's

---

[20] ibid, 30 December 1980.

pleasure in presenting 'what must be viewed as a very satisfying statement of accounts for the past year. Football is going through very serious financial times and because of that a small loss has to be viewed in some ways successful.'[21] He did not point out that the small loss of £1,200 was after the inclusion of players' transfer receipts of £17,000, and of a similar-sized profit on the sale of fixed assets, that lottery income and the distribution of the League pool provided £215,000 out of a total income of £370,000, that gate receipts were only 35% of wages or that current liabilities were six times as large as current assets and 35% larger than total assets even after the stadium had been included at a recent valuation. Chairmen of firms in few other industries would have expressed such satisfaction.

In May 1981 Bradford obtained former England defender Roy McFarland as player-manager from Derby. This was his first managerial post, but a new professionalism was soon apparent on the field. The dangers associated with financial pressures could also be seen in November 1981 when two cracked floodlight pylons forced the postponement of a League Cup game; the years of inadequate maintenance had taken their toll.

McFarland did what he was signed to do, and in the shortest possible time, but even the club's chairman was slightly rueful; while expressing his pleasure at promotion, the lack of hooliganism and the club's modest spending on transfer fees he also pointed out that 'success on the field has its price and you will see from the figures in the accounts the price the club has had to pay for its success'.[22]

League gates were up nearly 90%, the biggest improvement in the League, as Bradford finished second, but lottery receipts continued to fall and salaries and other expenses to rise, resulting in the worst financial results ever (if transfers are included). Short-term debt had also reached unprecedented levels.

Midway through the 1982-3 season McFarland revealed the extent of his personal ambition by breaking his contract and accepted an offer to return to Derby County, taking his assistant Jones with him, amid considerable public acrimony. City, who were later awarded £55,000 in compensation from Derby County by the judgement of a Football League committee, appointed Trevor Cherry from Leeds as player-manager.

In January a brewery announced a plan to build a new supporters' club on spare land near the Burlington Terrace entrance to the Spion Kop, as a belated replacement for the club closed seven years before.

In February, in a 90 mph wind the top section of a floodlight pylon keeled over, fortunately while the ground was empty. Spectators at the

[21] Bradford City AFC (1908) Ltd, Chairman's Report 3 September 1981.
[22] Bradford City AFC (1908) Ltd, Chairman's Report 12 December 1982.

Kop end in the season's highlight, the 0-0 draw with Manchester United in the League Cup, had already noticed ominous creaks from the flood-light towers in the blustery wind. In the consequent examination of the other pylons another was found to have a structural crack and had to be dismantled. This put an end to any further floodlit games that season.

The club finished in mid-table, and at the end of the season announced that their 'notorious' pitch was to undergo remedial treatment to improve its drainage. During the close season it was finances, not the pitch, which gained most attention when Leeds United issued a winding up notice for the £10,000 owed for Cherry, and the Customs and Excise presented a petition for £17,000 of unpaid VAT. The same week the players' pay cheques bounced. Astonishingly the club had refused an offer of £100,000 for centre-forward Campbell only three months before; although a desire to keep important players was laudable, in the context of the financial position in 1983 it implied a total lack of awareness of the gravity of the situation.

On 24th June a receiver was appointed by the City of Bradford Metro-politan Council as the holder of a mortgage secured by floating charge to look after the club's affairs. Accumulated debts were reported at £300,000. In fact the club owed £420,000 and had assets of only £70,000.

The Football League identified minimum conditions that any buyer of the new club would have to meet, if the club were to retain their place in Division Three:

> £350,000 to be paid in as Share Capital
> £50,000 to be guaranteed as security that the first season's fixtures will be completed
> £100,000 of League 'pool' fees to be withheld until the end of the season
> the old company's debts to the League to be paid in full
> the old company's preferential creditors to be paid in full
> the old company's taxation creditors to be paid in full
> the old company's League club creditors to be paid 70%
> the old company's other unsecured creditors to be paid 60%.

During the summer, rumours circulated chiefly concerning the willing-ness of the Council to assist the club by way of ground purchase and loan and whether the club would move to and share Odsal with Bradford Northern Rugby League club, thus escaping from a ground sited in a rundown inner city area. (Bradford Northern were not in much better condition; total home attendances for the season were only 74,000 and their assets of £145,000 were far less than the short-term liabilities of £425,000.)

In late July 1,500 supporters came to a meeting at Valley Parade and pledged £22,000. Less heartening was the news that personality clashes at board level were still important even in time of crisis; the chairman, Martin, was reported to have agreed to transfer his shares in the old company to J. Tordoff on condition that the previous chairman, Heginbotham, would not be a member of the new board.[23]

Further talks took place, and on 6th August 1983 Bradford City's 'fight for survival' was won; the City council were to loan the club £100,000, the public pledged over £50,000, including one £10,000 anonymous donor, and Tordoff and Heginbotham were to pay £375,000.

A new company Bradford City (1983) Ltd., had been formed from a £100 off the peg company, on 24th June 1983, its authorised capital increased and memoranda and articles of association redrafted to give the directors an absolute discretion to decline to register any transfer of shares. This was probably less necessary than hitherto; the issued share capital was £174,262; 75,006 to Heginbotham, 75,006 to Tordoff, 31 holdings of 250 shares, 19 of 500 and 7 of 1,000 shares each.

Any euphoria at saving City from extinction was sorely tested by the start of the 1983-4 season; Bradford won only one of their first fifteen matches and at the end of November were one from the bottom of Division Three. Campbell had been sold for £70,000 by the club's receiver in the summer; his reacquisition for just £20,000 from Derby in November both was good business and changed the results and shape of City's play. Campbell scored steadily, as he had always done at Valley Parade and provided sufficient distraction for twin centre-forward Hawley to score 22 goals as City climbed steadily to seventh. The club even declared a small profit. More importantly Cherry and Yorath reshaped their side within a clear wages policy and financial budget by buying cheaply and bringing younger players into the side who provided more ambition and pace, notably in attack. Campbell was now the single focus of attack and scored 23 goals; City combined a tight defence with fast breaking forwards and swept all before them. Indifferent early season form was followed by nearly three months without defeat which took them to top place at the end of November.

In late April City had gained promotion to Division Two; the local council had played their part with a loan 'plus a bit of creative accounting on the repayments', as they felt that a city 'misses something without a football team to represent it'. They were well pleased at promotion which would mean a 'great deal to all of Bradford, including business. The message will go out that Bradford is a successful place. The spin off could be tremendous'.[24]

On 11th May 1985 Bradford City were already champions of the Third Division, and 10,000 people, the largest crowd of the season, came to

---

[23] *Bradford Telegraph and Argus*, 26 July 1983.
[24] ibid, 24 April 1985, p. 16.

Valley Parade for the match against Lincoln to celebrate the club's triumph; from financial collapse to Division Two in two seasons was a magnificent achievement. The afternoon began with skipper Peter Jackson holding the Third Division trophy. After forty minutes of relatively uneventful play a small fire began in Block G of the main stand. The stand was full, all tickets sold on Friday. Within five minutes the small fire became a fireball that sped in the wind along the old wooden stand, trapped by the wooden roof, engulfing the whole structure. Exit towards the street was almost impossible, the narrow turnstiles were locked, exit was against the slope and thus there were no windows to jump from, the passageways were narrow and difficult to move along even under normal conditions. The only way out for most people was onto the pitch over a five-foot fence and a low surrounding wall. Mercifully there were no security fences along the front of the stand, but despite many acts of heroism, 56 people died, over 200 were seriously injured and no one who saw what happened would be unmarked.

Only at Ibrox in 1972 had more people died at a match, and then in very different circumstances, a crowd surge that the crush barriers could not withstand. Ibrox had also been the site of the first major soccer ground disaster in 1902 when part of a stand collapsed and 25 died. Thirty-three people died and 500 were injured when barriers collapsed at Burnden Park, Bolton in 1946. There have been many less serious accidents at Football League grounds, but they have almost invariably been caused by the collapse of barriers or parts of stands under pressure from large crowds.

There have also been stand fires before at football grounds, but usually they happened after matches or took place more slowly. Between the wars there were fires at Maine Road, Anfield, Southampton and Crewe. Since the war there have been six or seven serious fires, including two in West Yorkshire; at Huddersfield in 1950 the main stand caught fire on a Monday afternoon and a quarter of an hour after the alarm was given 'flames leapt high above the roof',[25] at Leeds in 1956 the main west stand burnt down overnight, but again without loss of life.

The 1975 Safety of Sports Grounds Act introduced a system of compulsory licensing, whereby designated grounds had to have a safety certificate issued by the local authority. In 1982-3 50 league grounds were designated – the 44 First and Second Divison clubs and other clubs that had been designated before relegation.

The Popplewell Inquiry investigated the circumstances connected with the disaster at Bradford and the measures that should be taken to prevent any similar occurrence in the future.

The particular and cruel irony at Bradford was that the work replac-

---

[25] *Huddersfield Examiner*, 8 April 1950.

ing the timber flooring with concrete was to have begun the following Monday as part of the necessary improvements due to the club's promotion to Division Two.

Some of the contributory factors were specific to the club; on 18th July 1984 the West Yorkshire Metropolitan Council wrote to City in connection with the club's application to the Sports Ground Trust for assistance with re-covering the main grandstand roof and identified the potential fire hazard from a discarded cigarette given the build-up of combustible materials in the voids beneath the seats.[26]

The Inquiry also found that 'any work or improvement or alteration was wholly related to finances that were available', and that to 'remedy the situation would have required greater expenditure of money and resources than was available to the club'.[27]

The investigation saw the problem facing Bradford as one common to most other clubs in the lower divisions, namely the 'problem of finance', but avowed that 'the public are entitled to expect that sports grounds will be reasonably safe'.[28]

Bradford, for a city of considerable size, had been relatively free from major disasters; not since December 1882 when the 225-foot chimney at 'Ripley's Mill' fell and killed 54 people had so many lives been lost.

The fire at Valley Parade was therefore perhaps the worst disaster in the history of the Football League, and in the history of the city of Bradford. The board of Bradford City (1983) Ltd. were inevitably left with ultimate responsibility for what happened; on the other hand what happened at Bradford in May 1985 had no real precedent.

If there were specific causes of the disaster that can be laid at the door of the club's directorate, equally there were underlying causes that go back to the entry of both clubs into professional football. From 1907 the supporters, particularly of the Manningham club that became Bradford City, preferred their own arrangements and traditions to a merger that would have rationalised facilities in a move to Park Avenue. Even when Park Avenue could no longer continue, antipathy between rival supporters, apparent municipal indecision and a preference for grand designs rather than more modest but achievable schemes allowed Park Avenue's ground to deteriorate to the point that it had to be demolished for reasons of public safety. The liquidation of Bradford City (1908) Ltd. brought about a closer relationship with the Metropolitan Council, and the trauma of the fire has inevitably

---

[26] *Committee of Inquiry into Crowd Safety and Control at Sports' Crowds*, (The Popplewell Inquiry) – Interim Report Cmnd. 9585, 1985, p. 20.
[27] ibid, p. 27.
[28] ibid, p. 28.

changed the position of the club in the local community, no doubt for the better.

None the less there were few, if any, consolations. Professional football developed in the city in its own way, and the city has paid its own terrible price. It is as well that Bradford prides itself on resilience as much as on its sense of identity; Stafford Heginbotham could still state after the 'most difficult year in the club's history' that 'we are, however, still in good shape and capable of surviving whatever adversities we are likely to encounter'.[29]

[29] Bradford City AFC (1983) Ltd., Chairman's Report 9 April 1986.

Conclusions

Bradford's two Northern Union clubs left commercial rugby when the popularity of the game declined in the early years of the twentieth century.

Manningham's entry into professional soccer, under the name Bradford City, was encouraged by the Football League, despite their total lack of experience, so as to establish soccer in the rugby-dominated West Riding textile district.

An intended merger of the two clubs in 1907 to combine City's developing experience and Park Avenue's well-appointed grounds was thwarted by the general members of Manningham who were staunchly protective of their own brief heritage.

Park Avenue could not earn enough from rugby to repay the debts owed on the development of their sports ground, and Bradford's two clubs thus came to compete for honours in a national sport where rivalries are more appropriate between, not within, urban areas.

Although Bradford is one of England's ten largest cities, it is one of the smallest to have had two League sides and the only one with additional competition from rugby league.

Both clubs achieved considerable success in the years before the Great War, particularly City, who won the FA Cup during a period of revived prosperity for the woollen and worsted trades, but the competition for spectator support within the city was a heavy burden in a competitive industry.

Did Bradford's two clubs find 'a game that would pay'? The desire to achieve success on the field in professional football knows no natural financial restraint, and football clubs as a whole have been willing to stretch their finances in a way that no commercially oriented firm would consider sensible. Thus normal business criteria provide no answer. Peter Robinson, secretary of Liverpool, when asked what his club's unexampled success in Europe had achieved, took his questioner not to the trophy cabinet but down the players' tunnel to inspect the stands and terraces as the club's investment in the future.

Playing football also brings its own rewards: employment and local renown for players, interest, excitement and a fund of shared experiences for spectators and for directors the peculiar pleasures and prestige of controlling a local asset.

Park Avenue had good facilities but were continually handicapped by moderate support and came to rely on a series of wealthy patrons. When the last of these, Herbert Metcalfe, could not provide sound judgement as well as money, the club soon collapsed.

Bradford City were held back by a ground that was never entirely adequate for professional soccer. No other Football League club has had to contend with the problems of a ground cut into a hillside; if the limitations from its conversion into a ground suitable for commercial rugby in 1886 were remedied by the redevelopment work in 1908, following promotion to the First Division, lack of success since the Great War left the ground in an increasingly shabby and dangerous condition.

Since the financial collapse of 1983, City's board has been more prepared than hitherto to apply the financial controls normal to other areas of business activity; this in conjunction with promotion and the effects of the fire has encouraged a more supportive attitude by the local council and the business community.

Valley Parade was re-opened in December 1986 after a £2.5m redevelopment, partly financed by West Yorkshire Metropolitan Council, which has given the club, belatedly, a twentieth-century ground with every conceivable safety feature and transformed facilities for those on terraces, in seats or in private boxes.

In England the very identity of clubs and their support has become inextricably connected with the precise location of their grounds. Bradford is a city not only of traditional industry and buildings but of traditional attitudes and loyalties as well. If loyalty is the source of support it can also be a barrier to progress, for professional team sports arouse feelings that divide as well as unite.

In Bradford internal distinctions seem to have been more important than the prospect of real success in a national competition. Park Avenue only entered the Southern League and then the Football League because the supporters of the Manningham club rejected a merger. On many occasions since then merger talks were held but failed, despite the convictions of chairmen like Briggs, Waddilove and Heginbotham that the city was too small to run two Football League teams and a Rugby League side.

Amalgamation at Park Avenue would have given Bradford a single football team to represent the city, and would have avoided the situation where many of Avenue's former supporters refuse even now to visit Valley Parade.[1] Fifty years ago Stanley Waddilove dreamed of a

---

[1] Stafford Heginbotham, private interview, April 1987.

'continental-style' ground that would provide soccer and rugby on alternate weeks in the winter with cricket in the summer; a stronger organisation at Park Avenue would almost certainly have persuaded Yorkshire County Cricket Club to move their headquarters there from Headingley and the establishment of a single football team during the formative years of the industry would have surely enabled the city to enjoy real success.

The search by Bradford's two clubs for 'a game that would pay' brought moments of success but increasingly became a struggle for survival all too typical of the city; it has left Park Avenue derelict and Valley Parade synonymous with tragedy while the rewards and honours of the football business have gone elsewhere.

Appendices

Appendix 1a: Annual Playing Performances: before 1903

Manningham F.C.

Northern Union

	P	W	D	L	F	A	Pts	Pos
1895-96	42	33	0	9	367	158	66	1 (22)

Yorkshire Senior Competition

	P	W	D	L	F	A	Pts	Pos
1896-97	30	21	4	5	291	129	46	2 (16)
1897-98	30	15	4	11	276	181	34	5
1898-99	30	15	2	13	222	212	30*	7
1899-1900	30	13	3	14	207	203	29	9
1900-01	30	9	1	20	115	258	19	12
1901-02	n/a	n/a	n/a	n/a	n/a	n/a	n/a	n/a

Northern Union Second Division

	P	W	D	L	F	A	Pts	Pos
1902-03	34	14	5	15	141	170	33	10 (18)

Bradford F.C.

Northern Union

	P	W	D	L	F	A	Pts	Pos
1895-96	42	18	9	15	254	175	45	11 (22)

Yorkshire Senior Competition

1896-97	30	15	3	12	170	157	33	7 (16)
1897-98	30	23	2	5	319	139	48	1= (lost play-off)
1898-99	30	21	0	9	330	139	42	3
1899-1900	30	24	2	4	324	98	50	1
1900-01	30	26	1	3	387	100	51*	1

Northern Union

1901-02	26	14	1	11	201	157	27*	6 (14)

Northern Union First Division

1902-03	34	16	5	13	220	161	37	7 (18)

(* 2 points deducted for a breach of professional rules)
(Note: the number of teams in the division is shown in parentheses)

Appendix 1b: Annual Playing Performances: 1903-15

Bradford City

Football League Division Two   F.A. Cup

	P	W	D	L	F	A	Pts	Pos	P	W	D	L	F	A	Reached Last:
1903-04	34	12	7	15	45	59	31	10(18)				–			
1904-05	34	12	8	14	45	49	32	8				–			
1905-06	38	13	8	17	46	60	34	11(20)	3	2	0	1	8	3	16
1906-07	38	21	5	12	70	53	47	5	3	2	0	1	3	1	16
1907-08	38	24	6	8	90	42	54	1	2	0	1	1	1	2	64

Football League Division One

	P	W	D	L	F	A	Pts	Pos	P	W	D	L	F	A	Reached Last:
1908-09	38	12	10	16	47	47	34	18 (20)	4	2	1	1	4	2	16
1909-10	38	17	8	13	64	47	42	7	2	1	0	1	5	4	32
1910-11	38	20	5	13	51	42	45	5	7	6	1	0	9	1	1
1911-12	38	15	8	15	46	50	38	11	8	3	4	1	9	3	8
1912-13	38	12	11	15	50	60	35	13	1	0	0	1	0	1	64
1913-14	38	12	14	12	40	40	38	9	2	1	0	1	2	1	32
1914-15	38	13	14	11	55	49	40	10	6	3	2	1	5	3	8

Bradford (Park Avenue)

Northern Union First Division

	P	W	D	L	F	A	Pts	Pos
1903-04	34	25	2	7	303	96	52	1=(18) (won play off)
1904-05	34	23	2	9	294	156	48	2

Northern Union League

	P	W	D	L	F	A	Pts	Pos
1905-06	34	19	2	13	371	199	40	12 (31)
1906-07	30	12	2	16	387	367	26	18 (26)

Southern League

	P	W	D	L	F	A	Pts	Pos
1907-08	38	12	12	14	53	54	36	13(20)

Football League Division Two   F.A. Cup

	P	W	D	L	F	A	Pts	Pos	P	W	D	L	F	A	Reached Last:
1908-09	38	13	6	19	51	59	32	16(20)				–			
1909-10	38	17	4	17	64	59	38	10	2	1	0	1	9	3	32
1910-11	38	14	9	15	53	55	37	12	2	1	0	1	6	5	32
1911-12	38	13	9	16	44	45	35	11	3	2	0	1	3	1	16
1912-13	38	14	8	16	60	60	36	13	5	3	1	1	7	7	8
1913-14	38	23	3	12	71	47	49	2	2	1	0	1	6	4	32

Football League Division One

	P	W	D	L	F	A	Pts	Pos	P	W	D	L	F	A	Reached Last:
1914-15	38	17	7	14	69	65	41	9(20)	3	2	0	1	2	1	16

Appendix 1c: Annual Playing Performances: 1915-19

Bradford City

Midland Section – Principal Tournament   Subsidiary Tournament –

	P	W	D	L	F	A	Pts	Pos	P	W	D	L	F	A	Pts	Pos
1915-16	26	12	4	10	52	32	28	4(14)	10	4	1	5	18	20	9	4(6)
1916-17	30	12	7	11	41	41	31	8(16)	6	0	3	3	5	13	3	16(16)
1917-18	28	8	4	16	34	55	20	13(15)	6	1	4	1	8	8	6	9(16)
1918-19	30	9	4	17	48	56	22	13(16)	6	1	1	4	4	15	3	4(4)

Bradford Park Avenue

Midland Section –
Principal Tournament   Subsidiary Tournament –

	P	W	D	L	F	A	Pts	Pos	P	W	D	L	F	A	Pts	Pos
1915-16	26	9	4	13	46	46	22	12(14)	10	6	0	4	27	17	12	2(6)
1916-17	30	14	6	10	51	32	34	5(16)	6	3	2	1	10	5	8	1(16)
1917-18	28	13	4	11	40	29	30	6(15)	6	1	1	4	8	12	3	15(16)
1918-19	30	15	7	8	53	41	37	5(16)	6	3	2	1	13	6	8	1(4)

Appendix 1d: Annual Playing Performances: 1919-39

Bradford City

Football League Division One   F.A. Cup

	P	W	D	L	F	A	Pts	Pos	P	W	D	L	F	A	Reached Last:
1919-20	42	14	11	17	54	63	39	15(22)	5	3	1	1	9	5	8
1920-21	42	12	15	15	61	63	39	15	2	1	0	1	3	5	32
1921-22	42	11	10	21	48	72	32	21	5	1	3	1	9	6	32

Football League Division Two

	P	W	D	L	F	A	Pts	Pos	P	W	D	L	F	A	Reached
1922-23	42	12	13	17	41	45	37	15	2	0	1	1	1	3	64
1923-24	42	11	15	16	35	48	37	18	1	0	0	1	1	2	64
1924-25	42	13	12	17	37	50	38	16	3	2	0	1	4	2	16
1925-26	42	13	10	19	47	66	36	18	1	0	0	1	0	1	64
1926-27	42	7	9	26	50	88	23	22	1	0	0	1	2	6	64

Football League Division Three (North)

	P	W	D	L	F	A	Pts	Pos	P	W	D	L	F	A	Reached
1927-28	42	18	12	12	85	60	48	6				–			
1928-29	42	27	9	6	128	43	63	1	2	1	0	1	2	2	32

Football League Division Two

	P	W	D	L	F	A	Pts	Pos	P	W	D	L	F	A	Reached
1929-30	42	12	12	18	60	77	36	18	4	2	1	1	7	4	16
1930-31	42	17	10	15	61	63	44	10	4	1	2	1	5	6	32
1931-32	42	16	13	13	80	61	45	7	1	0	0	1	0	1	64
1932-33	42	14	13	15	65	61	41	11	2	0	1	1	3	4	64
1933-34	42	20	6	16	73	67	46	6	1	0	0	1	2	3	64
1934-35	42	12	8	22	50	68	32	20	3	1	1	1	5	4	32
1935-36	42	15	13	14	55	65	43	12	3	2	0	1	4	2	16
1936-37	42	9	12	21	54	94	30	21	2	0	1	1	2	3	64

Football League Division Three (North)

	P	W	D	L	F	A	Pts	Pos	P	W	D	L	F	A	
1937-38	42	14	10	18	66	69	38	14	3	0	2	1	2	4	64
1938-39	42	22	8	12	89	56	52	3			–				

Bradford Park Avenue

Football League Division One   F.A. Cup

	P	W	D	L	F	A	Pts	Pos	P	W	D	L	F	A	Reached Last:
1919-20	42	15	12	15	60	63	42	11(22)	4	3	0	1	11	9	8
1920-21	42	8	8	26	43	76	24	22	2	1	0	1	1	1	32

Football League Division Two

	P	W	D	L	F	A	Pts	Pos	P	W	D	L	F	A	
1921-22	42	12	9	21	46	62	33	21	2	1	0	1	3	3	32

Football League Division Three (North)

	P	W	D	L	F	A	Pts	Pos	P	W	D	L	F	A	
1922-23	38	19	9	10	67	38	47	2(20)	3	1	1	1	3	5	32
1923-24	42	21	10	11	69	43	52	5(22)	1	0	0	1	0	4	64
1924-25	42	19	12	11	84	42	50	5	3	1	1	1	3	3	32
1925-26	42	26	8	8	101	43	60	2			–				
1926-27	42	24	7	11	101	59	55	3			–				
1927-28	42	27	9	6	101	45	63	1			–				

Football League Division Two

	P	W	D	L	F	A	Pts	Pos	P	W	D	L	F	A	
1928-29	42	22	4	16	88	70	48	3	4	2	1	1	5	8	16
1929-30	42	19	12	11	91	70	50	4	4	2	1	1	5	7	16
1930-31	42	18	10	14	97	66	46	6	3	2	0	1	3	1	16
1931-32	42	21	7	14	72	63	49	6	3	2	0	1	6	3	16
1932-33	42	17	8	17	77	71	42	8	2	1	0	1	6	3	32
1933-34	42	23	3	16	86	67	49	5	1	0	0	1	0	3	64
1934-35	42	11	16	15	55	63	38	15	1	0	0	1	1	4	64
1935-36	42	14	9	19	62	84	37	16	6	2	3	1	8	6	16
1936-37	42	12	9	21	52	88	33	20	1	0	0	1	0	4	64
1937-38	42	17	9	16	69	56	43	7	4	2	1	1	10	7	16
1938-39	42	12	11	19	61	82	35	17	1	0	0	1	1	3	64

Appendix 1e: Annual Playing Performances: 1939-46

Bradford City

Football League Division Three (North)								Regional League North East Division							
P	W	D	L	F	A	Pts	Pos	P	W	D	L	F	A	Pts	Pos
1939-40 3	0	1	2	3	6	1	–	19* 9	3	7	41	36	21	6(11)

*The twentieth fixture was not played.

North Regional League

							Ave	
1940-41	29	8	3	18	72	99	0.727	29(36)

Matches played varied between 20 and 38 so positions were decided by average points.

Football League-Northern Section								Football League-Second Competition							
1941-42	18	5	4	9	32	42	14	28(38) 14	6	1	7	28	35	13	–

Bradford City did not finish among the top 22 who qualified, in the second competition, for the Football League final official table.

Football League North-First Championship								Football League North-Second Championship							
1942-43	18	4	2	12	30	63	10	45(48) 16	7	2	7	29	29	16	31(54)

League War Cup-North

1943-44	10	1	1	8	11	26	3	54(56) 18	4	2	12	27	47	10	51(56)

The championship games in 1943-44 included those played in the League Cup.

Football League North-First Championship

1944-45	18	6	1	11	35	60	13	44(54) 20	8	3	9	43	46	19	38(60)

Football League Division Three   F.A Cup
North: East

1945-46	18	6	4	8	45	40	16	7(10)

Football League Division Three   Football League Division Three
North-Second Championship   North (East) Cup Qualifying
    Competition

1945-46	8	2	1	5	12	18	5	18(20)	10	4	3	3	27	22	11	3(10)

Bradford Park Avenue

Football League Division Two   Regional League North East
    Division

	P	W	D	L	F	A	Pts	Pos	P	W	D	L	F	A	Pts	Pos
1939-40	3	0	1	2	2	7	1	–	19*	10	2	7	44	38	22	3(11)

*The twentieth fixture was not played.

North Regional League

						Ave	
1940-41	31	9	7	15	64	74	0.864	22(36)

Matches played varied between 20 and 38 so positions were decided by average points.

Football League-Northern Section   Football League-Second
    Competition

1941-42	18	8	5	5	33	28	21	12(38)	19	5	6	8	35	40	16	18(22)*

*The final official table positions were decided on the basis of what the points would have been by averaging as if all teams had played 23 games.

Football League North-   Football League North-
First Championship   Second Championship

1942-43	18	8	7	3	46	21	23	10(48)	19	7	5	7	35	31	19	24(54)

League War Cup – North

1943-44	10	6	3	1	23	14	15	7(56)	20	11	4	5	50	30	26	10(56)

The Championship games in 1943-44 included those played in the League Cup.

Football League North-First Championship

1944-45   18   10   4   4   45   31   24   9(54)   22   10   4   8   49   39   24   24(60)

Football League (North)								F.A. Cup							Reached Last:
1945-46	42	17	6	19	71	84	40	14(22)	8	3	3	2*	16	16	–	8

*All rounds were played on a two-match aggregate basis.

Appendix 1f: Annual Playing Performances: 1946-58

Bradford City

Football League Division Three (North)								Ave. home attend.	F.A. Cup						Reached Last:
	P	W	D	L	F	A	Pts	Pos		P	W	D	L	F	A
1946-47	42	20	10	12	62	47	50	5(22)	9,800				–			
1947-48	42	15	10	17	65	66	40	14	10,100				–			
1948-49	42	10	9	23	48	77	29	22	10,400				–			
1949-50	42	12	8	22	61	76	32	19	13,100				–			
1950-51	46	21	10	15	90	63	52	7(24)	12,500				–			
1951-52	46	16	10	20	61	68	42	15	11,600				–			
1952-53	46	14	18	14	75	80	46	16	10,900				–			
1953-54	46	22	9	15	60	55	53	5	10,600				–			
1954-55	46	13	10	23	47	55	36	21	9,300	3	0	2	1	3	4	64
1955-56	46	18	13	15	78	64	49	8	10,000				–			
1956-57	46	22	8	16	78	68	52	9	13,300				–			
1957-58	46	21	15	10	73	49	57	3	12,500	1	0	0	1	0	1	64

Bradford Park Avenue

Football League Division Two

	P	W	D	L	F	A	Pts	Pos	Ave. home attend.	F.A. Cup P	W	D	L	F	A	Reached Last:
1946-47	42	14	11	17	65	77	39	16(22)	14,900	1	0	0	1	0	3	64
1947-48	42	16	8	18	68	72	40	14	17,700	2	1	0	1	3	3	32
1948-49	42	13	11	18	65	78	37	17	15,000	4	1	2	1	4	7	32
1949-50	42	10	11	21	51	77	31	22	15,900	1	0	0	1	0	1	64

Football League Division Three (North)

	P	W	D	L	F	A	Pts	Pos	Ave. home attend.	F.A. Cup P	W	D	L	F	A	Reached Last:
1950-51	46	23	8	15	90	72	54	6(24)	12,300	–						
1951-52	46	19	12	15	74	64	50	8	12,100	2	1	0	1	2	3	32
1952-53	46	19	12	15	75	61	50	7	9,900	–						
1953-54	46	18	14	14	77	68	50	9	9,100	1	0	0	1	2	5	64
1954-55	46	15	11	20	56	70	41	16	8,200	–						
1955-56	46	13	7	26	61	122	33	23	7,500	1	0	0	1	0	4	64
1956-57	46	16	3	27	66	93	35	20	8,500	–						
1957-58	46	13	11	22	68	95	37	22	9,000	–						

Appendix 1g: Annual Playing Performances: 1958-85

Bradford City

Football League Division Three

	P	W	D	L	F	A	Pts	Pos	Average home attendances
1958-59	46	18	11	17	84	76	47	11 (24)	11,300
1959-60	46	15	12	19	66	74	42	19	10,200
1960-61	46	11	14	21	65	87	36	22	7,400

Football League Division Four

	P	W	D	L	F	A	Pts	Pos	
1961-62	44	21	9	14	94	86	51	5(23)	6,700
1962-63	46	11	10	25	64	93	32	23(24)	4,000
1963-64	46	25	6	15	76	62	56	5	5,700
1964-65	46	12	8	26	70	88	32	19	4,200
1965-66	46	12	13	21	63	94	37	23	4,000
1966-67	46	19	10	17	74	62	48	11	5,700
1967-68	46	23	11	12	72	51	57	5	7,300
1968-69	46	18	20	8	65	46	56	4	7,200

Appendices

Football League Division Three

1969-70	46	17	12	17	57	50	46	10(24)	9,400
1970-71	46	13	14	19	49	62	40	19	6,000
1971-72	46	11	10	25	45	77	32	24	5,000

Football League Division Four

1972-73	46	16	11	19	61	65	43	16(24)	3,500
1973-74	46	17	14	15	58	33	48	8	3,800
1974-75	46	17	13	16	56	51	47	10	3,200
1975-76	46	12	17	17	63	65	41	17	2,900
1976-77	46	23	13	10	78	51	59	4	5,600

Football League Division Three

| 1977-78 | 46 | 12 | 10 | 24 | 56 | 86 | 34 | 22(24) | 5,100 |

Football League Division Four

1978-79	46	17	9	20	62	68	43	15(24)	3,900
1979-80	46	24	12	10	77	50	60	5	5,700
1980-81	46	14	16	16	53	60	44	14	2,900
1981-82	46	26	13	7	88	45	91*	2	5,400

Football League Division Three

1982-83	46	16	13	17	68	69	61*	12(24)	4,800
1983-84	46	20	11	15	73	65	71*	7	4,200
1984-85	46	28	10	8	77	45	94*	1	6,100

*3 points for a win

F.A. Cup   F.L. Cup

	P	W	D	L	F	A	Reached Last:	P	W	D	L	F	A	Reached Last:
1958-59	4	3	0	1	10	6	32							–
1959-60	8	4	3	1	16	14	16							–
1960-61	3	1	1	1	4	3	–	2	1	0	1	3	3	32
1961-62	3	2	0	1	3	4	64	1	0	0	1	3	4	–
1962-63	3	2	0	1	9	10	64	2	0	1	1	2	4	–
1963-64	1	0	0	1	1	2	–	1	0	0	1	3	7	–
1964-65	1	0	0	1	0	1	–	5	4	0	1	12	12	8
1965-66	1	0	0	1	2	3	–	1	0	0	1	0	1	–
1966-67	1	0	0	1	1	2	–	2	0	1	1	3	6	–
1967-68	2	1	0	1	9	4	–	1	0	0	1	0	2	–
1968-69	1	0	0	1	1	2	–	3	1	1	1	7	7	64
1969-70	4	2	1	1	7	8	64	5	3	1	1	6	7	16
1970-71	4	1	2	1	8	10	–	1	0	0	1	2	3	–
1971-72	1	0	0	1	1	5	–	2	0	1	1	2	3	–
1972-73	4	3	0	1	7	4	32	3	0	2	1	2	4	–
1973-74	5	3	1	1	9	7	32	1	0	0	1	1	2	–
1974-75	1	0	0	1	0	1	–	2	1	0	1	2	2	64
1975-76	6	5	0	1	11	4	8	2	1	0	1	2	3	–
1976-77	2	0	1	1	0	2	–	3	1	1	1	5	4	64
1977-78	1	0	0	1	0	1	–	2	0	1	1	2	5	–
1978-79	2	1	0	1	3	4	–	4	1	2	1	6	5	64
1979-80	3	2	0	1	6	3	64	1	0	0	1	0	2	64
1980-81	1	0	0	1	2	4	–	4	2	1	1	4	5	64
1981-82	1	0	0	1	0	1	–	6	2	2	2	11	9	32
1982-83	4	1	1	2	4	5	64	6	4	1	1	9	4	32
1983-84	2	0	1	1	2	4	–	2	0	1	1	1	2	–
1984-85	3	2	0	1	10	5	64	4	1	1	2	5	6	64

Bradford Park Avenue

Football League Division Four   Average home attendances

	P	W	D	L	F	A	Pts	Pos	
1958-59	46	18	7	21	75	77	43	14(24)	7,000
1959-60	46	17	15	14	70	68	49	11	6,500
1960-61	46	26	8	12	84	74	60	4	9,200
1963-64	46	18	9	19	75	81	45	13(24)	6,200

Football League Division Three

	P	W	D	L	F	A	Pts	Pos	
1961-62	46	20	7	19	80	78	47	11(24)	9,100
1962-63	46	14	12	20	79	97	40	21	7,400

Football League Division Four

1963-64	46	18	9	19	75	81	45	13(24)	6,200
1964-65	46	20	17	9	86	62	57	7	8,400
1965-66	46	21	5	20	102	92	47	11	5,300
1966-67	46	11	13	22	52	79	35	23	5,300
1967-68	46	4	15	27	30	82	23	24	3,600
1968-69	46	5	10	31	32	106	20	24	3,300
1969-70	46	6	11	29	41	96	23	24	3,100

Northern Premier League

1970-71	42	15	8	19	54	73	38	14(22)	2,200
1971-72	46	13	13	20	54	71	39	18(24)	1,400
1972-73	46	19	17	10	63	50	55	5	1,300
1973-74	46	9	15	22	42	84	33	21	700

	F.A. Cup							F.L. Cup						
	P	W	D	L	F	A	Reached Last:	P	W	D	L	F	A	Reached Last:
1958-59	2	1	0	1	4	3	–				–			
1959-60	3	2	0	1	12	7	64				–			
1960-61	2	0	1	1	0	2	–	3	1	1	1	3	3	64
1961-62	1	0	0	1	0	1	–	1	0	0	1	2	4	–
1962-63	1	0	0	1	0	1	–	3	1	1	1	5	4	32
1963-64	2	1	0	1	3	3	–	4	2	1	1	14	10	32
1964-65	1	0	0	1	2	3	–	1	0	0	1	0	1	–
1965-66	1	0	0	1	2	3	–	2	1	0	1	1	3	–
1966-67	3	2	0	1	7	6	64	4	1	2	1	5	6	64
1967-68	3	1	1	1	7	5	–	1	0	0	1	0	5	–
1968-69	1	0	0	1	0	3	–	1	0	0	1	0	3	–
1969-70	1	0	0	1	1	2	–	1	0	0	1	0	2	–
1970-71	1	0	0	1	0	1	–				–			
1971-72				–							–			
1972-73				–							–			
1973-74				–							–			

Appendix 2a: Annual Financial Results: before 1903

Manningham F.C. (£'s)

	1900-01 (Northern Union)	1901-02	1902-03
Gate receipts	1,275	685	670
Members' subscriptions	245	160	125
Players' wages	425	455	605
Ground repairs	125	60	60
Travel costs	140	100	140
Profit/(loss)	180	(200)	(660)

Bradford F.C. (£'s)

	1900-01 (Northern Union)	1901-02
Gate receipts	2,925	2,525
Members' subscriptions	510	420
Players' wages	1,050	1,000
Ground repairs	n/a	n/a
Travel costs	185	285
Profit /(loss)	960	400

Appendix 2b: Annual Financial Results: 1903-15

Bradford F.C. (£'s)

Cash Flows 1903-08 (£'s)

Donations	380
Cash generated by operations	3,855
Bank overdraft	565
Loans	780
	5,580

Investment in stands, terraces, equipment	3,045
Investment in transfer fees	2,535
	5,580

Selected Receipts, Expenses and Investments 1903-08 (£'s)

	1903-04 (Div. II)	1904-05	1905-06	1906-07	1907-08
Gate receipts	3,440	3,650	4,130	5,920	7,495
Members' subscriptions	430	1,065	1,240	1,260	1,960
Players' wages	2,150	3,090	3,250	3,560	3,990
Ground repairs	n/a	n/a	20	400	275
Travel costs	265	n/a	340	575	910
Profit/(loss)	105	15	85	390	1,330
Investment in:					
Stands,etc	1,175	–	165	70	1,635
Transfer fees paid/(rec)	970	405	540	(480)	1,100

Notes
1. Before 1903 £1,550 had been invested in land at Valley Parade, and approximately £630 on stands, terracing, equipment.
2. In 1907-8 expenses also included: secretary and clerks salary £245, trainer and groundsmen £225, referees and linesmen £115, gatemen £125, police £135, outfit £65.

Bradford City

Cash Flows 1908-15 (£'s)

Cash generated by operations	7,690
Bank overdraft	6,375
Share issues	3,610
	17,675

Investment in stands, terraces, equipment	11,365
Investment in (players') houses	800
Investment in transfer fees	4,050
Repayment of loans	1,460
	17,675

Selected Receipts, Expenses and Investments 1908-15 (£'s)

	1908-09 (Div. I)	1909-10	1910-11	1911-12	1912-13	1913-14	1914-15
Gate receipts	10,630	8,510	13,070	10,400	7,180	8,970	7,960
Season tickets	2,375	2,685	2,165	2,025	2,030	1,710	995
Players' wages	5,945	4,780	4,680	6,460	6,980	6,985	5,925
Ground repairs	250	615	240	205	320	415	330
Travel costs	970	1,115	1,325	1,245	1,000	1,285	1,000
Profit/(loss)	2,560	1,535	6,100	1,320	(1,625)	(580)	(1,060)
Investment in:							
Stands, etc	9,960	1,280	–	125	–	–	–
Transfer fees paid/(rec)	2,545	1,425	1,100	100	(2,835)	(960)	2,675

Notes
1. In 1911-12 Total receipts were £12,665; these included gate receipts and season ticket sales, programme sales £120 and sundry receipts £120.
2. In 1911-12 Total expenses were £11,345; match expenses comprised secretary and clerks salaries £425, trainers and groundsmen £350, referees and linesmen £110, gatemen £200, police £95, refreshments and training £265, outfit £110; administration costs were £2,085, and included subscriptions and fines £295, medical £130, insurance £445 and interest charges £365.

Bradford (Park Avenue) AFC Ltd

Cash Flows 1909-15 (£'s)

Cash generated by operations	4,720
Bank overdraft	3,440
Share issues	3,690
	11,850

Investment in stands, terraces, equipment	1,035
Investment in transfer fees	10,815
	11,850

Note
1. The investment in stands etc is unusually small because most of the ground development costs were borne by the combined Cricket, Athletic and Football Club prior to incorporation.

Appendices

Selected Receipts, Expenses and Investments 1906-15 (£'s)

	1906-07 (N. Union)	1907-08 (S. League)	1908-09 (F.L. Div. II)	1909-10
Gate receipts	1,330	4,225	n/a	n/a
Members' subscriptions or season tickets	475	1,200	n/a	n/a
Players' wages	985	3,760	n/a	n/a
Travel costs	235	1,110	n/a	n/a
Profit/(loss)	(570)	(1,360)	(500)	85
Investment in:				
Stands, etc.	n/a	n/a	n/a	100
Transfer fees paid/(rec)	–	n/a	n/a	3,340

	1910-11	1911-12	1912-13	1913-14	1914-15 (Div. I)
Gate receipts	n/a	6,350	5,650	8,325	6,400
Members' subscriptions or season tickets	n/a	1,460	1,275	1,180	1,150
Players' wages	n/a	4,580	4,410	4,485	4,835
Travel costs	n/a	550	610	775	745
Profit/(loss)	545	1,150	405	2,210	375
Investment in:					
Stands,etc	20	25	335	380	175
Transfer fees paid/(rec.)	950	3,115	(820)	1,150	3,080

The Bradford City Association Football Club (1908) Limited.

BALANCE SHEET, April 30th, 1915.

Capital and Liabilities.	£	s.	d.	£	s.	d.
SHARE CAPITAL :—						
Authorised :						
7,000 £1 Shares	7,000	0	0			
Issued :						
3,666 £1 Shares	3,666	0	0			
Less calls in arrear	95	0	0			
				3,571	0	0
Forfeited Shares ...				39	8	0
Sundry Creditors ...				1,739	15	0
Bank Overdraft ...	6,794	12	9			
Add charges to date	138	12	8			
				6,933	5	5
				£12,283	8	5

Property and Assets.	£	s.	d.	£	s.	d.
Freehold Land ...				1,553	14	4
Freehold Houses ...	800	0	0			
Less Mortgages and Interest thereon	430	4	10			
				369	15	2
Stands, Terracing, Fixtures, &c.				6,400	0	0
Sundry Debtors ...				472	2	5
Deposits				8	8	0
Cash in hand ...				12	8	3
REVENUE ACCOUNT :—						
Loss for Year ...	3,736	19	3			
(excluding depreciation)						
Less Credit Balance, April 30th, 1914, after writing £1,000 off Stands, Terracing, Fixtures, &c.	269	19	0			
				3,467	0	3
				£12,283	8	5

Signed on behalf of the Board,

W. N. POLLACK, *Director.*

ARTHUR LANCASTER, *Director.*

REPORT of the AUDITORS to the SHAREHOLDERS of the BRADFORD CITY A.F.C. (1908) LIMITED.

In accordance with the provisions of Sub-Section 2 of Section 113 of The Companies Consolidation Act, 1908, we report as follows:—

We have audited the Balance Sheet of the Bradford City A.F.C. (1908) Limited, dated the 30th day of April, 1915, above set forth. We have obtained all the information and explanations we have required, and in our opinion such Balance Sheet is properly drawn up so as to exhibit a true and correct view of the state of the Company's affairs, according to the best of our information and the explanations given us, and as shown by the books of the Company.

LONDON & YORKSHIRE BANK CHAMBERS,
2, TYRREL STREET, BRADFORD,
July 2nd, 1915.

SMITH & HAYWARD,
INCORPORATED ACCOUNTANTS,
Auditors.

The Bradford (Park Avenue) Association Football Club, Ltd.

BALANCE SHEET as at 30th April, 1915.

Capital and Liabilities.	£ s. d.	£ s. d.	Property and Assets.	£ s. d.	£ s. d.
Share Capital—			Players' Transfers...	7,409 10 0	
Nominal, £10,000 divided into			*Less* Amount written off to		
10,000 Shares of £1 each ...			Revenue Account	1,500 0 0	
Issued, 3,680 Shares of £1 each					5,909 10 0
(fully paid)	3,680 0 0		Sundry Debtors and Cash in Hand... ...		290 1 3
Forfeited Share Capital... ...	7 12 0		Dressing Room and Office Furniture, etc. ...		156 17 5
		3,687 12 0	Alterations and Improvements		
Sundry Creditors		441 3 11	to Stands and Ground:		
The London City and Midland Bank, Ltd....		3,437 8 10	30th April, 1914	532 19 11	
Dividend Unpaid		184 0 0	Further expenditure during year	175 0 0	
				707 19 11	
			Less Proportion written off ...	187 6 8	
					520 13 3
			Net Revenue Account—		
			Deficiency for the year ended		
			30th April, 1915	1,330 17 10	
			Deduct Credit Balance brought		
			from last year's account ...	466 18 0	
					863 19 10
		£7,750 1 9			£7,750 1 9

Signed on behalf of the Board,

A. H. BRIGGS ⎱ *Directors.*
W. H. ⎰

AUDITORS' REPORT.

We have audited the above Balance Sheet and have obtained all the information and explanations we have required. The amount paid, less the amount received, by the Company for Transfers of Players has been treated in "Players' Transfers Account," and the sum of £1,500 has been written off to the Revenue Account for the past year; and the Directors state that the value of the Transfers held by the Company on 30th April, 1915, exceeded the amount shown in the Balance Sheet.

Subject to the foregoing, in our opinion, such Balance Sheet is properly drawn up so as to exhibit a true and correct view of the state of the Company's affairs according to the best of our information and the explanations given us and as shown by the Books of the Company.

Bradford,
31st August, 1915.

ARMITAGE & NORTON,
Chartered Accountants.

Appendix 2c: Annual Financial Results: 1915-19

Bradford City
Cash Flows (£'s)

Bank overdraft	2,400
Cash lost on operations	2,400

Selected Receipts, Expenses and Investments (£'s)

	1915-16	1916-17	1917-18	1918-19
Gate receipts	1,680	1,200	1,060	3,470
Season tickets	50	10	20	20
Total expenses	2,630	2,880	2,180	3,810
Players' wages	0	0	0	0
Ground repairs	100	90	150	260
Travel costs	450	690	570	1,750
Profit/(loss)	(335)	(1,070)	(885)	(110)
Investment in:				
Stands,etc	0	0	0	0
Transfer fees				
paid/(rec)	0	0	0	0

Bradford (Park Avenue)

Cash Flows (£'s)

Bank overdraft	1,925
Loss on operations	1,925

Selected Receipts, Expenses and Investments (£'s)

	1915-16	1916-17	1917-18	1918-19
Gate receipts	n/a	1,135	1,365	3,185
Members' subscriptions	n/a	30	35	50
Wages	n/a	610	530	560
Travel costs	n/a	875	865	1,440
Profit/(loss)	n/a	(1,125)	(645)	530
Investment in:				
Stands, etc	n/a	0	0	0
Transfer fees	n/a	0	0	0

The Bradford City Association Football Club (1908) Ltd.

BALANCE SHEET, April 30th, 1919.

Capital and Liabilities.		£ s. d.	£ s. d.
SHARE CAPITAL:—			
Authorised :			
7000 £1 Shares	7000 0 0		
Issued :			
3704 £1 Shares	3704 0 0		
Less calls in arrear	95 0 0		
		3609 0 0	
Forfeited Shares ...		39 8 0	
Sundry Creditors ...		2236 6 10	
Bank Overdraft ...	9148 2 9		
Add charges to date	190 10 8		
		9338 13 5	
		£15713 8 3	

Property and Assets.		£ s. d.	£ s. d.
Freehold Land ...			1553 14 4
Freehold Houses ...	800 0 0		
Less Mortgages and			
Interest thereon	383 3 4		
			416 16 8
Stands, Terracing,			
Fixtures, &c.		6400 0 0	
Sundry Debtors ...		495 16 1	
Deposits		8 8 0	
Cash in hand ...		3 6 5	
REVENUE ACCOUNT:—			
Balance, April 30th,			
1918	6104 9 8		
Loss for Year ···	240 17 1		
			6345 6 9
			£15713 8 3

Signed on behalf of the Board,

ARTHUR LANCASTER, *Director.*
GEORGE GRANGE, *Director.*

REPORT OF THE AUDITORS TO THE SHAREHOLDERS OF THE BRADFORD CITY A·F.C. (1908) LTD.

In accordance with the provisions of Sub-Section 2 of Section 113 of The Companies (Consolidation) Act, 1908, we report as follows :—

We have Audited the Balance Sheet of the Bradford City A.F.C. (1908) Limited, dated the 30th, day of April, 1919, above set forth. We have obtained all the information and explanations we have required, and in our opinion such Balance Sheet is properly drawn up so as to exhibit a true and correct view of the state of the Company's affairs, according to the best of our information and the explanations given us, and as shown by the books of the Company.

SMITH & HAYWARD,

LONDON & YORKSHIRE BANK CHAMBERS,
2, TYRREL STREET, BRADFORD,
July 9th, 1919.

INCORPORATED ACCOUNTANTS,
Auditors.

The Bradford (Park Avenue) Association Football Club, Ltd.

BALANCE SHEET AS AT 30TH, APRIL, 1919.

Capital and Liabilities.	£ s. d.	£ s. d.	Property and Assets.	£ s. d.	£ s. d.
Share Capital—			Players' Transfers		5849 10 0
Nominal : £10,000 divided into 10,000 Shares of £1 each ...			Sundry Debtors		417 6 0
Issued, 3,680 Shares of £1 each (fully paid)	3680 0 0		Dressing Room and Office Furniture... ...		102 18 5
Forfeited Share Capital	7 12 0		Alterations and Improvements to Stands and Ground—Balance at 30th, April, 1915 ...		520 13 3
		3687 12 0	**Net Revenue Account—**		
Sundry Creditors		5962 0 1	Debit Balance at 30th, April, 1918 3462 12 10		
Dividend Unpaid (payment postponed by Resolution of Shareholders dated 10th September, 1915)		184 0 0	Deduct, Surplus for year 519 8 5		2943 4 5
		£9833 12 1			£9833 12 1

Signed on behalf of the Board,

A. H. BRIGGS,
P. PATERSON,   } *Directors.*

AUDITORS' REPORT.

We have audited the above Balance Sheet and have obtained all the information and explanations we have required.

No amount has been written off Players' Transfers Account nor Alterations and Improvements to Stands and Ground Account in the above Balance Sheet.

Subject to the foregoing, in our opinion, such Balance Sheet is properly drawn up so as to exhibit a true and correct view of the state of the Company's affairs according to the best of our information and the explanations given us and as shewn by the books of the Company.

Bradford,
3rd September, 1919

ARMITAGE & NORTON,
CHARTERED ACCOUNTANTS

Appendix 2d: Annual Financial Results: 1919-39

Bradford City

Cash Flows (£'s)

Donations	1,000
Cash generated by operations	2,870
Income from transfer fees	1,255
Mortgages	5,480
Loans	3,800
Share Issues	3,065
	17,470

Investment in land at ground	3,860
Investment in stands & terraces, equipment	7,740
Investment in (players') houses	800
Reduction in bank overdraft	5,070
	17,470

Selected Receipts, Expenses and Investments 1919-39 (£s)

	1919-20 (Div. I)	1920-21	1921-22	1922-23 (Div. II)	1923-24
Gate receipts	22,070	23,730	24,710	15,115	13,860
Season tickets	800	1,555	1,650	1,455	1,500
Players' wages	10,730	14,725	14,530	11,410	10,480
Travel costs	2,910	3,075	2,520	1,515	n/a
Ground repairs	0	730	1,185	310	n/a
Profit/(loss)	3,040	4,750	1,210	(2,040)	(1,850)
Investments in:					
Stands, terraces	2,140	1,400	1,200	–	–
Transfer fees paid/(rec.)	(4,580)	(2,210)	9,010	(2,170)	1,475

	1924-25	1925-26	1926-27	1927-28 (Div. III (N))	1928-29
Gate receipts	15,260	12,710	13,230	12,225	19,420
Season tickets	1,670	1,710	1,410	1,715	1,680
Players' wages	10,205	9,945	9,650	7,675	8,060
Travel costs	1,670	1,360	1,400	1,410	2,260
Ground repairs	240	860	n/a	n/a	130
Profit/(loss)	425	(2,170)	(430)	1,560	4,380
Investments in:					
Stands, terraces	–	–	–	–	1,800
Transfer fees paid/(rec.)	(1,050)	(340)	(1,160)	3,850	2,960

	1929-30 (Div. II)	1930-31	1931-32	1932-33	1933-34
Gate receipts	18,870	16,900	15,370	16,770	12,540
Season tickets	2,170	2,080	2,045	2,050	1,475
Players' wages	8,650	9,250	8,780	9,200	8,990
Travel costs	2,240	2,140	n/a	1,700	1,440
Ground repairs	130	500	325	n/a	n/a
Profit/(loss)	4,820	1,780	1,920	830	980
Investments in:					
Stands, terraces	1,200	–	3,860	–	–
Transfer fees					
paid/(rec.)	3,470	1,175	950	n/a	n/a

	1934-35	1935-36	1936-37	1937-38 (Div. III (N))	1938-39
Gate receipts	11,375	11,420	11,490	6,930	7,330
Season tickets	1,680	1,240	1,160	750	610
Players' wages	9,365	8,870	8,480	7,350	6,785
Travel costs	1,580	1,510	1,480	930	830
Ground repairs	410	n/a	640	215	260
Profit/(loss)	(2,720)	(3,390)	(2,135)	(4,780)	(3,975)
Investments in:					
Stands, terraces	–	–	–	–	–
Transfer fees					
paid/(rec)	(1,410)	(5,100)	(1,155)	(1,720)	(3,250)

Bradford (Park Avenue)

Cash Flows (£'s)

Share issue	6,320
Bank overdraft	9,955
Directors' loans	1,650
	17,925
Motor car	175
Operations and transfer fee losses	17,750
	17,925

Selected Receipts, Expenses and Investments (£'s)

	1919-20 (Div. I)	1920-21	1921-22 (Div. II)	1922-23 (Div. III)	1935-36 (Div.II) (N))	1936-37
Gate receipts	17,235	16,705	9,980	8,345	12,330	10,660
Season tickets	1,195	1,675	1,390	800	2,625	1,765
Players' wages	8,570	12,335	10,515	9,735	n/a	10,665
Travel costs	1,280	1,950	1,830	1,040	n/a	2,130
Profit/(loss)	6,995	990	(3,575)	(3,990)	n/a	(5,070)
Investment in: Stands,etc	–	–	–	–	–	
Transfer fees paid/(rec.)	1,730	(180)	4,230	(300)	n/a	2,000

Note:
Until 1938 Transfer expenditure was shown on the Balance Sheet to the extent that, in the director's opinion, the value of the transfers held exceeded the Balance Sheet amount; where this was not entirely the case transfers were charged against profits.

	1937-38	1938-39
Gate receipts	14,530	10,770
Season tickets	1,400	1,330
Players' wages	11,180	10,630
Travel costs	2,375	2,100
Profit/(loss)	(1,590)	(4,450)
Investment in: Stands,etc	–	–
Transfer fees paid/(rec.)	(1,185)	(4,730)

The Bradford City Association Football Club (1908) Ltd.

BALANCE SHEET. MAY 31st, 1939.

LIABILITIES.	£ s. d.	£ s. d.	ASSETS.	£ s. d.	£ s. d.
SHARE CAPITAL:—			Freehold Land (at cost)		5414 13 10
Authorised:—			Freehold Houses (at cost)		
7,000 £1 Shares ...	7000 0 0		As at May 31st, 1938	1652 10 0	
			Less Property realised	220 0 0	
Issued:—					
6,768 £1 Shares ...	6768 0 0			1432 10 0	
Less Calls in arrear	95 0 0		*Less* Loss on Property realised	220 0 0	
		6673 0 0			1212 10 0
Forfeited Shares ...		39 8 0	Stands, Terracing, Fixtures,		
Mortgage and Interest to date		5480 8 8	(at cost, *less* amounts		
Sundry Creditors ...		1526 5 3	written off):—		
Reserve for Accrued Liabilities		339 4 3	As at May 31st, 1938	5043 0 0	
Bank Overdrafts:—			*Less* Depreciation	252 0 0	
New Account ...	4051 12 1				4791 0 0
Old Account	258 2 8		Sundry Debtors ...		532 0 0
Accrued Charges ...	17 3 9		Deposits ...		35 15 0
		4326 18 6	Cash in hand ...		33 5 0
Loans and Interest to date		3797 18 5	Revenue Account (Adverse):—		
			Balance, May 31st, 1938	9167 11 6	
			Add Loss on Property realised	220 0 0	
			Deficiency for year	876 7 9	
				10263 19 3	
			Less further Donation from Supporters' Club towards Ground Purchase	100 0 0	
					10163 19 3
		£22183 3 1			£22183 3 1

Signed on behalf of the Board,

JOHN S. DRIVER,   } *Directors*
T. R. HILLIAM,

REPORT OF THE AUDITORS TO THE
MEMBERS OF THE BRADFORD CITY ASSOCIATION FOOTBALL CLUB (1908) LIMITED.

We report that we have audited the above Balance Sheet dated the 31st day of May, 1939, and have obtained all the information and explanations we have required. Nothing is included in this Balance Sheet in respect of the value of the Club's Players. Subject to the foregoing observation, in our opinion such Balance Sheet is properly drawn up so as to exhibit a true and correct view of the state of the Company's affairs according to the best of our information and the explantions given to us and as shown by the books of the Company.

1, PICCADILLY,
BRADFORD.
20th July, 1939.

SMITH & HAYWARD,
Incorporated Accountants,
Auditors.

THE BRADFORD (PARK AVENUE) ASSOCIATION FOOTBALL CLUB, LIMITED.

BALANCE SHEET as at 31st MAY, 1939.

Capital and Liabilities.	£ s. d.	Assets.	£ s. d.	£ s. d.
Nominal Capital : £10,000, divided into 10,000 Shares of £1 each ...		Dressing Room and Office Furniture and Motor Car, at cost, less depreciation		196 17 4
Issued Capital : 10,000 Shares of £1 each (fully paid)	10000 0 0	Sundry Debtors and Cash in hand		470 1 1
Forfeited Share Capital	7 12 0			666 18 5
Sundry Creditors : For Goods supplied and for liabilities accrued...	2083 9 6	Net Revenue Account :—		
Loans from Directors	1650 0 0	Debit balance from last year's Account 27528 5 8		
Midland Bank Limited	15316 11 0	Add, Deficiency for the year ... 862 8 5		28390 14 1
	£29057 12 6			£29057 12 6

Signed on behalf of the Board :

STANLEY WADDILOVE
H. J. WHITE } *Directors.*

AUDITORS' REPORT.

We have audited the above Balance Sheet and have obtained all the information and explanations we have required.

In our opinion such Balance Sheet is properly drawn up so as to exhibit a true and correct view of the state of the Company's affairs according to the best of our information and the explanations given to us and as shown by the books of the Company.

Bradford,
22nd June, 1939.

ARMITAGE & NORTON.
CHARTERED ACCOUNTANTS.

I hereby certify the above Balance Sheet and Auditors' Report to be true copies of the last audited Balance Sheet and the Auditors' Report thereon.

Dated this 19th day of October, 1939.

Appendix 2e: Annual Financial Results: 1939-46

Bradford City

Cash Flows (£'s)

Cash generated by operations	40
Income from transfer fees	2,375
Donations (inc. by loan creditors)	8,675
Share issues	10
	11,100
Mortgages and loans paid off	6,610
Improvement in cash position	4,490
	11,100

Selected Receipts, Expenses and Investments (£'s)

	1939-40	1940-41	1941-42	1942-43	1943-44
Gate receipts	2,330	1,080	2,220	3,035	3,420
Players' wages	2,705	885	785	885	1,080
Travel costs	305	290	375	460	545
Ground repairs	95	50	120	225	320
Profit/(loss)	(2,150)	(535)	320	670	750
Investments in:					
Stands, terraces	0	0	0	0	0
Transfer fees					
paid/(rec.)	500	0	0	0	0

	1944-45	1945-46
Gate receipts	5,910	5,390
Players' wages	1,190	4,200
Travel costs	810	1,860
Ground repairs	185	310
Profit/(loss)	3,155	(2,165)
Investments in:		
Stands, terraces	0	0
Transfer fees		
paid/(rec.)	600	(3,475)

Bradford (Park Avenue)

Cash Flows (£'s)

Surplus from operations	8,150

Investment in transfer fees	1,785
Purchase of dwelling houses	3,535
Repayment of directors' loans	1,265
Reduction of bank overdraft	1,925
	8,510

Appendices

Selected Receipts, Expenses and Investments (£'s)

	1939-40	1940-41	1941-42	1942-43	1943-44	1944-45
Gate receipts	3,270	1,290	3,355	3,825	6,010	7,930
Donations	1,580	190	240	n/a	n/a	n/a
Players' wages	3,715	700	870	n/a	n/a	n/a
Travel costs	365	375	545	n/a	n/a	n/a
Profit/(loss)	(1,765)	(490)	735	630	1,780	3,625
Investment in:						
Stands,etc	0	0	n/a	n/a	n/a	n/a
Transfer fees						
paid/(rec.)	(350)	0	0	n/a	n/a	(1,525)

	1945-46
Gate receipts	18,280
Donations	n/a
Players' wages	6,070
Travel costs	2,010
Profit/(loss)	4,445
Investment in:	
Stands, equipment	n/a
Transfer fees	
paid/(rec.)	3,660

Bradford City Association Football Club (1908) Limited
BALANCE SHEET, MAY 31st, 1946

LIABILITIES.	£ s. d.	£ s. d.
Share Capital —		
Authorised—		
7,000 £1 Shares ... 7000 0 0		
Issued—		
6,778 £1 Shares ... 6778 0 0		
Less Calls in Arrear 95 0 0		
	6683 0 0	
Forfeited Shares	39 8 8	
Sundry Creditors ...	309 2 6	
Accrued Liabilities and Reserves ...	2395 0 0	
Loans & Interest to date	2671 2 4	
	£12,097 12 10	

ASSETS.	£ s. d.	£ s. d.
Freehold Land (at cost)		5414 13 10
Freehold Houses (at cost) 1212 10 0		
Less Mortgage ... 2 16 3		
		1209 13 9
Stands, Terracing and Fixtures (at cost, less Amounts written off)—		
As at May 31st, 1945 3525 0 0		
Less Depreciation ... 176 0 0		
		3347 0 0
Sundry Debtors ...		185 12 10
Deposits		35 15 0
National Provincial Bank Limited—		
Cash in Hand		102 12 2
		93 15 6
Revenue Account (Adverse)		
As at May 31st, 1945 10,718 17 8		
Less Rebates from Loan Creditors ... 7905 4 9		
	2913 12 11	
Less Surplus for Year 1205 3 2		
		1708 9 9
		£12,097 12 10

Signed on behalf of the Board— J. RUSSELL ROSE,
ROBERT SHARP,
Directors.

REPORT OF THE AUDITORS TO THE
MEMBERS OF THE BRADFORD CITY ASSOCIATION FOOTBALL CLUB (1908) LIMITED.

We report that we have audited the above Balance Sheet dated the 31st day of May, 1946, and have obtained all the information and explanations we have required. In our opinion such Balance Sheet is properly drawn up so as to exhibit a true and correct view of the state of the Company's affairs according to the best of our information and the explanations given to us and as shown by the books of the Company.

1, Piccadilly, BRADFORD.
28th August, 1946.

SMITH & HAYWARD,
Incorporated Accountants
Auditors.

THE BRADFORD (PARK AVENUE) ASSOCIATION FOOTBALL CLUB, LIMITED.

BALANCE SHEET as at 31st MAY, 1946.

Capital and Liabilities.	£ s. d.
Nominal Capital : £10,000, divided into 10,000 Shares of £1 each ...	
Issued Capital : 10,000 Shares of £1 each (fully paid)	10000 0 0
Forfeited Share Capital	7 12 0
Provision for Deferred Repairs ...	1500 0 0
Sundry Creditors and Liabilities accrued	1425 5 0
Loans from Directors	387 7 6
Midland Bank Limited	13391 18 11
	£26712 3 5

Assets.	£ s. d.	£ s. d.
Dwelling Houses, at cost... ...		3537 14 0
Dressing Room and Office Furniture at cost, less depreciation ...		15 4 11
Sundry Debtors and Cash in hand		2172 5 4
		5725 4 3
Net Revenue Account :—		
Debit balance from last year's Account... ... ... 24681 3 1		
Deduct, Surplus for the year ... 3694 3 11		
		20986 19 2
		£26712 3 5

Signed on behalf of the Board :
STANLEY WADDILOVE
H. J. WHITE
} Directors.

AUDITORS' REPORT.

We have audited the above Balance Sheet and have obtained all the information and explanations we have required.

In our opinion such Balance Sheet is properly drawn up so as to exhibit a true and correct view of the state of the Company's affairs according to the best of our information and the explanations given to us and as shown by the books of the Company.

Bradford,
23rd October, 1946.

ARMITAGE & NORTON,
CHARTERED ACCOUNTANTS.

Appendix 2f: Annual Financial Results: 1946-58

Bradford City

Cash Flows (£'s)

Donations	19,970
Share issues	2,100
Loans and mortgages	7,635
Bank overdraft	2,775
	32,480

Cash deficits from operations	7,590
Investment in land	220
Investment in houses	6,020
Investment in stands, terraces, etc	11,245
Investment in transfer fees	7,405
	32,480

Selected Receipts, Expenses and Investments (£'s)

	1946-47 (Div. III (N))	1947-48	1948-49	1949-50
Gate receipts	15,490	15,940	19,945	20,390
Season tickets	n/a	790	960	2,000
Players' wages	8,320	11,185	14,270	16,740
Travel costs	1,905	2,775	3,400	3,640
Ground repairs	410	1,290	410	1,180
Profit/(loss)	3,130	(3,635)	(2,700)	(2,855)
Investments in:				
Stands, terraces	2,500	–	1,500	–
Transfer fees paid/(rec.)	3,885	4,915	(190)	3,200

	1950-51	1951-52	1952-53	1953-54
Gate receipts	23,140	22,920	20,875	20,300
Season tickets	2,730	3,385	2,640	3,805
Players' wages	16,830	19,995	14,090	14,250
Travel costs	3,890	4,090	3,550	3,230
Ground repairs	1,815	2,440	1,370	1,300
Profit/(loss)	(2,960)	(4,700)	430	1,070
Investments in:				
Stands, terraces	–	–	2,500	2,320
Transfer fees				
paid/(rec.)	(9,355)	1,220	(2,950)	(1,750)

	1954-55	1955-56	1956-57	1957-58
Gate receipts	17,890	21,000	25,475	31,200
Season tickets	3,980	2,370	2,590	2,620
Players' wages	13,890	13,490	15,580	21,800
Travel costs	3,285	3,090	4,400	3,690
Ground repairs	1,200	1,250	1,280	1,750
Profit/(loss)	(1,250)	1,130	2,270	965
Investments in:				
Stands, terraces	2,645	–	–	–
Transfer fees				
paid/(rec.)	3,500	200	1,230	3,500

Bradford Park Avenue

Cash Flows (£'s)

Share issues	1,345
Directors' loans	4,785
Bank overdraft	17,345
	23,475

Investment in stands, terraces, etc.	10,845
Investment in houses	6,040
Losses on operations	6,590
	23,475

Selected Receipts, Expenses and Investments (£'s)

	1946-47 (Div. II)	1947-48	1948-49	1949-50
Gate receipts	23,880	28,495	32,320	28,760
Season tickets	1,560	1,650	2,060	2,870
Players' wages	13,600	16,615	25,650	23,570
Travel costs	2,545	3,520	4,225	3,720
Ground repairs	2,365	1,755	3,005	1,835
Profit/(loss)	3,275	(390)	(7,900)	(10,075)
Investment in:				
Stands,etc	–	8,660	–	–
Transfer fees paid/(rec)	(3,380)	(8,390)	(12,930)	9,300

	1951-52 (Div. III (N))	1952-53	1957-58
Gate receipts	30,070	23,480	20,770
Season tickets	n/a	n/a	2,715
Players' wages	n/a	21,700	20,475
Travel costs	n/a	3,060	0,070
Ground repairs	n/a	1,170	1,685
Profit/(loss)	n/a	(10,700)	5,255
Investment in:			
Stands, etc.	n/a	–	–
Transfer fees paid/(rec.)	n/a	(650)	5,345

Appendix 2g: Annual Financial Results: 1958-85

Bradford City AFC (1908) Ltd Cash Flows 1958-83 (£'s)

Share issues	16,000
Loans	8,000
Cash generated on operations	43,000
Bank overdraft	86,000
	153,000

Investment in transfer fees	61,000
Investment in stands, buildings, equipment	55,000
Investment in motor vehicles	37,000
	153,000

Bradford City (1983) Ltd Cash Flows 1983-85 (£'s)

Share issues	174,000
Loans	63,000
Cash generated on operations	27,000
Bank overdraft	44,000
	308,000

Investment in stands, buildings, equipment	289,000
Investment in motor vehicles	19,000
	308,000

Selected Receipts, Expenses and Investments (£'s)

	1958-59 (Div. III)	1959-60	1960-61
Gate receipts	32,300	35,800	26,600
Season tickets	3,000	3,200	3,300
Share of League Pools	*	*	*
Lotteries, donations	4,800	5,400	6,000
Wages	23,200	24,800	25,600
Travel	5,000	5,100	5,100
Ground expenses	3,800	2,500	3,900
Profit/(loss)	2,350	5,800	(6,000)
Investment in:			
Stands, equipment	–	–	32,000
Transfer fees paid/(rec.)	2,500	(11,600)	(9,550)

Appendices

	1961-62 (Div. IV)	1962-63	1963-64	1964-65
Gate receipts	28,300	22,800	23,200	21,200
Season tickets	2,100	2,200	1,200	1,200
Share of League Pools	*	*	*	*
Lotteries, donations	6,300	5,600	6,500	15,800
Wages	27,300	28,800	27,900	26,500
Travel	4,500	5,800	4,700	5,400
Ground expenses	3,200	2,100	1,100	2,800
Profit/(loss)	(7,000)	(14,900)	(11,700)	(5,800)
Investment in:				
Stands, equipment	13,000	3,000	–	2,000
Transfer fees				
paid/(rec.)	(8,900)	(13,500)	(2,600)	(17,000)

	1965-66	1966-67	1967-68	1968-69
Gate receipts	23,000	32,500	44,600	46,600
Season tickets	1,300	1,300	2,100	2,700
Share of League Pools	*	*	*	*
Lotteries, donations	13,500	12,900	17,200	16,600
Wages	35,100	33,900	41,800	53,400
Travel	5,000	4,000	5,000	7,400
Ground expenses	1,700	2,500	2,600	3,900
Profit/(loss)	(12,400)	(5,250)	3,050	(10,300)
Investment in:				
Stands, equipment	(7,000)	5,000	5,000	14,000
Transfer fees				
paid/(rec.)	10,250	(4,300)	3,600	3,700

	1969-70 (Div. III)	1970-71	1971-72
Gate receipts	70,200	49,900	50,400
Season tickets	4,300	6,500	5,800
Share of League Pools	*	*	*
Lotteries, donations	16,600	15,200	18,400
Wages	50,900	57,600	56,300
Travel	7,900	8,500	9,000
Ground expenses	5,100	7,000	3,900
Profit/(loss)	15,600	(15,000)	(7,350)
Investment in:			
Stands, equipment	3,000	(35,000)	–
Transfer fees			
paid/(rec.)	4,200	3,600	(7,900)

	1972-73 (Div. IV)	1973-74	1974-75	1975-76	1976-77
Gate receipts	57,100	59,900	56,500	67,000	77,100
Season tickets	4,300	4,400	4,900	6,500	5,900
Share of League Pools	*	*	*	22,200	40,500
Lotteries, donations	19,400	16,900	18,000	16,300	6,300
Wages	72,500	71,800	67,800	56,400	94,800
Travel	9,900	8,700	8,500	7,300	11,900
Ground expenses	3,200	3,800	5,000	5,600	6,700
Profit/(loss)	(18,800)	(14,900)	(14,250)	32,450	(1,300)
Investment in:					
Stands, equipment	1,000	–	–	–	–
Transfer fees					
paid/(rec.)	(2,200)	11,400	(1,300)	–	28,250

	1977-78 (Div. III)	1978-79	1979-80	1980-81	1981-82
Gate receipts	85,900	75,300	114,400	91,900	162,000
Season tickets	11,300	14,200	11,000	17,900	25,000
Share of League Pools	35,900	45,100	88,500	76,800	89,200
Lotteries, donations	94,100	121,300	207,000	140,300	92,600
Wages	129,100	216,300	259,300	256,700	302,300
Travel	24,500†	24,100†	29,000†	20,700†	38,400†
Ground expenses	11,400	22,500	9,900	1,500	9,100
Profit/(loss)	25,250	(63,500)	38,450	(18,200)	(59,250)
Investment in:					
Stands, equipment	1,000	44,000	2,000	(28,000)	–
Transfer fees					
paid/(rec.)	56,900	(19,000)	45,000	(17,000)	6,000

	1982-83 (Div. III)	1983-84	1984-85
Gate receipts	n/a		
Season tickets	n/a		
Share of League Pools	n/a	502,000	621,000
Lotteries, donations	n/a		
Wages	n/a	312,000	419,000
Travel	n/a	n/a	n/a
Ground expenses	n/a	n/a	n/a
Profit/(loss)	(123,300)	4,300	(13,600)
Investment in:			
Stands, equipment	n/a	285,000	4,000
Transfer fees paid/(rec.)	n/a	n/a	n/a

* included in Gate Receipts
† including refreshment and training expenses.

Bradford (Park Avenue) – Cash flows 1958-74 (£'s)

Share issues	37,000
Loans	20,000
Sale of ground, equipment (net of previous expenditures)	68,000
Income from transfer fees	43,000
	168,000

Repayment of bank overdraft, loans etc.	68,000
Cash lost by operations	100,000
	168,000

Selected Receipts, Expenses and Investments (£'s)

	1958-59 (Div. IV)	1959-60	1960-61	1961-62	1962-63
Gate receipts	18,200	18,000	26,800	33,600	26,000
Season tickets	2,100	2,500	2,800	4,200	3,500
Share of League Pools	900	1,400	3,000	3,100	3,100
Lotteries, donations	14,800	14,500	14,600	14,000	12,200
Wages	22,800	25,900	26,600	29,500	31,000
Travel	4,500	5,500	5,200	6,700	7,000
Ground repairs	1,500	900	500	2,400	–
Profit/(loss)	500	(2,800)	6,300	2,900	0
Investment in:					
Stands, equipment	–	–	–	–	16,000
Transfer fees paid/(rec.)	4,600	(100)	(100)	(16,200)	4,900

	1963-64 (Div. IV)	1964-65	1965-66	1966-67	1967-68
Gate receipts	22,800	27,200	23,200	23,500	16,400
Season tickets	2,300	1,900	1,800	2,200	1,600
Share of League Pools	3,300	5,600	6,000	8,500	7,900
Lotteries, donations	11,200	11,400	7,100	15,300	14,300
Wages	31,200	32,300	36,800	44,400	41,300
Travel	5,500	4,400	3,800	5,300	4,200
Ground repairs	700	1,100	1,600	1,200	1,500
Profit/(loss)	(3,440)	1,500	(13,800)	(12,000)	(21,000)
Investment in:					
Stands, equipment	–	4,000	–	–	–
Transfer fees paid/(rec.)	3,000	500	(8,500)	(25,000)	2,100

	1968-69	1969-70
Gate receipts	17,400	17,000
Season tickets	1,000	1,300
Share of League Pools	7,500	9,100
Lotteries, donations	13,800	14,000
Wages	41,500	46,500
Travel	5,900	6,800
Ground repairs	1,700	1,500
Profit/(loss)	(21,700)	(26,600)
Investment in:		
Stands, equipment	–	–
Transfer fees		
paid/(rec.)	(13,400)	12,200

	1970-71 (N. Premier)	1971-72	1972-73	1973-74
Gate receipts	10,000	6,100	8,200	4,000
Season tickets	800	400	400	200
Share of League Pools	–	–	–	–
Lotteries, donations	12,300	13,200	11,800	5,500
Wages	28,700	13,200	14,700	9,600
Travel	3,400	1,800	3,000	1,100
Ground repairs	600	100	200	500
Profit/(loss)	(23,800)	(8,600)	(8,000)	(3,000)
Investment in:				
Stands, equipment	1,000	6,000	(95,000)	–
Transfer fees				
paid/(rec.)	(7,800)	(100)	–	300

BRADFORD CITY ASSOCIATION FOOTBALL CLUB (1908) LIMITED

Balance Sheet
as at 31 May 1982

	Note	1982 £	1982 £	1981 £	1981 £
EMPLOYMENT OF FUNDS	4		151,641		147,683
FIXED ASSETS					
CURRENT ASSETS					
Stock		2,500		2,467	
Debtors and Prepayments		80,348		40,030	
Cash in Hand		—		852	
		82,848		43,349	
CURRENT LIABILITIES					
Sundry Creditors and Accruals		213,192		105,986	
Directors Loans		17,267		17,599	
Hire Purchase Creditors		8,952		8,741	
Bank Overdraft	9	115,953		115,213	
Bank Loan	9	9,376		7,977	
Loans	10	275		775	
		365,015		256,291	
NET CURRENT LIABILITIES			(282,167)		(212,942)
			(130,526)		(65,259)
REPRESENTED BY:					
SHARE CAPITAL	6		24,719		24,719
RESERVES	5		(155,245)		(89,978)
			(130,526)		(65,259)

R. Martin   Directors
J. H. Garside

The accompanying notes form part of these accounts.

The Bradford (Park Avenue) Association Football Club, Limited

BALANCE SHEET as at 31st May, 1970

1969 £		Authorised £	Issued and Fully Paid £
15,152	**Share Capital:** Shares of £1 each	63,000	46,512
	Capital Reserves:		
7	Forfeited Share Capital re-issued	7	
7,730	Profit on Sale of Property	7,262	
			7,269
22,889			55,781
57,636	Deduct: Deficiency on Revenue Account ...		95,990
34,747	Net Deficiency, carried to Contra		42,209
	Life Membership Account as at 1st June, 1969 ...	269	
	Less: Transfer to Revenue Account	60	
269			209
	Company Membership Account as at 1st June, 1969	128	
128	Less: Transfer to Revenue Account	8	
			120
	Secured Liabilities: Lloyds Bank Ltd. (Secured on Park Avenue Ground and Buildings, East Bierley Ground and Personal Guarantee of Director and		
22,416	former Director)	30,751	
10,367	Building Society Mortgages on Houses	8,211	
			38,962
	Current Liabilities:		
19,108	Sundry Creditors and Accrued Charges	20,163	
—	Hire Purchase Creditor	67	
	Loans—		
8,649	Directors	500	
13,200	Others (including £4,100 at 8% per annum)	19,273	
4	Unclaimed Dividends	4	
			40,007
£74,141			£79,298

1969 £		Cost £	Aggregate Depreciation to Date £	£
	Fixed Assets:			
6,878	Park Avenue Football Ground, Offices and Stands	9,050	2,172	6,878
13,980	Dwelling Houses	11,312	—	11,312
25	Loudspeaker Equipment	559	534	25
400	Dressing Rooms and Office Furniture	845	445	400
3,596	East Bierley Ground	3,596	—	3,596
10,350	Flood Lighting	15,149	5,799	9,350
—	Motor Mower	175	17	158
35,229		40,686	8,967	31,719
	Current Assets: Sundry Debtors and Payments in			
4,153	Advance		5,173	
12	Cash in Hand		197	
				5,370
34,747	Net Deficiency, per Contra			42,209
£74,141				£79,298

NOTES:—

1. No provision has been made in the Revenue Account for Depreciation of Park Avenue Football Ground, Offices and Stands, Dressing Room and Office Furniture, Dwelling Houses, East Bierley Ground and Loudspeaker Equipment.

2. No liability for Corporation Tax arises on these accounts.

AUDITORS' REPORT TO THE MEMBERS OF
THE BRADFORD (PARK AVENUE) ASSOCIATION FOOTBALL CLUB LIMITED

We have examined the above Balance Sheet together with the annexed Revenue Account. In our opinion, the Balance Sheet and Revenue Account have been properly prepared in accordance with the provisions of the Companies Acts 1948 and 1967 and give a true and fair view of the state of affairs as at 31st May, 1970, and of the Loss for the year ended on that date.

5 Eldon Place,
BRADFORD 1.
7th December, 1970.

FIRTH, PARISH, CLARKE, HUSTWICK & CO.,
Chartered Accountants.

Appendix 3a: Directors and Managers: before 1903

Manningham FC

Committee 1886

W. Lister	Law stationer
T. Hartley	Joiner
J. Gill	Worsted spinner
J. Freeman	Solicitor
J. H. Iveson	Stuff warehouseman
A. W. McWeeney	Clerk
H. Archer	Cabinet maker
H. Jowett	Traveller
W. Midgeley	Wool warehouseman
J. Sunderland	Overlooker
W. I. Fawcett	Warehouseman
J. A. Clarkson	Architect and surveyor
H. Moxon	Working jeweller
F. Hartley	Stuff warehouseman
H. Summersgill	Accountants clerk

Appendix 3b: Directors and Managers: 1903-1915

Bradford City AFC

Committee 1907

W. N. Pollack	Yarn merchant
I. Newton	Licensed victualler
C. H. Marsden	Solicitor
J. Nunn	Gentleman
Dr. F. Lindsay-Woods	Physician
J. Lucas	Coal merchant
A. Lancaster	Wool merchant

Bradford City AFC (1908) Ltd

Directors 1908-15

W. N. Pollack	1908-1915/6	Yarn Merchant
C. H. Marsden	1908-1914	Solicitor
J. Nunn	1908-1927/8	Gentleman
Dr. F. Lindsay-Woods	1908-1910	Physician
I. Newton	1908-1909	Licensed victualler
J. Lucas	1908-1921/2	Coal merchant
A. Lancaster	1908-1921	Wool merchant
T. Paton	1909-1911/2	Chartered accountant
H. Hey	1910/11-1913	Worsted spinner
J. Gent	1911/12-1914	Wine and spirit merchant
J. A. Jowett	1913-1921/2	None

Secretary-Managers 1903-15

R. Campbell	1903-1905
P. O'Rourke	1905-1920

Bradford (Park Avenue) AFC Ltd

Directors 1909-15

A. H. Briggs	1909-1920	Spinner and manufacturer
J. Brunt	1909-1910	Schoolmaster
H. T. Coates	1909-1915	Stuff merchant
H. Geldard	1909-1922	Gentleman
F. Lister	1909-1912	Wool and waste dealer
T. H. Marshall	1909-1911	Leather merchant
P. Paterson	1909-1924	Presser
J. F. Rhodes	1909-1920	Traveller
A. Shepherd	1909-1912	Timber merchant
N. Sugden	1911-1912	Worsted spinner
W. Nixon	1911-1924	Insurance agent
E. Cohen	1911	Merchant
W. C. Parker	1912-1918	Manufacturer
C. L. Arnold	1912-1924	Worsted spinner
A. E. Briggs	1913-1924	Spinner and manufacturer

Secretaries and Managers 1907-15

E. R. Hoyle (Secretary) 1907-1913	
F. Halliday (Manager) 1907-1909	
G. Gillies (Manager) 1909-1911	
T. E. Malley (Manager) 1911-1924	(from 1913 Malley was Secretary-Manager)

Appendix 3c: Directors and Managers 1915-1919

Bradford City AFC

Directors

W. N. Pollack	1908-1915/6	Yarn merchant
J. Nunn	1908-1927/8	Gentleman
J. Lucas	1908-1921/2	Coal merchant
A. Lancaster	1908-1921	Wool merchant
J. A. Jowett	1913-1921/2	None
T. E. Power	1916/7-1926/7	Commission Agent
G. Grange	1918/9-1919/20	–

Secretary-Manager

P. O'Rourke	1905-1920

Bradford (Park Avenue) AFC

Directors

A. H. Briggs	1909-1920	Spinner and manufacturer
H. Geldard	1909-1922	Gentleman
P. Paterson	1909-1924	Presser
J. F. Rhodes	1909-1920	Traveller
W. Nixon	1911-1924	Insurance agent
W. C. Parker	1912-1918	Manufacturer
C. L. Arnold	1912-1924	Worsted spinner
A. E. Briggs	1913-1924	Spinner and manufacturer

Secretary and Manager

T. E. Malley (Secretary-Manager)	1913-1924

Appendix 3d: Directors and Managers 1919-39

Bradford City AFC

Directors

J. Nunn	1908-1927/8	Gentleman
J. Lucas	1908-1921/2	Coal merchant
A. Lancaster	1908-1921	Wool merchant
J. A. Jowett	1913-1921/2	None
T. E. Power	1916/17-1926/7	Commission agent
	1930/1-1934	
G. Grange	1918/9-1919/20	–
T. L. Dallas	1920/1-1927	Insurance broker
J. W. Driver	1920/1-1927	Manufacturer
A. Welch	1920/1-1927	Chartered accountant
E. Muff	1921/2-1922/3	Manufacturer
F. Obank	1922/3-1933/4	–
J. R. Gillyard	1925/6-1939	Stationer
A. Hey	1927/8-1928/9	Brewer
	1933/4-1946/7	
A. A. McDermott	1927/8-1928/9	–
F. B. Naylor	1927/8-1932/3	–
W. H. Sawyer	1927/8-1938	Journalist
A. Smith	1929/30-1931/2	–
T. E. Robinson	1928/9-1939	Manufacturer
J. S. Driver	1929/30-1937	Merchant
Coun. J. R. Rose	1934-1952	Engineer, Director
T. R. Hilliam	1937/8-1944/5	Topmaker

Secretary-Managers

P. O'Rourke	1905-1920
D. L. Menzies	1920-1925
C. M. Veitch	1925-1928
P. O'Rourke	1928-1929
J. G. Peart	1929-1934

Secretary

C. A. Maley	1934-1943/4

Managers

R. Ray	1934-1937
F. Westgarth	1937-1942

Bradford (Park Avenue) AFC Directors

A H. Briggs	1909-1920	Spinner and manufacturer
H. Geldard	1909-1922	Gentleman
P. Paterson	1909-1924	Presser
J. F. Rhodes	1909-1920	Traveller
W. Nixon	1911-1924	Insurance agent
C. L. Arnold	1912-1924	Worsted spinner
A. E. Briggs	1913-1924	Spinner and manufacturer
W. E. Collins	1920-1934 1935-1949	Director
J. A. Greenwood	1920-1933	Manufacturer
F. B. Greer	1921-1923	Veterinary surgeon
F. W. Brearley	1921-1935	Bank manager
Coun. J. Hoyle	1922-1927	Wool and noil merchant
S. Waddilove	1923-1931 1935-1955	Director
R. Ingram	1923-1927	Spinner and manufacturer
J. J. Newby	1925-1935	Wholesale draper
C. Smithies	1927-1930	Slate merchant
W. A. Berry	1927-1935	Printer
G. W. Copley	1928-1935	Wholesale fruiterer
G. Waddilove	1928-1931	Director
J. Lister	1932-1933	Wool merchant
C. H. Turner	1932-1935	Worsted spinner
C. Ambler	1933-1935	Worsted spinner
A. Ward	1933-1935	Accountant
Coun. H. J. White	1934-1953	Limewashing contractor
Lt-Col E. Waddilove	1935-1936	Director
Ald. J. W. Turner JP	1935-1956	Reed maker
J. Canning	1935-1952	Director of tyre firm
Ald. H. Hudson	1935-1950	Wool merchant
F. J. Barnes	1938-1940	–

Secretary-Managers

T. E. Malley	1913-1924
P. O'Rourke	1924-1925
D. Howie	1925
C. Ingram	1925-1934
W. Hardy	1934-1936
D. M. Steele	1936-1943

Secretary

G. H. Brigg	1934-1974

Appendix 3e: Directors and Managers 1939-46

Bradford City AFC Directors

A. Hey	1933/4-1946/7	Brewer
Ald. J. R. Rose	1934-1952	Engineer, Director
T. R. Hilliam	1937/8-1944/5	Topmaker
Ald. C. Barnett	1939-1952	Grocer, Managing Director
F. M. Gledhill	1939-1948	Butcher
Coun. G. A. Hirst	1939-1948	Gown and robe manufacturer
Coun. R. Sharp	1939-1949	Floor cover merchant

Secretaries

C. A. Maley	1934-1943/4
Coun. R. Sharp (Hon)	1944-1947

Managers

F. Westgarth	1937-1942
Coun. R. Sharp (Hon)	1942-1945
J. Barker	1945-1946

Bradford (Park Avenue) AFC Directors

Coun. H. J. White	1934-1953	Limewashing contractor
W. E. Collins	1935-1949	Director
S. Waddilove	1935-1955	Director
Ald. J. W. Turner JP	1935-1956	Reed maker
J. Canning	1935-1952	Director of tyre firm
Ald. H. Hudson	1935-1950	Wool merchant
F. J. Barnes	1938-1940	–
G. W. Watson	1944-1953	Consulting surgeon

Secretary-Managers

D. M. Steele	1936-1943
F. Emery	1943-1946

Secretary

G. H. Brigg	1934-1974

Appendix 3f: Directors and Managers 1946-58

Bradford City AFC Directors

A. Hey	1933/4-1946/7	Brewer
Coun. J. R. Rose	1934-1952	Engineer, Director
Ald. C. Barnett	1939-1952	Grocer, Managing Director
F. M. Gledhill	1939-1948	Butcher
Coun. G. A. Hirst	1939-1948	Gown and robe manufacturer
Coun. R. Sharp	1939-1949	Floor cover merchant
H. J. Holden	1948-1960	Builder, Director
H. Munro	1948-1962	Furnishing fabrics manufacturer
O. S. Wain	1948-1960/1	Clothier director
J. T. Badman	1949-1951/2	–
A. V. Harris	1949-1965	Timber merchant
W. M. Hird	1951/2-1961/2	Steeplejack firm owner

Secretaries

Coun. R. Sharp (Hon)	1944-1947
G. H. Jowett	1952-1956
J. Mellor	1956-1975

Managers

J. Milburn	1946-1947
A. V. Harris (acting)	1952
I. Powell	1952-1954/5
P. Jackson	1954/5-1961

Secretary-Manager

D. M. Steele	1947-1952

Bradford (Park Avenue) AFC Directors

W. E. Collins	1935-1949	Director
S. Waddilove	1935-1955	Director
Coun. H. J. White	1934-1953	Limewashing contractor
Ald. J. W. Turner JP	1935-1956	Reed maker
J. Canning	1935-1952	Director of tyre firm
Ald. H. Hudson	1935-1950	Wool merchant
G. W. Watson	1944-1953	Consulting surgeon
R. Kellett	1949-1960	Textile director
R. Collins	1951-1955	Director
C. R. Ambler	1951-1954	Wool company director
W. Hirst	1953-1957	Garage owner
G. Butler	1954-1962	Director
G. F. H. Phillips	1955-1964	Director
A. Pickles	1956-1966	Retired builder

Secretary

G. H. Brigg	1934-1974

Managers

F. Emery	1946-1951
V. Buckingham	1951-1953
N. Kirkman	1953-1955
J. Breedon	1955
R. Kellett (Hon. acting)	1955-1956
A. Young	1956-1958

Appendix 3g: Directors and Managers: 1958-85

Bradford City AFC (1908) Ltd Directors 1958-83

H. J. Holden	1948-1960	Builder, Director	b 1893
H. Munro	1948-1962	Furnishing fabrics director	b 1900
O. S. Wain	1948-1960/1	Clothier director	b 1888
A. V. Harris	1949-1965	Timber merchant	b 1905
W. M. Hird	1951/2-1961/2	Steeplejack firm owner	b 1891
C. K. O'Keefe	1959-1967	Wholesale fruiterer	b 1912
G. W. Briggs	1960/1-1964/5	Woollen company director	b 1910
E. L. Porter	1962/3-1974	Wetshop manager	b 1907
J. Kelly	1963/4-1965	–	
S. Heginbotham	1965-1974	Toy manufacturer	b 1933
G. D. Ide	1965-1974	Solicitor	b 1925

M. G. F. Dickens	1965/6-1970	Manager	b 1934
H. B. Metcalfe	1967-1975	Wholesale tobacconist	b 1928
P. J. W. Jones	1972-1974	Sales director	b 1939
R. Martin	1972-1983	Construction company director	b 1937
J. Dunne	1974-1981	Director	b 1938
K. D. Morrison	1974-1979	Supermarket director	b 1931
J. C. Tordoff	1974-1978	Motor firm director	b 1935
D. W. Wilkinson	1974-1977	Textiles director	b 1931
W. J. Davidson	1974-1978	Director	b 1933
J. H. Garside	1974-1983	Architect	b 1941
R. Stead	1974-1983	Director, licensee	b 1942
W. Roper	1975-1981	Textile director	b 1931
E. Sutcliffe	1978-1983	Insulation contractor director	b 1936
W. McGrath	1981-1982	Tool and gauge company director	b 1938

Secretaries

J. Mellor	1956-1975
C. S. Thompson	1975-1977
T. F. Newman	1977-1983

Managers

P. Jackson	1954/5-1961
R. E. Brocklebank	1961-1964
W. Harris	1965-1966
W. Watson	1966-1968
G. Hair	1968
J. Wheeler	1968-1971
B. Edwards	1971-1975
B. Kennedy	1975-1978
J. Napier	1978
G. Mulhall	1978-1981
R. McFarland	1981-1982
T. Cherry	1982-1983

Bradford City (1983) Ltd Directors 1983-85

S. Heginbotham	1983-1985	Toy manufacturer
J. C. Tordoff	1983-1985	Motor firm director
P. S. Flesher	1983-1985	Chartered accountant

Secretary

T. F. Newman	1983-1985

Manager

T. Cherry	1983-1985

Bradford (Park Avenue) AFC Directors 1958-74

R. Kellett	1949-1960	Textile director	
C. R. Ambler	1961-1964 1967-1969	Wool company director	b 1917
G. Butler	1954-1962	Director	b 1914
G. F. H. Phillips	1955-1964	Director	
W. Hirst	1959-1961	Garage owner	b 1904
A. Pickles	1956-1966	Retired builder	b 1894
J. Murphy	1959-1966	Demolition and haulage contractor	b 1910
L. Jackson	1961/2-1967	Bookseller's director	
J. L. Evans	1965/6-1968	Car firm owner	b 1898
M. F. Brown	1965/6-1974	Director	b 1913
G. Sutcliffe	1967-1974	Dairy owner	b 1912
J. Burkinshaw	1967-1974	Restaurant owner	b 1918
H. Metcalfe	1968-1970	Director	b 1907
S. Yeadon	1970	–	
T. Horsfall	1971-1974	Construction company director	b 1922

Secretary

G. H. Brigg   1934-1974

Managers

W. Galbraith	1958-1961
J. Scoular	1961-1964
J. Buchanan	1964-1967
J. Rowley	1967-1968
D. McCalman	1968
L. Brown	1968-1969
D. McCalman	1969-1970
F. Tomlinson	1970
T. Leighton	1970-1973
R. Ambler	1973-1974

Bibliography

Manuscript Sources

(The) Bradford City Association FC (1908) Ltd., Company Returns. (Founded 1908. Liquidation 1983). Companies House No. 98271.

Bradford City AFC (1983) Ltd., Company Returns. Companies House No. 1732784.

(The Incorporated) Bradford Cricket, Athletic and Football Club. Company Returns. (A Limited Company, liability of members limited by guarantee. Founded 1892. Defunct 1914. Dissolved 1932.) Public Records Office BT 31-15222/36101.

(The) Bradford (Park Avenue) Association FC Ltd. Company Returns. (Founded 1909. Liquidation 1974). Companies House No. 104075.

Bradford Rugby Union FC, Sundry Papers, Bradford Reference Library.

Bradford Skating Rink Company. Company Returns, Companies House No. 11,117.

Halifax Skating Rink Company. Company Returns, Companies House No. 10257.

Halifax Town Association FC Ltd. Company Returns, Companies House No. 116844.

Holbeck Football and Athletic Club Limited. Company Returns, Public Records Office BT31-7363/52183.

Huddersfield Athletic Club, Huddersfield Cricket and Athletic Club, Sundry Papers, Huddersfield Reference Library.

Huddersfield Town's Directors Minute Books (by courtesy of G. Binns, Secretary).

Leeds City Association Football Club Company Limited. Company Returns, Public Records Office BT 31-17428/84163.

Leeds Cricket, Football and Athletic Co Ltd. Company Returns, Companies House No. 28301.

Manningham Football Club. Company Returns. (A Limited Company, liability of members limited by guarantee. Founded 1886. Liquidation 1908). Public Records Office BT 31-3700/23007.

Newspapers

Athletic News
Bradford Daily Telegraph
Bradford Observer
Bradford Telegraph and Argus
Halifax Courier
Huddersfield Daily Examiner

Illustrated Weekly Telegraph (Bradford)
The Times
Yorkshire Observer
Yorkshire Post

Published sources relating to Bradford: books etc.

Briggs, Asa, *Victorian Cities*, London 1968.
Dewhurst, I., *Yorkshire through the Years*, London 1975.
Hird, H., *Bradford in History*, Bradford 1968.
Jenkins, D. and K. Ponting, *British Wool Textile Industry 1770-1914*, London 1982.
Jeremy, D. J. (ed.), *Dictionary of Business Biography*, London 1985.
Lockwood, E., *Colne Valley Folk*, London 1936.
Mellor, G. J., *The Cinemas of Bradford*, Bradford 1983.
Mitchell, B. and P. Deane, *Abstract of British Historical Statistics*, Cambridge 1962.
Mitchell, B. and H. G. Jones, *Second Abstract of British Historical Statistics*, Cambridge 1971.
Reynolds, J., *The Great Paternalist: Titus Salt and the Growth of Nineteenth-Century Bradford*, Bradford 1983.
Richardson, C., *Geography of Bradford*, Bradford 1976.
Ryder, J. and H. Silver, *Modern English Society*, London 1970.
Walton, J and J. Walvin, *Leisure in Britain 1780-1939*, Manchester 1986.
West Yorkshire Metropolitan County Council, *Structure Plan Survey Report*, Wakefield 1983.
Wright, D. G. and J. A. Jowitt, *Victorian Bradford*, Bradford 1981.

Published sources relating to Bradford: articles

Ashworth, W. 'Changes in the Industrial Structure 1870-1914', *Yorkshire Bulletin of Economic and Social Research*, XVII, 1965.
Oxtoby, G. H., 'The Wool Textile Industry', *Yorkshire Bulletin of Economic and Social Research*, 1970.
Pankhurst, K. V., 'Fluctuations in Wool Prices 1870-1953', *Yorkshire Bulletin of Economic and Social Research*, 1955.
Pearce, C., 'The Manningham Mills Strike', *University of Hull Occasional Paper*, 1975.
Reynolds, J. and K. Laybourn, 'The Emergence of the ILP in Bradford', *International Review of Social History*, 20, 1975.
Thomas, Joan, 'Later Developments in the Clothing Industry', *Leeds Journal*, September 1954.

Published sources relating to football, sport: books etc.

Arnold, A. J., I. Benveniste and A. Collier, *Cross Subsidisation in the English Football League*, Department of Economics, University of Essex, Discussion Paper No. 302, November 1986.
Bailey, P., *Leisure and Class in Victorian England*, London 1978.
Blyth, Denis, *Memorable Matches Bradford City AFC*, Milnthorpe, Cumbria, 1981.
Bradford Cricket Club, Bradford 1973.

Bradford Northern Rugby League FC, *Souvenir History of Odsal Stadium*, Bradford 1981.

Cashman, R. L. and M. McKenna (eds), *Sport: Money, Morality and the Media*, Sydney 1980.

Chadwick, S., *Northern Union*, Huddersfield 1946.

———— *Through 56 Years*, Huddersfield 1951.

Commission for Industrial Relations Report No. 87, *Professional Football*, 1974.

Committee of Inquiry into Crowd Safety and Control at Sports Grounds (The Popplewell Inquiry) – Interim Report, Cmnd 9585, 1985.

Committee of Inquiry into Crowd Safety and Control at Sports Grounds (The Popplewell Inquiry) – Final Report, Cmnd 9710, 1986.

Cunningham, Hugh, *Leisure in the Industrial Revolution*, London 1980.

Department of Education and Science, *Report of the Committee on Football* (The Chester Report), London 1968.

Dickinson, F. T., *Milestones 1911-37: History and Records of Halifax Town AFC*, Halifax 1937.

Dunning, E. (ed.), *The Sociology of Sport: A Selection of Readings*, London 1971.

Dunning, E. and K. Sheard, *Barbarians, Gentlemen and Players: A Sociological Study of the Development of Rugby Football*, 1979.

Gibson, A. and W. Pickford, *Association Football and the Men who Made It*, London 1906.

Halifax Town AFC Official History, Halifax 1923.

Hartley, M., *History of Bradford PA*, Bradford 1978.

Headingley Football Club 1878-1978, Leeds 1979.

Holmes, R. S., *The History of Yorkshire County Cricket 1833-1903*, London 1904.

Howkins, A. and J. Lowerson, *Trends in Leisure 1919-39*, State of the Art Review, SSRC, London 1979.

Inglis, S., *The Football Grounds of England and Wales*, London 1983.

Ludlam, C. H., *The Complete History of Bradford Northern*, Bradford 1969.

Mason, Tony, *Association Football and English Society 1863-1915*, Brighton 1980.

Political and Economic Planning, *Planning*, Vol. XVII, No. 324, *The Football Industry*, London 1951.

Political and Economic Planning, *English Professional Football*, London 1966.

Report of the Committee of Enquiry into Structure and Finance (Chairman Sir N. Chester), Lytham St. Annes 1983.

Rothmans Football Yearbooks 1970/1 to 1985/6, London 1970-1985.

Rothmans Rugby League Yearbook 1982/3, Aylesbury 1982.

Sawyer, W. H., *Bradford City AFC – The Jubilee Story 1903-53*, Bradford 1953.

Shearman, Montague, *Athletics and Football*, London 1887.

Smout, T. C., *Search for Wealth and Stability*, London 1979.

Tischler, S., *Footballers and Businessmen: The Origins of Professional Soccer in England*, New York 1981.

Walvin, J., *The People's Game*, London 1975.

Warters, D., *Leeds United – the Official History of the Club*, Norwich 1979.

Published sources relating to football, sport: articles

Baker, W. J. 'The Making of a Working Class Football Culture in Victorian England', *Journal of Social History*, XIII, No 2, 1979.

Bird, P., 'The Demand for League Football', *Applied Economics* Vol. 14, No. 6, 1982.

Dunning, E. and K. Sheard, 'The Bifurcation of Rugby Union and Rugby League: A Case Study of Organisational Conflict and Change', *International Review of Sports Sociology*, II, 1976.

Edwardes, C., 'The New Football Mania', *Nineteenth Century*, XXXII, 1892.

Jones, S. G., 'The Economic Aspects of Association Football in England 1918-39', *British Journal of Sports History*, 1,3, 1984.

———— 'The Leisure Industry in Britain 1918-39', *Service Industries Journal*, 5, 1, 1985.

Schofield, J.A., 'The Development of First Class Cricket in England', *Journal of Industrial Economics*, XXX, No. 4, 1982.

Sigsworth, E. M., 'Leeds and its Industrial Growth: 22 Sport (1)', *Leeds Journal*, March 1957.

———— 'The Rise of Football', *Leeds Journal*, May 1957.

P. J. Sloane, 'The Economics of Professional Football – The Football Club as a Utility Maximiser', *Scottish Journal of Political Economy*, June 1971.

Tomlinson, A., 'Explorations in Football Culture', *Brighton Polytechnic Working Papers* (unpublished), 1983.

Vamplew, W., 'Sports Ground Disorder in Britain 1870-1914: Causes and Controls', *Journal of Sport History*, Vol. 7, 1980.

Veitch, C., 'Play up! Play up! and Win the War! Football, the Nation and the First World War 1914-15', *Journal of Contemporary History*, 20, 1985.

Wheeler, R. F., 'Organised Sport and Organised Labour: The Workers' Sports Movement', *Journal of Contemporary History*, XIII, No 2, 1978.

Wilders, M. G., 'The Football Club Manager – A Precarious Occupation?', *Journal of Management Studies*, 1976.

Index